SEVEN YEARS TO SAVE THE PLANET

THE QUESTIONS ...AND ANSWERS

SEVEN YEARS TO SAVE THE PLANET

THE QUESTIONS ...AND ANSWERS

BILL McGUIRE

WEIDENFELD & NICOLSON

First published in Great Britain in 2008
by Weidenfeld & Nicolson
10 9 8 7 6 5 4 3 2 1

A CIP catalogue record for this book is available from the British Library.

ISBN: 978 0 297 85336 7

Printed and bound in the UK

Weidenfeld & Nicolson
The Orion Publishing Group Ltd
Orion House
5 Upper St Martin's Lane
London WC2H 9EA

An Hachette Livre UK Company

The Orion Publishing Group's policy is to use papers that are natural, renewable and recyclable products and made from wood grown in sustainable forests. The logging and manufacturing processes are expected to conform to the environmental regulations of the country of origin.

For my son Fraser, and all of his generation,
who will reap the whirlwind

CONTENTS

INTRODUCTION: WHY SEVEN YEARS?

We live at a pivotal time in human history. While most of us go about our daily business oblivious to the unprecedented environmental changes taking place around us, our world is poised at a critical tipping point beyond which we will bequeath to our children and our children's children a world of environmental degradation, economic breakdown and social chaos. A ruined planet, sweltering beneath a carbon-soaked atmosphere, plundered of its resources and shorn of many of its iconic (and not so iconic) species will be our legacy. Unless, that is, we take drastic and immediate action to diminish our emissions of the greenhouse gases that are inexorably transforming a generally benign climate into a volatile maelstrom. Have we the means and the will to change course? The picture does not look good. Already we are experiencing some of the milder consequences of a changing climate. Increased bouts of torrential rain, more heat waves, and larger numbers of Atlantic hurricanes are symptomatic.

To prevent the full-blown effects of 'dangerous climate change'[1], governments, businesses and individuals need to rethink radically their policies, their values and how they live their lives. Most climate scientists agree that a rise in global average temperature of just 2°C above pre-industrial values would almost certainly be sufficient to have dangerous, pervasive and long-lasting repercussions for both our planet and our civilisation. Just how close we are to committing ourselves to such a rise is reflected in the title of this book. Temperatures have already climbed more than 0.7°C and because warming lags somewhat behind the accumulation of greenhouse gases in the atmosphere, another 0.6°C or so rise is already 'in the system', leaving us less than 1°C away from crossing the critical threshold. The UN Intergovernmental Panel on Climate Change (IPCC) in its 2007 Fourth Assessment Report, which draws on the work, knowledge and experience of 2,500 climate scientists from around the world, recognises that global greenhouse gas emissions must be cut back by between 50 and 80 per cent by 2050 for there to be any possibility of avoiding dangerous climate change. Even this, however, may not be enough. A new study warns that even a 90-per-cent cut in emissions by the middle of the century will not prevent crossing of the 2°C threshold. Achieving little short of a zero-carbon world by 2050 is a huge task, and one that may simply be impossible to achieve.

Nothing short of swingeing cuts in emissions, starting now, stands any chance of staving off climate chaos, and nothing less than a global war-footing will make this happen. Emissions can only be brought under control in time if every government, business and individual accepts responsibility for their actions and takes up the challenge to create a low-carbon world. Reducing emissions must take precedence over economic growth; if it does not, then 30, 50 or 100 years from now the world economy may no longer exist in any coherent and recognisable form. The IPCC highlights the desperate urgency of the problem, noting that in order to have any chance of preventing dangerous climate change, and all that this entails, worldwide emissions will have to peak by 2015 and fall thereafter. We have just seven years to save the planet, at least as we have come to know it – a tiny and rapidly closing window of opportunity within which to counteract the polluting activities of more than 200 years of industrialisation.

Seven Years to Save the Planet opens with an examination of where exactly we are now with respect to climate change: what it is, how human activities are causing it, and how it is already changing our planet. Part two looks ahead to the planet our children and grandchildren will inhabit, and to the predicted impacts of unfettered climate change on their lives and their world. Part three focuses on what all of us can do as individuals to help bring emissions to heel, while part four looks at what others are doing, and should be doing, to tackle climate change, including national governments, big businesses and the scientific community. The finale addresses the $64,000 question – is it already too late? Are we doomed, whatever we do, to a world of climate mayhem, economic collapse and social breakdown, or is there still time to build a successful and sustainable future?

PART 1: WHERE ARE WE NOW?

Six and a half billion of us cling tenaciously to the surface of a tiny, rapidly spinning ball of rock as it hurtles through space. The skin of the rock is broken into pieces that jostle and scrape against one another as they float erratically on a semi-molten stratum. Here and there magma bursts through onto the surface, while some of the pieces founder and slide down into the hot interior. The rocky sphere is periodically pounded by other rocks and icy fragments as it flashes through a solar system filled with debris. Only a frail gaseous envelope allows us to breathe while, at the same time, providing a last shield against some of the smaller rocks and the intense cosmic radiation coming from the sun and other stars, but even this is in constant turmoil as it speeds across the rock's stormy, water-covered exterior. Changes in the geometry of our planet's orbit, rotation and geophysical circumstances trigger dramatic swings in temperature – from ice age to balmy paradise and back again. You would think that our existence on Earth was already precarious enough, but now our own polluting activities are destabilising our future and threatening the very fabric of our civilisation. In the course of a few centuries we are returning to the Earth's atmosphere virtually all of the carbon that has been locked away by geological processes over hundreds of millions of years – and all of this started just down the road from where I live.

The small English village of Cromford in Derbyshire, resting quietly on the banks of the river Derwent a few kilometres from my home, has a great deal to answer for. In 1771, Richard Arkwright built the first mechanised cotton mill here and almost single-handedly launched what we now know as the Industrial Revolution. Little did Arkwright know that his water-powered spinning frame – a development of the more famous spinning jenny – would almost overnight galvanise and transform a British economy previously built solely upon manual labour.

In a matter of decades, textile production, iron-making, coal refining and a host of other processes embraced machine technology, powered by steam. As production rose and trade expanded the infrastructure followed: a profusion of new roads, canals and railways blasted through the hills and bridged the valleys of Britain. In the nineteenth century, industrialisation spread rapidly across Western Europe and North America, and its march across the face of our planet continues today.

In 2005, global industry used oil, coal and gas totalling over nine billion tonnes oil equivalent[2] to make 67 million cars and vans and 105 million bicycles, to fly a couple of billion people around the planet, and to provide the infrastructure for nearly two billion mobile phone users and 400 million internet-connected computers.

When Cromford Mill opened 236 years ago, the concentration in the Earth's atmosphere of carbon dioxide, the most ubiquitous greenhouse gas, was around 280 parts per million (ppm). This is more or less what you would expect for a planet experiencing the natural amelioration of the climate known as an interglacial, squeezed between the ice age that ended around 10,000 years ago and the one to come. Approaching 250 years later, however, this figure has increased dramatically to more than 380 ppm. Without drastic action, just a few decades from now, the level in the atmosphere of carbon dioxide and other greenhouse gases, such as methane, will be so high as to make dangerous climate change certain. Before taking a look at how this is likely to make itself felt, it is worth taking time to examine how both natural and human influences have impinged upon the climate, and how our ideas about what is happening to our current climate have changed over time.

WHAT IS CLIMATE CHANGE?

The Earth's climate is naturally variable and has experienced wild swings throughout its 4.6-billion-year history. More than 600 million years ago, glaciers pushed from the poles to the equator, enclosing the planet in a thick, icy carapace. In complete contrast, 55 million years ago, the Earth basked in some of the highest temperatures in its history, with sweltering continents and bath-water oceans. Nearer our time, ice ages have alternated with warmer interglacials – including the latest, within which our civilisation has developed and thrived. Now temperatures are on course to climb far higher than is normal for an interglacial, and human activities are the cause.

I doubt if the difference between weather and climate has ever been explained more succinctly, or more amusingly, than by the great American writer and humorist Mark Twain, who accurately noted that 'climate is what we expect; weather is what we get'[3]. Nowhere is this truer than in the UK, where we expect pleasantly warm, dry(ish) summers and mild, wet winters, but get everything from blistering heat waves and parching droughts to flash floods, blizzards and even tornadoes.

The climate, both of the Earth as a whole and of its constituent regions, is constantly changing in response to an enormous range of factors. These include the disposition of the land masses, as movement of the planet's tectonic plates carries them on a slow-motion dance across the surface of the Earth, sometimes from the equator to one or other of the poles and back. Over the course of the last 600 million years, for example, the voyages of the chunk of crust upon which Great Britain is located have led to a climate that has variously encompassed tropical, desert, polar and temperate conditions. Other influences that may lead to a changing regional or local climate include adjustments in the relative distribution of neighbouring land and water, and proximity to oceans and mountain belts.

While the climate of different parts of the planet can change over time, so can that of the whole Earth. This may be a consequence of adjustments in the geometry of the planet's orbit about the sun, changes in the radiation output of the sun itself, or variations in the composition of the Earth's atmosphere. Over the 4.6-billion-year history of our world, the climate has swung wildly from baking to frigid. One of the most extreme climates held the Earth in its grip between about 630 and 850 million years ago, during a period appropriately known as the Cryogenian. At this time, a combination of a weaker sun and low greenhouse gas levels in the atmosphere resulted in a global freeze, with huge ice sheets pushing southwards from the poles towards the equator and leading to so-called 'snowball Earth' conditions. While the details of exactly how much of the planet was covered by ice at this time remain a matter for debate, the most extreme models propose that the entire planet was covered in an icy carapace more than a kilometre thick.

In total contrast to 'snowball Earth', our world 55 million years ago was baking under some of the highest temperatures in its history. The end of the Palaeocene period and the start of succeeding Eocene times saw the planet heating up in one of the most extreme and rapid global warming events in geological history. This episode of abrupt climate change, known as the Palaeocene–Eocene Thermal Maximum, or PETM, has attracted considerable interest in the last few years, not surprisingly as it could quite easily provide an analogue to current global warming.

If this proves to be true, then we really are in trouble. The PETM spawned a sauna world of sweltering continents and bath-water oceans, with sea-surface temperatures climbing by 5–8°C and even the Arctic waters reaching sub-tropical temperatures. Extinctions occurred both in the oceans and on land, while sea levels climbed by 20 metres. The reason for this extreme temperature hike is yet to be corroborated, but it seems likely to have resulted from a giant methane 'burp' sourced by solid gas deposits, known as clathrates, stored in sea-floor sediments. Flooding of the atmosphere with this potent greenhouse gas is charged with locking in the sun's heat, and sending temperatures soaring.

For the last couple of million years, the Earth has been in the grip of alternating periods of cold and warm – ice ages and interglacial periods, within the latest of which our civilisation has developed. The temperature changes that accompanied the repeated cycles of ice-sheet growth and decay typically occurred slowly, over many thousands of years. On occasion, however, the climate changed extremely rapidly, rather like flipping a switch. Such so-called abrupt climate change may, at times, have involved the planet's climate switching from cold to warm, or vice versa, in just a few decades. Most notably, around 12,700 years ago, just as our world was becoming accustomed to growing post-glacial warmth, it was plunged – within a decade or so – into a period of bitter cold that lasted 1,300 years. This freezing episode, known as the Younger Dryas, saw average UK temperatures fall like a stone, with glaciers re-forming in upland areas. The reason remains uncertain, but it is suspected to be a consequence of a major slowdown or shutdown in the Gulf Steam and associated currents that carry warm waters from the tropics to high latitudes.

No other abrupt climate change event of the scale or rapidity of the Younger Dryas has occurred since – until now. Over the past century, and particularly in the last few decades, a new episode of rapid climate change has been initiated, with temperatures climbing quickly from 'normal' interglacial values. This time, however, the hike has little to do with nature, and is almost entirely the result of human activities artificially enriching the atmosphere with greenhouse gases.

CAN WE BE CERTAIN THAT THE EARTH IS HEATING UP?

The Earth is undergoing a period of very rapid and pronounced warming, which has driven up temperatures by 0.74°C over the last 100 years. The heat has really been on since the 1990s, with 11 of the hottest years ever recorded occurring in the last 13 years. Warming has been particularly strong on land and across the polar regions, where ice melting is accelerating dramatically. Heat waves and drought are on the rise, growing seasons are getting longer and frost and snow are far less common than in the past. Our planet is now within 1°C or so of its highest temperature in the last million years.

There is no doubt whatsoever that global temperatures are rising, and fast. In its fourth assessment report, the IPCC states that warming of the climate is 'unequivocal'. The evidence to support this is overwhelming, with both atmosphere and oceans warming rapidly, widespread melting of snow and ice, and an acceleration in the rate of sea-level rise. Over the last 100 years, the Earth's global surface temperature has climbed by 0.74°C, but the rate of warming over the past 50 years, and particularly since 1990, has risen dramatically – to such an extent that 11 of the hottest years ever recorded have occurred in the last 13 years. Going back much further, the widely debated 'hockey stick' graph, which combines proxy records of past temperatures, such as ice-core and tree-ring data, with the more recent instrumental record, shows how northern-hemisphere temperatures have changed over the past millennium, showing a sharp rise in temperatures during the twentieth century – rather like the curl at the end of a hockey stick.

This warming is not evenly distributed. On land, warming has been more rapid than in the seas, particularly in the northern hemisphere and especially during winter and spring. The icy wastes of the polar regions have warmed faster still, with average arctic temperatures, for example, rising at twice the rate for the world as a whole over the last 100 years. While the oceans have warmed less, they have been heated right down to an astonishing three-kilometre depth in places. Fortunately, in the course of this, they have also absorbed 80 per cent of the heat resulting from global warming; something they will not be able to do forever.

In the UK, the average central England temperature was reasonably stable throughout much of the twentieth century, but it has jumped by 1°C since 1980. The 1990s was the warmest decade since records began far back in the 1660s, but is virtually certain to be overtaken by the current decade. The hottest year ever was 2006, followed by 2007 (provisionally), 1999 and 1992, with seven of the ten hottest years occurring since 1995. 2006 and 2007 broke several records: July 2006 was the hottest month on record, while September 2006 was the warmest September and April 2007 the warmest April since observations began. For the period January to November 2007, UK temperatures were 1.4°C up on the long-term average. This should come as no surprise to those of us who have been around for a while, who can hardly have failed to notice that we now experience far fewer frosts and cold snaps than in earlier decades. Air frosts across the UK have fallen by a third since 1961, while in Scotland the frost-free season is already a month longer than it was in the swinging sixties. Snow is rapidly becoming a rarity in many parts of the UK, most particularly in southern

England, where the number of days of lying snow has plummeted by three-quarters since the early 1960s.

The summers are getting significantly hotter too, with 25°C exceeded twice as often in the 1990s as in the first half of the twentieth century. One consequence is that hosepipe bans and drought orders – unheard of 50 years ago – are now an accepted part of our lives, with more than 13 million people affected across England and Wales in 2006. The growing season is also getting longer, and is now extended by around a month compared to a century ago. Even the chilly waters that bathe our coasts are affected, although the 0.7°C rise so far is hardly enough to make Skegness the new Cannes.

In addition to the rise in average temperatures, extreme highs are also becoming more common. July 1995 in Chicago, for example, saw daytime temperatures reach 41°C, with night-time temperatures as high as 29°C. More recently, the baking summer heat wave of 2003 shattered temperature records across the UK and Europe, and was probably the hottest summer for 500 years.

The most worrying aspect of global warming, however, is undoubtedly the degree to which it is affecting polar regions. The Arctic and Antarctic seem to be extremely sensitive to the increasing concentration of greenhouse gases in the atmosphere, and temperatures at these high latitudes are already climbing far faster than elsewhere on the planet. On the Antarctic Peninsula, they have risen 2.5°C in the last 40 years. At the other end of the Earth, Siberia and Alaska are warming faster than almost anywhere else, with a 3°C rise over the same period. Across the Arctic as a whole, temperatures have risen by an average of 0.4°C a decade since the 1960s: a rate of increase unprecedented since the last ice age. With the ice sheets of Greenland and Antarctica together holding sufficient water to raise sea levels by 70 metres, the impact of warming in these regions is of critical importance. Already, the break-up of the Greenland Ice Sheet is seen as a real threat to the world's coastlines – the resulting seven-metre rise in sea level being sufficient to drown most coastal towns and cities.

ISN'T OUR CLIMATE NATURALLY VARIABLE?

Even in the last few thousand years, our planet's climate has exhibited natural variations. Since the end of the last ice age, 11,500 years ago, the world has been in an interglacial known as the Holocene, during which temperatures have oscillated in response to changes in the sun's activity, variations in ocean currents and large volcanic eruptions. The last 1,000 years have seen both the Medieval Warm Period, during which Vikings colonised Greenland, and the Little Ice Age, which saw bitter winters in Europe and frost fairs on the River Thames. Unlike current global warming, however, neither phenomenon appears to have affected the whole planet.

Our dynamic planet is constantly changing. The continents creep across its surface at the speed our fingernails grow; life-forms evolve, prosper and fade into extinction; the climate – both globally and locally – swings from one extreme to another. Arguably, the biggest swings in climate happened over the last couple of million years as ice sheets swept down from the poles on numerous occasions, only to retreat again as temperatures climbed during the warmer interglacial periods. Following the end of the last ice age, 11,500 years ago, the world entered the current interglacial, which we know as the Holocene.

On the whole, the Holocene climate can best be described as mild, and it has been sufficiently stable to provide the perfect conditions for human life to thrive. Nonetheless, significant variations can be recognised that demonstrate that even during relatively stable periods, our planet's climate is constantly restless. Between about 9,000 and 5,000 years ago, during the so-called Holocene Thermal Maximum (HTM), our planet was pleasantly balmy, with temperatures in Siberia climbing by up to 9°C and Arctic temperatures higher than they are at present. Following the end of the HTM, temperatures gradually declined until around 2,000 years ago. Since this time, the climate has oscillated between warmer and colder, resulting in climate phases known as the Medieval Warm Period (MWP) and the Little Ice Age (LIA). The MWP saw higher temperatures between the late ninth and early fourteenth centuries, which allowed new vineyards to spring up across the UK, and purportedly encouraged Viking emigrants to settle parts of Greenland. The succeeding LIA, which lasted until the second half of the nineteenth century, involved a modest cooling of the northern hemisphere, perhaps by only around 1°C, but this was sufficient to bring bitterly cold winters to Europe and North America. Iceland was frequently ice-locked, contributing to a famine that cut the population in half, while in Switzerland glaciers remorselessly advanced, engulfing farmsteads and burying high mountain communities. New York harbour froze, and, in the winter of 1622, part of the Bosphorus – which separates Europe from Asia – was also ice-bound. In the UK, exceptionally cold winters permitted frost fairs on a frozen River Thames, provided the background to a number of Dickens' gloomier works, and fostered Britain's continued fascination with snowy Christmases.

To those of a sceptical bent, the changes to the climate that we see around us today appear little different to those natural variations associated with the Medieval Warm Period or the Little Ice Age, but there are important differences. Although the current warming is clearly global in extent, both the MWP and the LIA seem either to have affected different hemispheres at different times or to have been confined predominantly to the northern hemisphere.

A definitive cause for the Medieval Warm Period, which affected the north a few hundred years before making itself felt south of the equator, remains to be established, but one possibility is that it was at least in part a consequence of the redistribution of heat around the planet due to changes in ocean currents. The underlying cause of the Little Ice Age is somewhat better understood: it is thought to have resulted from of a combination of reduced output from the sun and the cooling effect of an explosive burst of volcanic activity. For much of the time that the northern hemisphere shivered during the LIA, the sun's activity seems to have been depressed, firstly during a period known as the Spörer Minimum, and later by the better known Maunder Minimum. In addition, major volcanic eruptions contributed to the reduced temperatures by pumping out large volumes of sulphur particles, which act as a very effective sunscreen once distributed throughout the stratosphere. Two volcanic events stand out: firstly the 1783 Laki eruption in Iceland, which wafted a sulphurous fog across Europe, causing temperatures the following winter to plunge by 3°C; secondly, the huge 1815 eruption of the Indonesian volcano Tambora – the greatest eruption for 1,000 years, which reduced northern hemisphere temperatures by around 0.7°C, and resulted in the so-called 'year without a summer' in 1816. Crops were lost to snow and frost across Europe and eastern North America, with resulting shortages of grain leading to bread riots, famine and disease, in what has been described as the last great subsistence crisis in Europe.

Episodes of regional or hemispherical climate change, as represented by the Medieval Warm Period and Little Ice Age, are very different from the global ramping up of temperatures that have characterised the twentieth century and particularly the last few decades. With no significant increase in the sun's activity, continued warming can only be explained by the rapid increase in the level of carbon dioxide and other greenhouse gases in the atmosphere.

ARE WE SURE THAT HUMAN ACTIVITIES ARE CAUSING CLIMATE CHANGE?

There is no doubt that current warming is the result of greenhouse gas emissions arising from human activities. The problem was foretold as far back as the 1890s, when Swedish chemist Svante Arrhenius calculated that a doubling of the concentration of carbon dioxide in the atmosphere would result in a 5°C rise. While Arrhenius thought that this would not happen until around 4000 AD, however, it now looks like we could double emissions before 2100. Global warming cannot be explained by changes in solar activity, with the sun relatively stable over the course of the twentieth century. Like it or not, mankind's polluting activities are the only explanation.

The only uncertainty about current climate change is how big a problem it is going to be, for us and for the countless species we share the planet with. In terms of the underlying cause, there is absolutely no doubt that human activities are responsible. In its 2007 assessment, the IPCC reports that there is a 'very high confidence' that human activities since

1750 have had an overall warming effect, and goes on to recognize that most of the global temperature increase observed since the mid-twentieth century is very likely the result of greenhouse gas emissions arising from our polluting lifestyles. The use of terms such as 'very likely' leaves the door open for climate change deniers to decry – 'ah, so it isn't certain then?' It must always be remembered, however, that IPCC assessments are highly politicised, with representatives of all UN countries having the opportunity to pore over each sentence, demanding rewording and even removal if they are not satisfied. As a consequence of this, the final product is inherently conservative and optimistic. Left to themselves, many jobbing climate scientists involved in the accumulation of the data that went into the report would undoubtedly prefer the words 'very likely' to be replaced by 'unequivocally'.

The idea that human activities are driving global warming should come as no surprise at all. The Swedish chemist Svante Arrhenius calculated in the 1890s that a doubling of the level of carbon dioxide in the atmosphere would result in a global temperature rise of about 5°C. Considering that he was working alone, without access to super-computers and their modelling capabilities, this is a remarkably accurate prediction, with current models for a doubling of carbon dioxide forecasting a temperature rise of close to 4°C. Arrhenius was way out, however, in his prediction of how long it would take for human activities to double the amount of carbon dioxide in the atmosphere. While he guessed it would be reached somewhere around 4000 AD, it looks as if this dubious landmark will be achieved, without drastic emissions cuts, sometime before 2100.

Arrhenius's work underpins probably the simplest and best answer to those climate sceptics and deniers who would have us believe that (a) global warming is not happening or (b) if it is happening it is the result of natural variations in the climate. We know that carbon dioxide and other greenhouse gases, such as methane, warm up the atmosphere, and we can calculate how much warming will result from any particular level of greenhouse gases. We can therefore look at how much warming of our planet there has been and match it with the rise in atmospheric greenhouse gases to find out if they agree – and they do. Current warming of the planet is a consequence of increased greenhouse gas concentrations in the atmosphere brought about by mankind's polluting endeavours – end of story.

This simple answer is also supported by the fact that alternative models have no basis in scientific fact. The sun cannot be held responsible as there has been no significant increase in its activity capable of driving rapid warming, in particular over the last few decades when temperatures have really started to accelerate. Similarly, the idea touted in a recent, and justifiably derided, UK television programme, that current warming is due to the interaction of cosmic rays with the atmosphere, does not stand up under rigorous scientific analysis. Another argument proposes that the amount of carbon dioxide in the atmosphere, even without added emissions, is just too small to have any impact on temperatures, which is simply untrue. The total amount of atmospheric carbon dioxide is irrelevant; it is the increase that is important – carbon dioxide levels are up 37 per cent since pre-industrial times, methane up 248 per cent, and other greenhouse gas concentrations in the atmosphere up sharply too.

Computer models of the climate are clever enough now to rule out alternative causes for recent warming, being able not only to predict how the climate is affected by greenhouse gas levels in the atmosphere, but also to examine the effects of other important factors such as changes in solar activity or the effects of large volcanic eruptions. Both of these are likely to have had some influence on the twentieth century temperature curve, but neither can explain the very rapid warming of recent decades. Computer models that take into account just solar output and volcanic activity simply do not predict the current warming, whereas adding in the observed greenhouse gas rise results in a close match with a high degree of certainty.

The simple fact is that we and our activities are causing climate change, and the sooner we recognise this, the sooner we can concentrate on the important job of tackling the problem.

HOW ARE GREENHOUSE GASES WARMING THE PLANET?

Our world is a natural greenhouse. Visible radiation from the sun passes easily through the atmosphere, to heat up the surface and produce long-wave, infra-red radiation. This is unable to make the return trip because it is very efficiently absorbed by so-called 'greenhouse gases'. This natural 'greenhouse effect', which sees heat trapped in the lower atmosphere, is being augmented by emissions from human activities that have driven up carbon dioxide levels in the atmosphere from 280 parts per million (ppm) in pre-industrial times to 384 ppm in 2007. Today, we add 26 billion tonnes of carbon dioxide to the atmosphere every year – that is nearly four tonnes for every man, woman and child on the planet.

In order to keep the surface warm, the Earth's atmosphere acts in exactly the same way as a greenhouse. Visible radiation from the sun travels relatively unimpeded through the atmosphere, where it heats up the Earth's surface, producing long-wave, infra-red radiation. This radiation is very efficiently absorbed by water vapour, carbon dioxide, methane and other greenhouse gases in the Earth's atmosphere. As a consequence, heat is trapped in the lower atmosphere rather than being released back into space. Such a natural 'greenhouse effect' is vital to life on Earth as it helps to insulate the surface from the frigid cold of outer space and evens out the temperature variations between day and night. If taken to extremes, however, it can become life's nemesis. On our sterile sister planet, Venus, for example, the thick, carbon dioxide atmosphere keeps surface temperatures at a blistering 483°C – a salutary warning if ever there was one.

The increase in concentration of greenhouse gases in the Earth's atmosphere, which is driving contemporary climate change, is primarily a consequence of fossil fuel burning, although cement production also has an impact, currently accounting for around five per cent of emissions. These activities, along with accompanying land-use changes, especially deforestation, are pushing up atmospheric concentrations of carbon at an alarming rate. On pre-industrial Earth, the concentration of carbon dioxide in the atmosphere was about 280 ppm; now it is 384 ppm and climbing at more than two parts per million every year. This equates to a total mass of around three trillion tonnes of carbon dioxide[4] currently present in the Earth's atmosphere – more usually expressed as 3,000 Giga-tonnes[5]. To this we are adding about 26 Giga-tonnes every single year – or nearly four tonnes per person.

While carbon dioxide is the primary culprit in the warming of the atmosphere, other gases must also take some of the responsibility – namely methane, nitrous oxide, ozone, chlorofluorocarbons (CFCs), hydrofluorocarbons (HFCs), and even humble water vapour. At around two parts per million in total, methane makes up a tiny proportion of the Earth's atmosphere, and far less than carbon dioxide. It is, however, a much more potent greenhouse gas. Although a methane molecule will only stay in the atmosphere for a decade or so, compared with more than a century for a molecule of carbon dioxide, it will, in that time, have a warming impact a third as great as a carbon dioxide molecule in the course of its much longer lifetime. Like methane, ozone, chlorofluorocarbons, hydrofluorocarbons and nitrous oxide also punch above their weight in terms of trapping heat. Even plain old water vapour, although not a very strong greenhouse gas, makes an important contribution to warming just through its sheer volume in the atmosphere – and its concentration is climbing at around one per cent every decade.

Because of the big differences in concentration, potential for trapping heat, and atmospheric lifespan, comparing the global warming capabilities of the different greenhouse gases is far from straightforward. To make things simpler, climate scientists attach Global Warming Potential (GWP) values to the various greenhouse gases, whereby – for example – carbon dioxide is 1 and methane is 23. Multiplying the GWP of a gas by its concentration in the atmosphere results in a carbon dioxide equivalent, which is used as a basis for grouping together all the greenhouse gases, as it were, under one banner. Today, the basket of greenhouse gases, taken together, adds up to a carbon equivalent atmospheric concentration of at least 430 ppm, compared with 384 for carbon dioxide alone.

WHATEVER HAPPENED TO GLOBAL COOLING AND GLOBAL DIMMING?

It doesn't seem long ago that the big worry was global cooling and the imminence of the next ice age; a concern that arose largely from the fact that the Earth cooled slightly between the 1940s and the early 1970s. Climate scientists now know that this cooler episode was the result of industrial pollutants in the atmosphere masking the true warming trend. Global dimming, the fall-off in the amount of the sun's energy reaching the Earth's surface between the 1950s and 1970s, was also a consequence of industrial pollution. This trend has reversed since the 1990s as the atmosphere has become cleaner, causing 'global brightening', which is bad news for climate change.

While concern over global warming was growing in scientific circles during the 1970s, this rarely penetrated into public perception – indeed, most of the popular talk of the time was of global cooling and the imminent arrival of the next ice age. In the UK, such talk was bolstered by a succession of bad winters in the late 1970s and early 1980s, leading to a flurry of press interest in the return of the glaciers. In the scientific community, an episode of global cooling was recognised, with temperatures showing a slight fall from the 1940s to the 1970s, after which they began to rise rapidly. Although expounded by some as evidence that we would soon be overwhelmed with ice, climate scientists can now explain the brief cooling episode in terms of an increase in industrial atmospheric pollution, including sulphur, aerosols and soot. These tiny particles are very effective at absorbing and reflecting solar radiation, thereby reducing the amount of the sun's energy reaching the Earth's surface, and causing temperatures to slump. The particles also act as nuclei for cloud droplets. If there are many particles, clouds are formed that consist of a large number of smaller droplets, as opposed to a smaller number of larger ones. Such clouds tend to be more reflective, so enhancing the cooling effect.

Notwithstanding the recent cooling blip, we are certainly in an interglacial period, so under normal circumstances the ice could be expected to return in anything from several to a few tens of millennia. New research suggests, however, that the huge quantities of greenhouse gases we are pumping into the atmosphere may cause us to skip anything from the next ice age up to the next five. This would mean that we might have to wait half a million years before conditions allow the ice sheets to start to form once more.

Industrial pollution, in the form of soot, smoke and chemical aerosols, is also held responsible for another phenomenon, known as global dimming, which caused a bit of kerfuffle in the climate science community and the media a couple of years ago. On occasion, the dimming idea was presented as an alternative explanation of what was happening to the Earth's climate. In reality, however, global dimming and global warming are actually linked, but in such a way that forecasts for future temperature rises may be even more conservative than expected.

The global dimming idea relates to the gradual reduction, by a percentage point or two every decade since the 1950s, in the amount of solar radiation reaching the Earth's surface. Apart from a couple of dips arising from the huge quantities of sulphur pumped into the atmosphere by the 1982 eruption of El Chichón (Mexico) and the 1991 Pinatubo (Philippines) blast, however, the trend has reversed itself since the early 1990s, with progressively more solar radiation now making it through to the surface. The cause can easily be established by looking at the concentration of sulphur aerosols in the atmosphere, which has headed consistently downwards over the last fifteen years or so. Mainly as a result of 'cleaner air acts', which have led to the introduction of more efficient and less polluting technologies and reduced sulphur emissions, our atmosphere is getting cleaner – and with the sunlight-blocking haze fading away, global dimming has been superseded by global brightening.

Cleaner air is great for everyone, but this is bad news for global warming. Meinrat Andrae of the Maz Planck Institute in Mainz, Germany and his colleagues warn that the warming effect of greenhouse gas emissions has been kept partly in check by the 'parasol' of other atmospheric pollutants from industry responsible for global dimming, a situation they liken to driving with one foot on the accelerator and the other on the brake. As the atmosphere is cleaned up and the moderating influence of the parasol is lost, Andrae and his fellow researchers warn that the end result could be temperatures at least 6°C warmer by the end of the century.

DOES CLIMATE CHANGE JUST MEAN A WARMER WORLD?

Climate change means far more than just a warmer planet. It means wholesale, dramatic and insidious modifications to our world that will affect everyone and everything on Earth. The consequences of failure to prevent dangerous climate change make bleak reading: more and bigger storms; increased floods and droughts; desertification of large parts of the planet; collapse of the polar ice sheets; massive landslides and meltwater breakouts in mountainous terrain; huge releases of methane from permafrost and sea-floor sediments; catastrophically rising sea levels; perhaps even the slowdown or shutdown of the Gulf Stream. Ultimately, large, rapid sea-level rises could even trigger more volcanic eruptions, earthquakes, underwater landslides and tsunamis.

We use the term 'climate change', rather than 'global warming', because a rise in the planet's actual temperature is only one effect of increasing the concentration of greenhouse gases in the atmosphere. In fact, the warming of our world is an insidious process that will, one way or another, affect everyone and everything on the planet. So far-ranging are the potential impacts of a dramatically changing climate that there is nowhere to run to and nowhere to hide, either for us or for the countless species with which we share this small and fragile planet. Human society can at least attempt to adapt to the new conditions, but for many animal and plant species the changes are happening too fast. If temperatures reach 4°C above pre-industrial levels, they will have climbed higher in 100 years than in the previous 15,000. Climate change, in concert with the myriad other ways in which human activities impact upon ecosystems, means that we are currently seeing a massive rise in the rate of extinctions – sometimes of species that we have never even catalogued or seen.

As you would expect, a warmer planet means less ice and snow. Already, ski resorts are confronting a bleak future, with ice-bound mountain faces starting to crumble, and glaciers in the Alps, Himalayas, Andes and elsewhere in rapid retreat. Polar areas are warming much faster than the rest of the planet, so the ice here is melting and breaking up even more rapidly. The consequence is an increase in the rate of sea-level rise, with the potential – eventually – to inundate all coastal towns and cities. As climate change really begins to bite, the vast areas of permafrost that stretch across Arctic Canada and the seemingly infinite frozen wastes of northern Siberia will also start to melt, pumping out increasing quantities of the potent greenhouse gas methane. This is one example of what climate scientists call a positive feedback mechanism, which sees rising temperatures causing something to happen that raises temperatures even further. Other positive feedback mechanisms are also expected as the Earth warms: and it looks as if the soils, the forests, and the oceans – which up to now have absorbed about half of all human emissions – are already becoming less effective carbon sinks. This means that they are taking up less carbon; a situation that may culminate in their eventually becoming carbon sources, actually adding carbon dioxide to the atmosphere and giving warming an added boost.

The melting of polar ice could also trigger changes in ocean current systems, particularly in the North Atlantic. Here, concerns have been voiced for some time that the freshwater pouring into the Arctic Ocean from the melting Greenland Ice Sheet, and from rejuvenated Canadian and Siberian rivers, may be sufficient to slow or shut down the Gulf Stream and associated currents that provide Ireland, the UK, and much of western Europe with a balmier climate than they have any right to expect, given that they share latitudes with Siberia and Labrador. Any dramatic slowing of the currents could have us reaching for our thermal underwear rather than our sunscreen.

In Iceland, the loss of the Vatnajökul Ice Cap is sure to spur those dormant volcanoes beneath into action, while right across the planet, the increased load of sea-water pushing down on the margins of the continents could bring a rise in the level of geological activity, including volcanic eruptions, submarine landslides and tsunamis. If the oceans warm sufficiently the huge quantities of solid methane that are currently stored in sea-floor sediments may also be transformed to gas, leaking into the atmosphere in burps and belches in yet another positive feedback effect.

As rapidly rising greenhouse gas emissions bounce our world's climate out of its reasonably stable state, it should come as no surprise that the weather will become more unpredictable too. Increased storminess is already being reported for both the tropics and the UK, and more extreme precipitation is on the rise. On the whole, climate change is predicted to see wet places getting wetter – not good news for western Scotland or the English Lake District – and dry places getting drier – bad news for southeast England, the South West United States, much of the southern Mediterranean and Australia.

Clearly, a warmer planet is just one of the many ramifications of dangerous climate change, but rising temperatures are the main driver behind the other contents of the climate-change portfolio. Ultimately, and without urgent action, it will bring about not only these physical effects, but also their concerted product – a struggling global economy and a rapidly unravelling social fabric.

IS THE GULF STREAM FALTERING?

The Gulf Stream and its northward extension, the North Atlantic Drift, play a critical role in preventing the UK and much of Europe experiencing the bitter winter weather of other regions at comparable latitudes, such as northern Canada and eastern Siberia. But are the currents beginning to falter? Recent measurements have revealed highly erratic behaviour that could be a warning of sudden and dramatic change: one that could herald a ruinous deterioration of the European climate and have widespread ramifications across the world. Such is the level of concern over the future behaviour of the Gulf Stream that a new UK monitoring system, known as Rapid Watch, will be keeping an eye on things until at least 2014.

While outrageously exaggerated in the typical Hollywood mould, the disaster movie *The Day After Tomorrow* bore a real and worrying message: our rapidly changing climate is likely to have a number of unexpected and no doubt nasty surprises in store for us. Some parts of the world may get much colder, although the idea that we will be plunged into a new ice age within weeks is pure fiction.

Any cooling effect arising from climate change is likely to be closely linked to the behaviour of the worldwide system of ocean currents known as the Thermohaline Circulation (THC) or Global Conveyor, which transfers vast quantities of heat throughout all the major ocean basins. The system is driven by changes in temperature and saltiness, both of which affect the density of the water, and therefore its tendency to sink or remain at shallow levels. The THC is largely propelled by ocean current behaviour in the North Atlantic, where the Gulf Stream and its extension, the North Atlantic Drift (together making up the Atlantic Thermohaline Circulation or ATHC) carry the hot-tub waters of the Gulf of Mexico as far north as the Arctic Circle. As they approach higher latitudes, evaporation due to winds blowing across the sea surface cools these warm waters, and also makes them saltier and therefore denser. Under the freezing conditions of the Arctic, sea ice forms, expelling salt and increasing the saltiness and density of the surrounding water to such a degree that it starts to sink, eventually returning southwards in a current known as the North Atlantic Deep Water or NADW, which connects with the rest of the Global Conveyor.

The Gulf Stream and its associated currents are 60 times more powerful than the Amazon River. They also transport a staggering amount of heat northwards every year, roughly equivalent to the thermal output of a million large power stations – 100 times the amount of energy used each year by our entire civilisation. Unlike much of the heat we generate, that carried north by the Gulf Stream is put to good use, helping to maintain a relatively benign climate in the UK and northwest Europe, with temperatures up to 8°C higher than in comparable latitudes such as northern Canada or the Kamchatka Peninsula of eastern Siberia. The North Atlantic Drift provides the balmy conditions that allow palms and other sub-tropical plants to thrive in western Ireland, southwest England and parts of western Scotland, and keeps Norway's Lofoten Islands ice-free despite their location within the Arctic Circle.

A weakening of these currents has been linked in the past with a deterioration of the North Atlantic climate, and most global climate models predict that the current warming may have a weakening effect at some point in the future. Recent evidence, however, has led to worries that this process may already have started, consigning the inhabitants of Europe to life in a bubble of cold within a world that continues to heat up. Concerns were first voiced just a few years ago, with evidence that a combination of increased precipitation, melting of sea ice and Greenland glaciers and greater northward flow of freshwater from Siberian and Canadian rivers – all consequences of climate change – were conspiring to reduce the salinity of the North Atlantic Drift. If this caused a large enough fall in density, the waters would no longer sink, so short-circuiting the ATHC by stopping or slowing the flow of the NADW. On top of this, observations made by Faeroe Island and British scientists suggested that the return of deep, cold water between Greenland and Scotland had already slowed by 20 per cent.

Scariest of all, in 2005, Harry Bryden and his team at the UK's National Oceanography Centre in Southampton published evidence for a 30-per-cent slowdown in the North Atlantic Drift. This huge drop seemed to have happened very recently – since 1992 – and was portrayed, in some sections of the media, as a portent of freezing conditions to come. A new system of monitoring buoys, installed by the UK, has shown, however, that the circulation varies enormously and erratically during the course of a year. Bryden and his colleagues just happened to measure the circulation at a low point, from which it has since recovered. The question is, though, has the ATHC always behaved in such a highly irregular manner, or could this indicate some form of destabilisation prior to a dramatic slowdown or even shutdown? Scientists were certainly surprised when the new monitoring system flagged up the cessation of part of the circulation for ten days in November 2004. Lloyd Keigwin of the Woods Hole Oceanographic Institution in Massachusetts described this event as 'the most abrupt change in the whole [climate] record'. He was probably also voicing the concerns of many other scientists when he posed the question 'How can we rule out a longer shutdown in the future?' Perhaps the UK's new Rapid Watch project, a £16-million network of sensors set to monitor current changes to 2014, will provide the answers.

IS THE WORLD GETTING STORMIER?

Climate change models predict stormy times ahead, but it looks as though they are already with us. As the atmosphere warms, so do the oceans, with the surface waters of the Atlantic heating up by 0.7°C over the past century. Since the mid-1990s alone, warmer seas have been responsible for a 40-per-cent increase in Atlantic hurricane activity and, according to some scientists, the most powerful tropical cyclones now occur twice as often as they did 30 years ago. Europe and the UK, too, have been taking a pounding in recent decades, with more storms and bigger waves, and a damage cost measured in the tens of billions of Euros.

The current debate about how climate change will affect our future weather is almost as stormy as the predictions themselves. Over the last couple of years a battle has raged among US hurricane researchers about whether the recent increase in the number of powerful tropical cyclones is driven by human-induced climate change or whether it is part of a natural cycle. The protagonists have not yet come to blows, at least not in public, but some are refusing to speak to one another or appear on the same podium at scientific conferences. All quite childish really, but important nevertheless, as at stake is proof that climate change is already beginning to have a major impact on the world's weather systems.

Just eight years ago, the general consensus in the research community was that a doubling (from pre-industrial times) of carbon dioxide levels to around 550 ppm would not affect the frequency of storms at all, and only push up their severity by ten per cent or so. In the last few years, however, unprecedented hurricane activity, particularly in the Atlantic, has resulted in a number of leading hurricane researchers breaking ranks. 2004 was one of the worst seasons on record, with five hurricanes making landfall in the United States, four of them hitting Florida alone. The following season was the most active ever, with 15 hurricanes – including Katrina, which devastated New Orleans, taking over 2,000 lives and costing more than US$100 billion in damage and destruction.

The quarrel centres on whether this unprecedented activity is climate change driven or not. Veteran hurricane forecaster Bill Gray of the University of Colorado and his team are convinced that the recent flurry of storms is part of a natural cycle that saw a similar upsurge in activity between 1940 and 1960, and that could keep going for another ten years or so before dying down again. Others, such as Kevin Trenberth of the National Center for Atmospheric Research in Boulder, Colorado, Kerry Emanuel of MIT, and Peter Webster of the Georgia Institute of Technology in Atlanta, see the hand of climate change at work. All link the accelerating activity to warmer seas feeding more powerful storms, pointing to the fact that average Atlantic sea-surface temperatures have climbed 0.7°C over the last century. According to Emanuel, the destructive capacity of Atlantic storms has almost doubled over the last 30 years. This idea gets support from Peter Webster and his colleagues, who reveal that twice as many of the most powerful category 4 and 5 storms are now running amok across the planet as three decades ago. With more scientists joining their ranks, a new consensus is developing around the idea that climate change is making itself felt through the formation of bigger and badder tropical cyclones, with rising sea surface temperatures the main driver. The latest research, recently published in the journal *Nature* by my

UCL colleague Mark Saunders, provides more support for a climate change link by showing that warmer seas were responsible for a 40 per cent hike in Atlantic hurricane activity between the mid-1990s and 2005.

As well as getting bigger and blusterier, tropical cyclones also seem to be venturing beyond their traditional hunting grounds, which are the tropical North Atlantic, tropical northwest-, northeast- and southeast Pacific, and the Indian Ocean. In 2003, Hurricane Caterina struck the north coast of Brazil, confounding scientists who thought that hurricanes could not form in the South Atlantic. In the North Atlantic, too, storms are moving further afield, and in October 2005, Hurricane Vince was accorded the honour of being the first hurricane to strike Spain. The Atlantic hurricane season seems to be getting longer as well. Traditionally it lasts from the beginning of June to the end of November, but the final storm of the 2005 season did not peter out until January 2006, and in 2007, the season lasted from early May until mid-December.

Europe also seems to be coming under increasing attack. Last October the UK marked the twentieth anniversary of the Great Storm of 1987, which battered much of southern England and brought down around 15 million trees. Although it was vaunted at the time as an extreme event that might be expected to happen every 200 years or so, another major storm arrived just three years later, taking more than 100 lives in the UK, Denmark and Germany. In all, 55 severe windstorms have rampaged across the region since 1970, causing damage costing tens of billions of Euros. Research by the UK Met Office shows that Britain is now twice as stormy as it was 50 years ago, although further observations are needed to confirm whether this upward trend is likely to continue. If it does, then we are in for stormy weather indeed. Increasing windiness is also agitating the sea around our shores, with average wave heights around the southern and western coasts of the UK a metre higher now than they were in the 1970s. The biggest waves have increased their height by a third to an alarming ten metres – a trend that, if it continues, will make sailing and windsurfing rather more exciting in the future.

ARE FLOODS BECOMING MORE COMMON?

As our planet heats up, those parts of the world familiar with rain are already seeing more of it. 2007 was the year of the flood, with torrential rains and storm surges affecting tens of millions of people across the UK, Mexico, India, Bangladesh, Africa and elsewhere. The annual number of floods has shot up from around 100 in the early 1990s to 250 or so during the early years of the new millennium, partly through climate change driving more extreme rainfall events and storms, and partly due to exacerbating human activities such as deforestation and urbanisation.

2007 was the year of the flood. In the UK, torrential summer rains brought almost unprecedented flooding across northeast and central England, with the inundation of 55,000 homes and businesses causing damage costing over six billion Euros. Impressive as this sounds, other countries fared far worse. In Africa, two million people suffered the most devastating floods in 35 years, with 650,000 losing their homes, while across Pakistan, India, Nepal and Bangladesh, monsoon floods disrupted the lives of an extraordinary 20 million people and left 1,500 dead. Catastrophic floods were also reported in Korea, China, Indonesia,

Argentina, Haiti, Mexico and Nicaragua. The widespread flooding of 2007 should not come as a total surprise, with the Dartmouth Flood Observatory in the USA reporting that the annual number of floods worldwide has climbed rapidly from around 100 in the early 1990s to more than 250 in the first few years of the new millennium.

Since 1990, more than a thousand river-flood-related disasters have taken well over 100,000 lives across the world, and made life a misery for billions. In China alone, where flooding on the Yangtze, Yellow and other rivers dwarfs anything seen elsewhere on the planet, biblical floods in 1991 and 1998 each affected more than 200 million people. 2005 was another bad year, when floods in the Yangtze basin took close to 2,000 lives and displaced an incredible 14 million people.

There have always been devastating river floods, but it seems now that there are even more of them. This is only to be expected, partly because a changing climate has pushed up by four per cent the number of extreme rainfall events at mid- to high latitudes, but also because there are now many more people living in areas where floods are a problem. Furthermore, changes to land use, such as deforestation and increasing urbanisation, are also conspiring to increase run-off and enhance the flood threat. Just think how many people have paved over their gardens in your street, stopping water from infiltrating into the ground. In London, an astonishing two thirds of front gardens have been transformed into hard standing, adding up to an area of 30 square kilometres.

Because there are human factors at play, it is extremely difficult to pinpoint the role of climate change in increased flooding, but it seems that it is making a significant contribution. Global climate models predict that, on the whole, climate change will lead to wet places getting wetter and dry places getting drier. They also forecast that rainfall will become more intense – in other words, more rain will fall over a shorter period. The signs are that we are already seeing this, with a disproportionate number of extreme[6] floods across the world occurring in the last few decades of the twentieth century. A continuation of this trend will ensure that the flood threat associated with many of the world's great river systems will increase dramatically. If coastal as well as river flooding is taken into account, then more than half a billion people worldwide are already at risk from the most severe flooding.

South Asia has a particular problem, with major coastal and river flooding now a perennial occurrence. In 2005, the Indian city of Mumbai was hit by record monsoon rains, with nearly 1.5 metres of rain swamping the region and taking more than a thousand lives. Two years later, in 2007, the monsoon rains brought even more devastation, with an estimated 45 million people affected in India alone. The same year also brought massive flooding to Bangladesh, where a huge storm surge driven by Cyclone Sidr took 3,000 lives and touched around 22 million.

Major flooding also seems to happen almost every year in the developed world. Following the unprecedented 2002 floods that inundated Prague and many German and Austrian cities, the spring of 2006 saw a River Danube swollen by snow-melt and torrential rains reach a 100-year high and burst its banks to flood much of Serbia, Bulgaria and Romania. In the USA, the great Midwest floods of 1993 drowned hundreds of towns and 15 million acres of farmland across seven states, and destroyed 10,000 homes. Rainfall in the region rose by up to 20 per cent over the twentieth century, and this trend is expected to continue. Hurricanes also bring vast amounts of rain. In 1998, Hurricane Mitch dumped a third of a metre of water on Honduras and Nicaragua in just a few days – triggering more than a million mudslides. As the world warms, it seems that hurricanes are getting wetter, and those hitting the USA already unload seven per cent more rain than they did 100 years ago.

Rainfall patterms across the UK are changing too. Since 1900, the frequency of intense rainfall has increased in winter and decreased in summer. This trend is predicted to continue, leading to progressively wetter winters and – notwithstanding 2007 – drier summers. Against a broad background of summer drought, the southern UK, in particular, can also look forward to more and bigger flash floods, spawned by electrical storms. The torrent that nearly washed away the Cornish town of Boscastle in August 2004 is surely just a forerunner of many similar events to come.

IS DROUGHT AN INCREASING PROBLEM?

It is likely that droughts have increased across many parts of the world since the 1970s, and today over 80 million people are in their grip. Africa, unsurprisingly, faces a bleak future of increasingly meagre rainfall and rivers reduced to trickles. Drought conditions and water resource problems are now also endemic in the western USA, while Australia is struggling with its worst drought in 1,000 years. Bigger and badder droughts mean that the Mediterranean region will find it increasingly difficult to find enough water to quench the thirst of a growing population and tourist trade, while the southern UK might have to resort to cloud seeding or towing icebergs from the Arctic to keep its reservoirs topped up.

A quick check of my research centre's online Global Drought Monitor reveals that on the morning of 18 December 2007 more than 87 million people woke to a world gripped by extreme drought. While this figure will vary from month to month and year to year, climate change is driving the numbers of those affected by extreme water shortages inexorably upwards. It seems intuitive to link higher temperatures with drier conditions, droughts and wildfires, and for many parts of the world, this is just what climate change is already bringing. In its Fourth Assessment Report, the IPCC notes that it is likely that drought has increased in many areas since the 1970s, with rainfall declining across the Mediterranean, the Sahel region, southern Africa and parts of southern Asia. Areas that are especially badly hit by drought at the moment include Australia, Spain and California – where Los Angeles last year experienced its driest year since 1877, with temperatures approaching those more typical of Death Valley, and the tinder-dry conditions across the state sparked some of the worst wildfires on record.

The western USA as a whole has had real water supply problems in recent years, with rainfall far below normal across eight states stretching from Arizona in the south to Montana in the north. Reservoirs in the region are half full, if that, and increasing water demand may mean they will never be full again. There is enormous concern that agriculture will fail across the region as water becomes increasingly scarce, bringing persistent dustbowl conditions such as those that devastated the southern plains in the 1930s. Then, a combination of ever-deepening drought and over-ploughing led to the loss of the topsoil, which blew across the region in great dust storms, burying fields and towns alike. By 1934, the drought was the worst in US history, stretching across 75 per cent of the country and affecting more than half of all states. By 1936, 140,000 square kilometres of formerly cultivated land had been destroyed for future crop production, while many times more had lost its topsoil. Looking ahead, higher temperatures will mean that soil moisture levels fall across much of the region, intensifying drought conditions. Farming and ranching already use 50 per cent of the region's water resources, leading to the pumping of more and more groundwater and the steady depletion of aquifers – a practice that clearly cannot be maintained as climate change progressively dries out the soils.

The majority of Australia is already desert, with most of the country's population living in the more hospitable coastal areas. Rising temperatures, however, are sure to make life even here increasingly difficult. The country is currently experiencing the 'Big Dry': the worst drought in 1,000 years, which has brought bone-dry conditions to six of Australia's seven states and territories, and to all of its major cities. This is hardly surprising with flows of the Murray-Darling river system, which provides three quarters of Australia's water, down almost 50 per cent. This is likely to be the start of a longer-term trend that will make this already-parched country even more desiccated.

Europe is not immune either: 2005 and 2006 were particularly bad years, especially in the south, where conditions were the worst since records were first kept 60 years ago. Ninety-seven per cent of Portugal experienced severe drought conditions, with water shortages leading to the destruction of many crops, while Spain also suffered to the extent that emergency boreholes had to be drilled for water. Across the Mediterranean, in Morocco and Tunisia, the parching conditions drove hungry farmers and their families from rural areas to the cities. Southern Europe is unlikely to benefit as much from increased winter rainfall as the north, and higher temperatures will mean even worse droughts.

In the UK, 2006 was an especially bad year. The southeast was held in the grip of one of the worst droughts for hundreds of years, with chalk streams no longer flowing and water hosepipe bans in place across the region. The problem is that winters are not as wet as they were, and any rain in the summer months either evaporates or is sucked up by plant life. The south east of England has always been pretty dry, but it is now one of the driest areas in Europe, with – according to one water company – less available water per head than Egypt or Sudan. In just a few decades, summers here could be around 2°C hotter and more than 30 per cent drier. Even with more winter rains, soil moisture levels will be on the way down, while the population and the demand for water will be inexorably on the up. Water metering will certainly be the norm in the decades ahead, but water companies are also examining more drastic solutions, including a national water grid, a system of canals, cloud seeding and even towing icebergs down from the Arctic.

WHAT IS HAPPENING IN THE ARCTIC?

The gigantic masses of ice locked up at the Earth's poles are crumbling at an ever-faster rate. In the Arctic, temperatures have risen by almost twice the global average over the last century. Every year, warmer summers melt more and more of the Greenland Ice Sheet's surface, and in just the last couple of years two of its biggest glaciers have doubled the speed at which they are moving towards the sea. The warmer climate has allowed a return of sheep farming to Greenland, and the multi-nationals are also moving in, attracted by the region's gold, oil and aluminium deposits.

You can actually hear the Greenland Ice Sheet tearing itself apart as it slides off the underlying crust at ever-increasing speeds. Harvard University seismologist Göran Ekström and his colleagues were puzzled by unusual seismic signals they were picking up, until they realised that they originated in breaking ice rather than breaking rock. Now, they have been able to explain the 'ice-quakes' as being due to the crumbling of Greenland's glaciers as they speed seawards on a bed of meltwater. The quakes are small, in the 4–5 magnitude range, but their numbers have been increasing – from between 6 and 15 a year in the 1990s to 32 in the first 10 months of 2005. The chunks of ice that are breaking up and slipping may be as large as Manhattan and as thick as the Empire State Building is high, and they reflect the astonishing acceleration of some of Greenland's largest glaciers in just the last few years.

With a staggering volume of 2.85 million cubic kilometres, the Greenland Ice Sheet is the second largest body of ice on Earth, and holds six per cent of the planet's freshwater. It covers an area only a little smaller than Mexico, and contains enough water to raise global sea level by more than seven metres. With the Arctic region warming at twice the rate of the rest of the planet, it looks as if the ice sheet is already beginning to fall apart. The area affected by summer melting has increased by 16 per cent over the past 27 years, and now amounts to more than a third of the entire surface area of the ice sheet. The melt line is also steadily climbing, and in 2002 and 2005 reached 2,000 metres above sea level. Around the margins of the ice sheet, the situation is even more worrying, with the total annual ice loss, even allowing for snowfall in the interior, more than doubling in the last decade from 96 cubic kilometres in 1996 to 239 cubic kilometres in 2006. This means that, on average, Greenland is now losing more than a cubic kilometre of ice – or a trillion litres of water – every 40 hours. Its contribution to global sea-level rise has tripled in less than ten years, and is likely to continue rising rapidly.

IPCC estimates of how fast sea level will rise during the twenty-first century are based upon slow, incremental melting of the great polar ice sheets, including that of Greenland, but do not consider the possibility that the ice sheets may physically break up. Top-down melting of Greenland's three-kilometre-thick ice carapace would take thousands of years to accomplish, but another mechanism seems to be intervening that could secure its disappearance in just a few centuries. Instead of the enormous amount of water produced by summer melting remaining at the surface and refreezing, or slowly percolating downwards, it is pouring down crevasses that rapidly channel it to the base of the ice sheet. In the words of climate scientist Richard Alley, of the University of Pennsylvania, 'we used to think it would take 10,000 years for meltwater at the surface of an ice sheet to penetrate to the bottom, now we know it takes 10 seconds'.

With meltwater lubricating the contact between the ice and the underlying bedrock, many of the glaciers that carry ice from Greenland's interior towards the sea are moving more quickly than expected. In just the last couple of years, two of Greenland's biggest glaciers – the Helheim and the Kangerdlugssuaq – have doubled their speed to around 14 kilometres a year; in 1998, the Jakobshavn glacier showed a similar acceleration. Together, these three glaciers drain nearly a fifth of the entire ice sheet, and there is real concern that others could follow, leading to wholesale collapse. Even if such a collapse does not happen this century, it is highly likely that temperature rises over the next few decades will trigger a tipping-point that will commit us to ice-sheet collapse and a sea-level rise of several metres in the centuries ahead.

What is bad for the rest of the world may not necessarily be so bad for the 55,000 inhabitants of Greenland. Today, sheep are grazing around the retreating margins of the ice sheet for the first time since the Vikings abandoned their settlements at the start of the Little Ice Age. With the growing season already a month longer, vegetable plots are popping up too, and in the summer of 2007 Greenlanders had their first taste of fresh, home-grown broccoli. The avaricious eyes of the multi-nationals are now turning towards this vast island, with gold already being mined, oil companies planning offshore surveys, and designs on the board for three aluminium smelters. All of this is good for Greenland's economy in the short term, perhaps, but bad for climate change. And notwithstanding access to fresh broccoli, all is not rosy for the inhabitants even now. The Inuit community, who rely for a living on hunting for seals and other Arctic wildlife, face extinction as their food source disappears. In 2005, there was not even kill enough to feed the thousands of dogs used by the hunters, and the government had to fly in emergency supplies of dog food to save them from starving.

WILL THE ARCTIC OCEAN SOON BE ICE FREE?

Much of the Arctic Ocean is permanently frozen, even at the height of summer. In the 1970s, the area of this persistent ice field never fell below seven million square kilometres – an area about the size of Australia. The summer of 2007, however, saw the sea ice extent slashed by 40 per cent. The most recent forecasts predict that summer sea ice will vanish altogether in as little as five or six years, opening up the Northwest and Northeast passages to trade, and bringing the oil and gas companies swarming to the region. More trade and more oil will push up emissions ever further, while the replacement of white ice with dark sea will lead to the absorption of more of the sun's energy, and even more warming.

Sometimes the pace of climate change is truly staggering. Just a few years ago, recognising that the permanent Arctic sea ice was beginning to suffer increasingly from local temperature hikes, climate scientists were warning that the Arctic Ocean could be ice free by 2070 to 2100. In 2006, following another rise in the rate of ice loss, one group suggested that this could happen by 2030. Late in 2007, however, Wieslow Maslowski and his US-Polish research team issued the prediction that the Arctic Ocean could be ice free in summer by 2013 – just five years from now. Such is the rapidity with which climate change is overtaking our forecasts.

In the summer of 2002, the absence of ice at the North Pole attracted much media attention, and interest has been high ever since. Three years later, in 2005, the ice cover was a record 20 per cent down during September, a reduction equivalent to an area twice the size of the state of Texas. Even more dramatically, 2007 saw a 40-per-cent reduction in ice cover – an area more than equal to the size of Texas and Alaska combined. At just over four million square kilometres, compared with a summer average of nearly seven million, this is the smallest ice extent in modern times.

Already, greedy eyes are turning to the region, with plans to exploit new opportunities once the ice cover has waned sufficiently. One reason for this interest is trade, with ice-free summers opening up new shipping routes: the Northeast Passage, connecting the Atlantic and Pacific Oceans via the seas north of Siberia, and the almost-mythical Northwest Passage, linking the Atlantic and Pacific via a route through the currently ice-bound islands of northern Canada. In fact, way ahead of predictions, satellite images released by the European Space Agency revealed that the Northwest Passage was ice-free and navigable in 2007, perhaps for the first time since 1497, or even earlier. Sixteenth-century English explorer Martin Frobisher failed to find a way through, and his compatriot Henry Hudson – of Hudson Bay fame – was also unsuccessful. Tragically, an expedition put together in 1845 by Rear Admiral Sir John Franklin vanished, with the loss of all 129 crew[7]. At last, in 1905, the famous Norwegian explorer Roald Amundsen managed to navigate the passage in a small herring boat – only, however, by making the most of shallow waterways that would not be navigable by today's giant tankers and cargo ships. With the route likely to be regularly ice-free from now on, large ships will soon be able to make their way through using deeper channels. The opening of the Northwest Passage will cut the journey time between

Europe and East Asia by one third, so proving extremely attractive to shipping companies looking to reduce time and costs.

With the rapid loss of the ice cover, plans are being quickly put in place to exploit oil and gas reserves beneath the Arctic Ocean, which the United States Geological Survey estimates hides a quarter of undiscovered deposits, including up to 375 billion barrels of oil. Exploitation by oil and shipping companies is already throwing up a number of territorial disputes between countries that have claims to parts of the region. Norway and Russia are at loggerheads over the Barents Sea, while Canada is stepping up its military presence along the Northwest Passage (which it regards as falling within its territorial waters) as a deterrent to the USA, which is keen to take advantage of the new route. The disputes came to a head in 2007, with a Russian publicity stunt that saw the country's red, white and blue flag planted by a mini-submarine on the sea floor at the geographical North Pole. The exploit was designed to bolster Russia's claim, made in 2001, to much of the Arctic and its energy resources. This is based upon their contention that a range of submarine mountains, known as the Lomonosov Ridge, which extends to the North Pole, is actually an extension of Siberia's continental shelf. As such, under international law, they claim, this entitles the country to ownership of a huge area of the Arctic Sea, and everything in it and under it. Not surprisingly, the claim has been challenged by those other nations who have an interest in the region and its resources, namely the USA, Canada, Denmark and Norway.

While the loss of Arctic sea ice and the opening of the Northwest, and eventually Northeast, passages might be good for business, this is the last thing the climate needs. Any advantage gained through shorter passage times resulting in lower emissions are likely to be completely outweighed by the significant growth in trade that opening of the passages is likely to encourage. Predicted knock-on effects include more intense storms battering the UK and Europe and an even drier American west. Even worse, not only will more trade and more oil mean more emissions, but the replacement of white ice by dark ocean will mean that more of the sun's energy will be absorbed rather than reflected, pushing up temperatures even higher.

WHAT ABOUT ANTARCTICA?

Like the Greenland Ice Sheet, half a world away, the gigantic West Antarctic Ice Sheet is also on the move. As ice shelves as big as Luxembourg snap off and shatter into a million icebergs, they release the pent-up glaciers behind, which then speed up their flow towards the sea. When the Larsen-A ice shelf collapsed in 1995, adjacent glaciers accelerated to four times their previous speed. Two major glaciers are now discharging into the Amundsen Sea three times faster than they were a decade ago, and complete melting of these alone would raise global sea levels by more than a metre.

In its 2001 report, the IPCC described the West Antarctic Ice Sheet (WAIS) as a 'slumbering giant'. More recently, Chris Rapley, the former Director of the British Antarctic Survey, who now heads up London's Science Museum, has referred to it, rather ominously, as an 'awakened giant'. Believe me, this is not a giant that we want to see fully awake and *compos mentis*. The entire Antarctic Ice Sheet (west and east) has a volume of 25 million cubic kilometres, which makes it almost nine times the size of the Greenland Ice Sheet. Around ten per cent of this total volume is contained in the West Antarctic Ice Sheet.

In common with the Arctic region, Antarctica is being transformed rapidly by climate change. In the Antarctic Peninsula, the finger of land that points towards the Falkland Islands, summer temperatures have shot up by 5°C, with the result that nearly 90 per cent of the peninsula's glaciers are shrinking rapidly. Because prevailing Antarctic temperatures are lower than those of Greenland, summer melting of the West Antarctic Ice Sheet's surface is not such a big problem. The WAIS does, however, appear to be highly susceptible to melting caused by a completely different mechanism. Unlike the Greenland Ice Sheet, which is entirely on land, the WAIS rests on bedrock, much of which is below sea level. At the very edge, where the ice sheet is floating, melting will not make a contribution to sea level rise, because ice actually takes up more space than an equivalent mass of liquid water. Further inland, however, there is enough ice to raise global sea levels by five metres or so – if it all melts. Climate scientists are increasingly concerned that the warming waters of the Antarctic Ocean may cause collapse of the margins of the WAIS, and that this will destabilise the entire ice mass. Already, there are real signs that this is starting to happen.

Over the last 50 years, 13,500 square kilometres of the floating ice shelves that buttress the WAIS glaciers along the eastern side of the Antarctic Peninsula have been lost – amounting to an area larger than the Lebanon or Jamaica. This includes the Larsen-A shelf, which disintegrated into a fleet of icebergs in 1995, and the Luxembourg-sized (3,250-square-kilometre) Larsen-B ice shelf, which broke off and broke up over a period of just a month in 2002. Ice shelf loss is now allowing the glaciers that were previously held back to speed up. Five out of the six glaciers that fed the Larsen-A shelf have accelerated since its loss, some by up to four times their previous speed. Loss of the huge Larsen-B ice shelf is of particular concern as it seems that the event is unprecedented since the end of the last ice age, and if the pattern of break-up continues as expected, the next one to go should be the larger Larsen-C shelf, immediately to the south.

Ice is being lost elsewhere too, most notably around the Amundsen

Sea, on the western side of the Antarctic Peninsula. The Pine Island and Thwaites glaciers are now discharging ice into the sea three times as fast as they were ten years ago – a total volume of 110 cubic kilometres every year. Both glaciers are in direct contact with the sea and appear to be very sensitive to warming of the waters around the Peninsula. Although the southern ocean here has warmed by just a few tenths of a degree since the 1950s, even this seems to be sufficient to get the glaciers sliding faster. As the southern ocean is warming faster than other oceans, prospects for the survival of the WAIS, in the longer term, are not good. If just the Pine Island and Thwaites glaciers, alone, melted in their entirety, this would raise global sea levels by more than a metre.

In total, Antarctica lost about 150 cubic kilometres of ice a year between 2002 and 2005, mostly from the WAIS. In the decade to 2006, in fact, the rate of ice loss from West Antarctica as a whole was up 59 per cent, and loss from the Antarctic Peninsula was up 140 per cent. At present, this contributes a tiny amount – just half a millimetre a year – to global sea-level rise, but it would be no surprise to see this rate increase many times over the next 100 years.

ARE SEA LEVELS ALREADY RISING FASTER?

Visit the seaside before it visits you. Sea levels rose by about 20 centimetres in the last century and are currently climbing at about one centimetre every three years. Each one-millimetre rise translates, on average, into a 1.5-metre retreat of the shoreline, which is already threatening many low-lying nations. Even as I write this, the inhabitants of Papua New Guinea's Cartarets Islands are beginning to look for lives elsewhere on the planet, and over the next 30 years, the population of the South Pacific island of Tuvalu will be transferred, bit-by-bit, to New Zealand.

Around 20,000 years ago, when much of the Earth's water was locked up in the great ice sheets that spread across North America, Europe and Asia, sea levels were an astonishing 130 metres lower than they are now. As the post-glacial climate warmed, they have progressively risen – sometimes steadily, sometimes in bursts of several metres in just a few centuries. Now, as a result of our polluting activities, it looks as if we are on the verge of another such burst. For most of the last 5,000 years or so, sea levels have been rising at the rate of about one millimetre a year. Over the last 150 years, however, this doubled to two millimetres a year and then, since 1993, jumped again to three millimetres. According to the IPCC Fourth Assessment Report, by 2100 sea levels will be between 18 and 59 centimetres higher than they are today. This estimate, however, does not take account of any physical breakup of the polar ice sheets, and some climate scientists feel that a more likely rise will be one or two metres, or even more. From the safety of even a few tens of metres above the sea this may not sound like much. If your town or country sits less than a metre above sea level, however, it is a shocking statistic. On average, every one-millimetre rise in sea level sees the shoreline retreat by a metre and a half, guaranteeing a retreat of at least 100 metres by 2030 – a devastating prediction if you live on a low-lying island that is just a few hundred metres across.

Two tiny, uninhabited South Pacific Islands in the Kiribati archipelago, Abanuea and Tebua Tarawa, vanished beneath the waves in 1999, and already entire communities are being forced to move as a result of rising sea levels. The Papua New Guinea government has just launched a plan to evacuate the 980 people living on the six minuscule Cartarets Islands. Life on these islands, which together are about as large as 80 football pitches and sit barely 1.5 metres above sea level, is no longer viable as saltwater intrusion has poisoned the coconut palm, breadfruit and vegetable plots, leaving the inhabitants reliant on emergency aid. Now, every time a storm is forecast, the islanders fear for their lives, and just a decade ago a storm surge completely inundated one island and destroyed shoreline homes on others. The soon-to-be-abandoned islands are doomed, and may disappear beneath the waves as soon as 2015.

Other inhabited islands, too, face the threat of inundation in the immediate future. The South Pacific island of Tuvalu has perhaps attracted the most attention, mainly as a result of its government's much-publicised intention in 2002 to sue industrialised countries that it held responsible for climate change – which it has now abandoned. Tuvalu is one of the smallest and most remote nations on the planet. It is made up of just nine atolls, the widest of which is a few hundred metres across and all of which are already being encroached upon by rising seas. The total area of the islands is just 26 square kilometres, about the same as the heart of London, and most of their land is less than two metres above sea level. With salt water seeping ever further inland during high tides, the picture looks far from rosy.

In 1998, the government of Tuvalu had a stroke of luck that has helped the country develop a voice on the international stage, particularly in relation to the climate change threat to small island states. The Californian IT company Idealab bought the rights to Tuvalu's internet domain address. Because this is '.tv' it is highly sought after by entertainment companies. In return for being able to sell '.tv' domain names, therefore, Idealab agreed to pay Tuvalu's government $4 million a year for the next 20 years. This unlooked-for income has doubled the country's GDP, enabled it to join the United Nations and funded measures to tackle the impact of climate change on its people. Ultimately, however, rising sea levels seem certain to lead to abandonment of the islands. Already the government has approached other countries about taking its 12,000 or so citizens, with mixed responses. Australia, per head of population one of the biggest emitters of greenhouse gases on the planet, has so far ignored Tuvalu's pleas for help, as has that other great polluter, the United States. New Zealand has been more forthcoming, agreeing to take 75 citizens of the islands every year for the next 30 years.

Across the tiny island states of the Pacific, it is not just rising sea levels that are the problem. The Red Cross reports that weather-related disasters have increased by an extraordinary 65 times in the last three decades as a result of cyclones, floods and droughts, making life extremely difficult. Under such circumstances, it may well be that the island populations just drift away long before the seas doom them to watery graves.

WHICH OTHER PARTS OF THE WORLD ARE THREATENED BY RISING SEAS?

Close to 150 million people live less than one metre above sea level. The Maldives are doomed to disappear beneath the waves, as are the highly populated deltas of the Bengal, Nile, Yangtze and Mississippi rivers. By the middle of the century, one sixth of Bangladesh could be permanently under water, displacing 13 per cent of the country's population. In the developed world, rising sea levels mean serious problems for New York, while the Thames Barrier, as it currently stands, will probably keep London safe until 2030 – but, according to some, only just.

With 145 million people currently living within one metre of sea level, the imminent threat from rising water is not just confined to the Pacific Ocean, or to small nations. The world's great river deltas are also susceptible, including the Bengal delta in Bangladesh, which supports a population of nearly three and a half million. The Mekong (Vietnam), Nile (Egypt), Yangtze (China) and Mississippi (USA) deltas are also in danger. River deltas are highly exposed to rising sea levels, because most are sinking in their own right due to upriver dams cutting off their supply of sediment or because of oil or water extraction. Even before Hurricane Katrina struck with such devastating force in 2005, subsidence was causing tens of square kilometres of wetlands in the Mississippi delta to be claimed by the sea every year. Sediment starvation and oil extraction have resulted in much of New Orleans now residing below sea level, and future rises are likely to make the city unviable. Realising this, the US government has recently announced a plan to depopulate large areas of the most exposed coastline, in an effort to provide a natural barrier to future hurricanes and rising sea levels. The plan involves buying up more than 17,000 homes. Such managed retreat policies are far from popular with those who have to move, but they are the only sustainable means of managing the threat from remorselessly rising seas, and will become increasingly commonplace.

The situation is even worse on the Bengal delta, where cyclone-driven storm surges took 300,000 lives in 1970, a further 138,000 in 1991, and more than 3,000 in 2007. Largely because of groundwater abstraction, some parts of the delta are subsiding at a rate of 2.5 centimetres a year. By the middle of this century, if not earlier, the sea could reclaim around one sixth of the land area of Bangladesh, leaving some 13 per cent of the country's population with nowhere to farm or live. By 2030, neighbouring India could also lose up to 2,000 square kilometres of its land area, along with 150,000 livelihoods.

Out in the Indian Ocean, prospects seem little better for the third-of-a-million inhabitants of the 1,196 islands that make up the Maldives. The 2004 tsunami, which caused serious damage on 69 islands and forced the evacuation of 20, provided a salutary warning of how sea levels pushed up by climate change will eventually claim this nation of islands. Like the most threatened Pacific states, the Maldives rarely rise more than one or two metres above sea level, and stand to be increasingly battered by bigger storm surges driven by more powerful cyclones as well as suffering from encroachment by the sea and saltwater contamination of water tables.

Developed countries are not immune to sea-level rise, and the same rule of thumb applies with respect to encroachment: a one-millimetre rise leads, on average, to a 1.5 metre retreat of the shoreline. While coastal defences may be able to cope at first, the inexorable rise of the sea will require a serious rethink of policy in the next few decades. Given the prohibitive cost of building fortresses against the ocean, managed retreat and relocation will inevitably become a more attractive option, although this will be costly in its own right – as well as hugely unpopular and disruptive. Already, a decision has been taken to allow the sea to reclaim nearly 200 square kilometres of rural England over the next 15 years. In the USA, studies have shown that by 2030, some parts of New York and its environs, including the Lower Manhattan shoreline and much of downtown Jersey City, could be at risk of inundation. In the UK, the Thames Barrier, which protects London from the sea, is designed to keep the capital safe until 2030, but concerns have been voiced that by this date it will only be 50 per cent effective. It is worth noting that the barrier was raised just four times between its opening in 1983 and 1989, but is now operated a number of times each year to protect the capital from tidal surges.

Notwithstanding inundation, there is also an insidious and often ignored threat from sea-level rise that will shortly prove equally devastating. As the sea rises, so salt water infiltrates into the freshwater aquifers that supply dozens of the world's great coastal cities, making the water unusable. More than two billion people depend on underground water, and no defences can protect coastal aquifers from the sea. Already, salt water has penetrated five kilometres beneath the Philippine capital, Manila, while Shanghai, Mumbai, Bangkok, Jakarta, Lima, Karachi, Lagos and Buenos Aires can all expect saltwater contamination in coming decades. Ultimately, starved of essential fresh water, these cities could be abandoned long before the sea overtops their defences.

WHAT ABOUT MOUNTAINOUS REGIONS?

Across the planet, climate change is playing havoc with mountains. As the world's glaciers retreat ever more rapidly, the billions of tonnes of resulting meltwater present a growing, and potentially catastrophic, threat to nearby towns and cities. In the Himalayas, millions live within range of giant, glacial lakes that are growing and must eventually burst their banks. In the Alps, the ice that holds the mountains together is starting to melt, causing rock faces to break apart, and bringing the prospect of massive landslides crashing onto alpine communities.

Like the polar regions, the world's mountains are taking more than their fair share of grief from climate change. Nowhere is this more apparent than on Tanzania's iconic Mount Kilimanjaro – the dormant, snow-capped volcano that towers almost 6,000 metres above the floor of the East African Rift Valley. This mountain is important to the region in two main ways. Firstly, the congruence of snow and a tropical climate is rare and constitutes a major attraction for visitors. Secondly, meltwater from the ice fields that top the peak feeds streams that supply communities living around the base of the mountain with fresh water.

Soon, however, the mountain will lose its snowy cap altogether. Between 1912 and 2000, global warming contributed, along with other factors, to the loss of 82 per cent of the ice fields. Since then the ice has begun to disintegrate even more rapidly and Lonnie Thompson of Ohio State University, who has been monitoring the rate of ice loss, expects the mountain to be entirely free of ice sometime between 2015 and 2020. This is expected not only to cause a downturn in local tourism, but also to increase the burden of drought as streams fed by the ice falter.

Right across the world, mountain ranges are beginning to suffer as atmospheric temperatures climb, chipping away at the snow and ice that enhances their beauty, supports fragile ecosystems, sustains a recreation industry, supplies potable water and even helps to hold the mountains together. Glaciers in mountainous regions are in retreat everywhere we look. In Africa, most will have disappeared in the next couple of decades, including those in Rwanda and Uganda that feed the headwaters of the Nile. In Montana's Glacier National Park, originally named for its 150 spectacular glaciers, only 27 remain, and these could all be gone by 2030. The Alps lost half of their glacier mass between 1850 and 1990, snow and ice cover in the eastern Himalayas has shrunk by 30 per cent since the 1970s, and Alaska's Exit glacier, a major visitor attraction, has retreated an incredible 300 metres in just ten years. The Patagonian glaciers of South America are probably melting faster than any others, and between 1975 and 2000 contributed nearly ten per cent of the rise in sea level caused by melting mountain glaciers.

Inevitably, the disintegrating glaciers are making mountainous environments far more dangerous, both to visitors and to those who make a living there. In 2006, ice loss from Switzerland's Grindelwald glacier destabilised a huge chunk of the Eiger, and left another Wembley-Stadium-sized rock mass precariously poised. In the Himalayas, where two thirds of the glaciers are retreating, meltwater has pooled in at least 44 huge lakes in Nepal and Bhutan that could burst their weak debris dams at any time – sending deluges of icy water tumbling into the inhabited valleys far below. Temperatures in the region have already risen by about 1°C since the 1970s, and as they continue to climb, the accelerating melting of thousands of glaciers will lead to the accumulation of many more meltwater lakes. It is only a matter of time before one of these discharges into a populated area, with catastrophic results.

Rising temperatures are causing a problem in the Alps too, by melting the permanently frozen soil and rock that is keeping many of the mountain faces from disintegrating. In 2003, falling rock claimed 50 lives in the Alps, and many mountain routes had to be closed for safety reasons, while collapse of part of a ridge on the Matterhorn stranded nearly a hundred climbers. Since the 1970s, temperatures in the Alps have climbed by more than 2°C, and the increasing warmth is starting to melt the permafrost that binds otherwise-unstable rock masses together. North-facing slopes seem to be most vulnerable, as they largely miss out on the extremes of temperature change that affect those that face south, and have therefore been unaffected by melting for centuries or millennia. Narrow ridges and arêtes that are heated from both sides also seem to be at risk of future destabilisation and collapse. Thermometers inserted into boreholes have revealed that temperatures inside some Swiss mountains are just a couple of degrees below freezing, and climbing at half a degree or more every 15 years. A rise in the number of rock falls, landslides and mudflows seems inevitable, as does the failure of entire mountainsides with the potential to bury alpine villages and ski resorts under millions of tonnes of rock within seconds. Even without the help of climate change, this has happened before on a number of occasions. In 1806, the collapse of the Rossberg peak in Switzerland's Goldau Valley flattened four villages and killed more than 500 people, while in 1881, again in Switzerland, the Plattenbergkopf mountain fell onto the village of Elm, taking 115 lives. Most recently, in 1991, 30 million cubic metres of rock crashed down into a busy valley just ten kilometres from the Swiss ski resort of Zermatt, amazingly taking no lives. Undoubtedly, these are the forerunners of more and bigger landslides to come.

HOW ARE ANIMALS AND PLANTS SUFFERING?

Our changing climate is already putting stress on many animal and plant species, pushing some into decline and forcing others to seek new homes. As waves of warmth roll towards the poles, sea creatures, birds, insects and plants follow in their wake. As North Sea cod and haddock head north, red mullet and squid move in to take their place in temperate waters. In the UK and Europe, termites, poisonous spiders and disease-carrying mosquitoes will replace declining butterfly species. The mosses and lichens of the Arctic tundra are vanishing beneath burgeoning bushes and trees, while traditional wild flowers struggle to outrun the baking summers that are creeping inexorably northwards.

Climate change is already driving plant and animal species to new pastures, to expand their ranges polewards or – for the unlucky ones – to extinction. The most obvious changes so far have taken place in the oceans, where there are far less barriers to movement than there are on land. Water temperatures in the North Sea are 1°C higher than 25 years ago, attracting Mediterranean and sub-tropical species such as the colourful rainbow wrasse, and sightings of leatherback turtles, striped dolphins and humpback whales are now commonplace. UK fishermen are increasingly finding squid, octopus, sardines, anchovies and even seahorses among their catch. John dory, sea bass and red mullet are also becoming more common, and with a commercial red mullet fishery now operating in the Thames Estuary, it can't be long before mullet and chips appears on the menu at fish and chip shops across the capital. Meanwhile, many of the UK's native species are heading further north. The North Sea cod and haddock are just two of 18 species that have shifted their distributions northwards in the last 30 years – both by close to 100 kilometres.

These movements can play havoc with entire marine ecosystems. In the spectacularly rich fishing grounds of the Bering Sea, between Alaska and eastern Russia, a 3°C rise in temperature has led bottom-dwelling marine organisms north, followed by the gray whale and other predators such as walruses. The movement of these species away from the traditional native hunting grounds is threatening the livelihoods of local subsistence communities. The alternative scenario is just as grim. In the North Sea, fish and crustacean larvae that have not headed north now emerge two whole months earlier than they would have done 40 years ago, leading to a dearth of food for fish and seabirds. The absence of a food supply when they most need it almost certainly contributed to 2004 being the worst breeding season on record for many British sea birds, which left virtually no chicks fledged and thousands of dead birds strewn across the shores of Scotland and elsewhere.

Birds are themselves having to change their behaviour to accommodate climate change. In the UK, breeding species moved north, on average, by almost 20 kilometres between 1970 and 1990, and new species like the Mediterranean cattle egret are taking a look around with a view to breeding here in the future. Scavenging black kites and colourful European bee eaters have also made recent attempts to breed, and both are likely to be completely at home in the UK by 2030. It is equally likely, however, that rising temperatures will by then have driven the snowy owl, ptarmigan, snow bunting, dotterel, and Scottish Crossbill from our shores. The same huge reorganisation of species is happening everywhere: worldwide, animals and plants have recently shifted their ranges by around six kilometres a decade towards the poles, and six metres or so uphill.

Not to be left out, insects are also on the move or in decline. A quarter of British butterflies are shifting north, while new species, such as the European swallowtail, appear from the south. Warmer summers and milder winters will push many unpleasant creepy-crawlies towards the poles, too – into the UK, northern Europe, the northern United States and Canada. The UK can expect ticks, poisonous spiders and scorpions to make themselves at home in decades to come – already, the false black widow spider, known for its excruciating bite, is known to over-winter in parts of Dorset. At the same time, rare indigenous species are likely to be wiped out as more common, established UK species expand their territories. In France, termites are already heading north, while mosquitoes carrying dengue fever and West Nile virus will become a regular feature of the sweltering European and UK summers of the future.

Plant life is also changing dramatically, and nowhere more so than in the cold wastes of the Arctic tundra, where within decades, the vast carpet of lichen and moss will be increasingly replaced by bushes and trees. Because this darker vegetation absorbs more sunlight, the change will result in another positive feedback effect, contributing to increased warming that will far outweigh the additional carbon dioxide sucked up by the new arrivals. Further south, 80 per cent of European plants are leafing, flowering and fruiting earlier, while in the UK the number and distribution of plant species has changed hugely in just the last 20 years. Milder conditions have seen orchids and ferns spread north and west, while the mountain pansy and the lesser butterfly orchid are already in decline. It seems that plants that have tiny seeds, such as the ferns, have been able to move the greatest distances, as their seeds can be carried far by the wind. As temperatures rise, there are concerns that plants that produce heavier seeds, including many of Britain's traditional wild flowers, may not be able to change their distribution quickly enough to survive.

ARE CARBON LEVELS STILL RISING?

Both the concentration of greenhouse gases in the atmosphere and the level of emissions are continuing to climb rapidly. The concentration of carbon dioxide in the atmosphere rose more between 1970 and today than between the Industrial Revolution and 1970; global carbon dioxide emissions were 35 per cent higher in 2005 than in 1980, and they are now rising four times faster than they were in the 1990s. With emissions climbing far more rapidly than expected, and faster than accounted for in the IPCC climate scenarios, the worse-case global temperature rises of up to 6.4°C by 2100 may actually be optimistic.

With climate change already having a big impact across the board, you might think that cutting back on emissions should be at the top of everyone's agenda. Depressingly, however, this is not the case. Both the concentration of greenhouse gases in the Earth's atmosphere and the level of emissions due to human activities are continuing to rise rapidly. In fact, concentrations of carbon dioxide in the atmosphere may now be higher than at any time in at least the last 800,000 years, and the rate of increase is on the up, from an average of 0.9 ppm a year in the decade to 1970 to an annual average of two parts per million since 2001.

By 2005, global carbon dioxide emissions stood at 28.19 billion tonnes (7.9 billion tonnes of carbon) – 35 per cent higher than in 1980, and a massive 28-per-cent increase on 1995. During the 1990s, carbon dioxide emissions rose by an average of 0.8 per cent each year. By comparison, the annual rate of increase in the first five years of the new millennium was 3.2 per cent – a fourfold increase. So far this century, carbon dioxide emissions have climbed a whopping 35 per cent faster than expected. Half of this extra rise is attributed to the burning of fossil fuels, but, most disturbingly, the other half seems to be the result of a progressive reduction in the natural ability of the land and the oceans to soak up carbon dioxide from the atmosphere. This is a trend that can be expected to accelerate as positive feedback mechanisms conspire to pump up the level of greenhouse gases in the atmosphere, and – at the same time – global temperatures.

In contrast to levels of carbon dioxide, atmospheric levels of methane have actually fallen over the last 20 years, for reasons that are not certain, and this is taken to suggest that methane emissions due to human activities are not currently rising. Levels of chlorofluorocarbons (CFCs), the aerosol chemicals responsible for opening up the Antarctic ozone hole, are also falling following international agreement on the phasing out of their use under the terms of the 1989 Montreal Protocol. Nitrous oxide concentrations in the atmosphere continue to rise, while hydrofluorocarbon (HFC) levels are increasing at an alarming rate. This is worrying, because although the absolute concentration of these gases in the atmosphere is tiny, they are 10,000 times more potent than carbon dioxide.

The rises in emissions are occurring across the board, in both developed and developing countries, and in the energy, transport and other sectors. About 26 per cent of greenhouse gas emissions now (2004) come from the generation of electricity and heat; industry accounts for another

20 per cent, while the transport sector is responsible for 13 per cent. Deforestation and the loss of carbon from soil decay after (often illegal) logging may account for up to 16 per cent, with the remainder coming from residential and commercial buildings (eight per cent), agriculture, forestry, land-use and waste.

The richest seven per cent of the world's population are now responsible for half of all carbon dioxide emissions from burning fossil fuels, while the poorest three billion people produce just seven per cent of emissions. In the developing world, however, India, Brazil and, in particular, China, are beginning to make their mark. Both India and China doubled their emissions between 1995 and 2005, and in 2006, China overtook the USA to become the world's biggest producer of greenhouse gases. Now, just four countries – China, the USA, Russia and Japan – are responsible for half of all energy-related greenhouse gas emissions.

Not only are emissions still heading through the roof, but they are doing so faster than predicted in the IPCC's computer models. These look ahead and try to predict what our climate will be like up to the year 2100, based upon a range of different 'emissions scenarios' known as SRES (after the IPCC Special Report on Emissions Scenarios). The trouble is that these scenarios were published seven years ago, using data that are nine years old. At the current rate of change, that means that they are seriously out of date. For example, they assume that so-called carbon intensity – the ratio of carbon emissions to the world's GDP – will progressively get better. In fact, while energy efficiency measures led to a drop in carbon intensity in the 1990s, it has actually increased since 2000, mainly as a result of rapid, energy-inefficient economic growth in India and China. The scenarios also fail to address the degree to which natural carbon sinks such as the oceans are already struggling to keep up with emissions growth. In the past, such sinks have sucked up around half of all carbon emissions, but this figure is now falling. As a consequence, carbon dioxide levels in the atmosphere are climbing more rapidly than predicted. The bottom line is that the IPCC scenarios, which forecast temperature rises as high as 6.4°C by 2100, are hopelessly optimistic.

HAS THE KYOTO PROTOCOL HELPED TO SLOW CLIMATE CHANGE?

The Kyoto Protocol has the admirable goal of stabilising greenhouse gas concentrations in the atmosphere at a level that will prevent dangerous climate change. In actual fact, however, when the Protocol ends in 2012, it will have made little impact on either global carbon emissions or rising temperatures. The Protocol has had some successes, helping to launch carbon as a commodity, introducing carbon trading, and developing a scheme to encourage 'green' projects in developing countries, although not without problems and criticism. Now, however, there is an almost universal consensus that a new and more hard-hitting approach is needed to tackle climate change after Kyoto ends in 2012.

The Kyoto Protocol represents the global community's first attempt to slow the rise in greenhouse gas emissions, committing 41 of the most highly industrialised states (known as Annex 1 countries) to reducing their greenhouse gas emissions by five per cent below 1990 values by 2012. The fact that the Annex 1 countries are together responsible for less than two-thirds of the total emissions from developed countries indicates that a number of industrialised countries have refused to ratify the protocol – most notably the USA, which accounts for around a quarter of global emissions, and Australia, which has higher emissions per head of population than any other major state. One hundred and thirty-seven developing countries, including India and China, have also ratified the Protocol, but none of these nations is obliged to reduce emissions.

Although an average emissions cut of 5.2 per cent is the overarching aim of the agreement, different targets have been allocated to different countries, depending upon their economic situation and other factors – and some are even allowed to increase their greenhouse gas emissions. The European Union as a whole, for example, is obligated to reduce its emissions by eight per cent, but specific targets vary from country to country, with Portugal, on the one hand, permitted to increase its emissions by 27 per cent while Germany, on the other, is required to cut its emissions by 21 per cent.

The Kyoto Protocol is based on a 'cap and trade' mechanism, meaning that although there are caps on the emissions of Annex 1 countries, it is perfectly acceptable for these countries to 'trade' emissions in order to meet national obligations. One way in which industrialised countries can do this is via the protocol's Clean Development Mechanism (CDM), which allows them to 'buy' carbon credits by investing in sustainable projects in developing countries, such as energy from waste power plants or wind farms, which will reduce greenhouse gas emissions in those countries. These carbon credits can then be counted towards the industrialised country's emissions reductions. Understandably, the CDM has proved to be highly contentious and has been attacked as providing an easy way out for the industrialised countries, by allowing them to meet their emissions reduction targets without actually tackling the problem at home.

The CDM took a considerable amount of flak in a recent investigation in the UK's *Guardian* newspaper, which presented evidence for the mechanism being contaminated by 'gross incompetence, rule-breaking and possible fraud by companies in the developing world'. According to the report, some project validation and verification companies were not up to the job, projects were being approved that produced absolutely no emissions savings, and many of the projects would have gone ahead anyway, even without the CDM. In other words, they were not delivering any additional savings in greenhouse gas emissions. So far, just 100 million tonnes' worth of carbon credits have been issued, a total comparable to just a couple of months' worth of UK emissions. Worst of all, by allowing industrialised countries and their corporations to purchase carbon credits for supporting projects that would have happened anyway, in place of acting to cut emissions at home, the CDM could actually be encouraging more greenhouse gas emissions.

In a second initiative to encourage carbon trading, the Kyoto Protocol allows countries to band together to form emissions trading groups – an opportunity that the European Union was quick to take advantage of. In January 2005, the EU launched its Emissions Trading Scheme (ETS), designed to cap emissions on large greenhouse gas emitters within the Union, such as power stations and industrial plants. Under the scheme, national governments receive allowances that they then divide among industrial installations, permitting them to emit a certain amount of greenhouse gas. If an installation exceeds its allocation, it can use the ETS mechanism to buy further allowances. Like the CDM, the ETS has suffered from teething problems and been strongly criticised – in particular, because national governments were given emissions allowances that were needlessly large.

The Kyoto Protocol was originally planned as a multi-stage mechanism that would ultimately achieve 'the stabilization of greenhouse gas concentrations in the atmosphere at a level that would prevent dangerous anthropogenic interference with the climate system'. Doubts about its ability to accomplish this, however, are likely to ensure that the

Protocol, which only came into force in February 2005, will be short-lived and will almost certainly be laid to rest on the last day of 2012. As for its legacy – assuming, rather optimistically, that all the Annex 1 nations meet their targets – this would slow the global temperature rise by somewhere between 0.02°C and 0.28°C by 2050. Hardly a cause for celebration.

Kyoto is just the first step on a long and rocky road that may, or may not, lead to the successful curtailment of greenhouse gas emissions and climate change. While not, in its own right, contributing much in the way of greenhouse gas reduction or slowdown in global warming, Kyoto has at least provided mechanisms for tracking and trading carbon emissions, and for supporting 'green' projects in the developing world, even if these are less effective than they should be. It has also promoted carbon as a commodity and ensured that climate change is a key policy consideration of most of the world's governments. There is now, however, a general consensus that a more inclusive approach, with more clout and more ambitious goals, is needed post-2012, if there is to be any chance of preventing dangerous climate change.

BALI AND BEYOND – WHAT NEXT?

In December 2007, 187 national representatives met on the Indonesian island of Bali to debate the nature of the climate change agreement that will succeed Kyoto. While all signed up to a statement which recognised that 'deep cuts in global emissions will be required', the USA and others insisted that the targets proposed by the EU, of a 25–40 per cent reduction by 2020, were removed from the final agreement. This hardly bodes well for a satisfactory outcome when delegates meet in Denmark in 2009, and seems to suggest that there is little chance of the new agreement supporting the necessary 90-per-cent (at least) cuts by the middle of the century.

While Kyoto has accomplished little in terms of either slowing emissions or bringing rising temperatures under control, it has been successful in making the heads of government of more than 90 per cent of the world's nations acknowledge that climate change is a real problem. Most countries probably signed up to the agreed emissions cuts in good faith even though it now looks as if some targets will be missed by a very long way. With Kyoto commitments ending in a little over five years, thoughts are rapidly turning to what might follow. In this respect, the gathering of 187 national representatives on the Indonesian island of Bali in December 2007, for the latest UN Climate Change Conference, marked the first tentative step towards developing an emissions reduction plan that might have some real authority. Bali was undoubtedly a meeting about a meeting, but it had critical importance nevertheless. With the USA, China and India not bound, for one reason or another, by Kyoto, it was vital that all three were kept on board and coddled, coerced or bulldozed into agreeing a so-called 'road map' that should ultimately lead to a binding and all-inclusive international agreement. Failure at this early stage would have made it much more difficult to have a seamless transition when Kyoto comes to an end.

As I write this, the meeting has been over for barely a week and, depending upon who you listen to, it has been a resounding success, or a total failure, or something in between. Admittedly, in order to keep the USA and others on board, the EU had to withdraw its insistence that reduction targets of 25 to 40 per cent reduction by 2020 should be agreed at this early stage in the negotiation process. But then again, the USA is still on board – despite the usual recalcitrant brinkmanship – and has signed up to an action plan that recognises that 'deep cuts in global emissions will be required'. Keeping the USA onside is recognised as a major challenge, especially when the stage is reached where specific emissions targets and timelines need to be agreed. The challenge might be a little easier after the 2008 presidential elections, however, and US democrats have already indicated that they will be fully on board if the party should win the coming election. Perhaps by the time you read this they already have. With time of the essence, however, and the Bali road map needing to be translated into a binding agreement by 2009, the US election is proving to be a thorn in the side of those having to put the climate deal together. The new President will have little time to get to grips with the details of the negotiations and their implications before being required to put pen to paper, while other critical nations, most importantly China, may hold back until they see which way the incoming administration will jump.

This could slow progress to such a degree that everything might not be ready for the new agreement to come into force on 1 January 2013.

Whether the 'road map' agreed in Bali will ever lead to a worthwhile agreement is questionable: it is currently so vague that there is no guarantee it will lead anywhere useful at all. Plans have been agreed to improve the transfer of green technologies to developing countries, and to provide more money to allow them to start to launch projects that help in adapting to climate change. The critical importance of preventing deforestation in developing countries – which causes one fifth of all carbon dioxide emissions – was recognised, but no concrete plans were proposed to stop this happening. In fact, the Bali road map lacks clarity in a way that the final agreement simply cannot afford to, if there is to be any possibility of preventing dangerous climate change. The target emissions reductions of 25–40 per cent by 2020 must be adhered to – and far closer to 40 per cent than 25 per cent. Already, however, the USA, Japan, Canada and Russia are saying that they will resist such stringent targets, even though the science says that emissions need to be slashed by at least 90 per cent by the middle of the century to prevent the worst. This sounds like a very tall order, but Norway, New Zealand and Costa Rica have already committed themselves to zero emissions by 2050. Germany, one of the world's industrial powerhouses, is also well on the way, with plans in place to cut emissions by 40 per cent within 13 years. Even UK Prime Minister Gordon Brown is considering signing the country up to an 80-per-cent cut by 2050, although this would require drastic, across-the-board changes in current government policies, many of which are far from climate friendly.

Clearly, coming to an agreement that incorporates stringent enough targets is going to be extremely difficult. It is a struggle, however, that has to be won. Anything less than a binding, inclusive treaty that requires massive emissions cuts will mean that we have lost any chance of preventing climate chaos. When the representatives of national governments gather again in Poland in 2008 to hammer out the details, and in Denmark a year later to construct a final agreement, they will hold in their hands nothing less than the future of our descendents' world.

PART 2: WHAT WILL CLIMATE CHANGE MEAN FOR MY CHILDREN AND THEIR CHILDREN?

Within just a few decades, it is likely that climate change will have begun to affect everyone's day-to-day lives, and even the most oblivious or sheltered of us will no longer be able to ignore its impact. If we are serious about preventing dangerous climate change, then stringent carbon reduction measures will also impinge increasingly upon our everyday lives. Trying to pin down the sort of world our children and their children will inhabit, however, is extremely difficult, firstly because there is enormous leeway in predictions and forecasts made about how severe the consequences of climate change will be in 2050 and beyond, and secondly because how bad things will get will depend to a huge degree on what action – if any – we take over the next few decades. If we fail to stabilise greenhouse gas emissions within a decade or so, we would expect a rise of at least 2°C – and probably much more – by 2100. This would almost certainly be sufficient to set in motion the wholesale melting of the Greenland Ice Sheet and commit future generations to a sea-level rise of several metres. Until quite recently, the hope was that if carbon emissions could be capped by international agreement at 550 ppm, just about double what they were in pre-industrial times, we could avoid the worst, but the latest research suggests that this is far too high a level to prevent dangerous climate change. It now seems that we need to try and prevent carbon emissions topping 450 ppm if we are to avoid the most drastic consequences, and even this might be far too much.

NASA climatologist Jim Hansen and his colleagues argue that a global average temperature rise of just 1°C above the level in the year 2000 could be sufficient to unleash the consequences of dangerous climate change. With temperatures predicted to climb by at least 0.2°C every decade, this would mean that the more extreme effects of climate change could start to become apparent in just a few decades. To avoid temperatures reaching this additional 1°C yardstick, Hansen and his fellow researchers warn that the concentration of carbon dioxide in the atmosphere must be kept at a level no higher than 450 ppm. Given the rate at which the gas is currently accumulating in the atmosphere, this is a figure that will be achieved by 2040, or even earlier if emissions increase or the land and oceans become less effective at soaking up carbon. According to the results of a UK Met Office study presented at the Bali conference, even this may not be enough. The depressing conclusion of the study is that the climate may be so sensitive to the flooding of the atmosphere with extra greenhouse gases that there is only a 20-per-cent chance that holding carbon dioxide concentrations at 450 ppm will prevent a 2°C temperature rise. Indeed, as we go to press, Hansen and his colleagues have lowered their safe limit to 350 ppm.

In any case, prospects for keeping below even the 450 ppm threshold are not good. The International Energy Agency predicts that worldwide demand for electricity will double by around 2030, with most of this increase met by fossil fuels. Over this period, they suggest, the equivalent of around 4,300 coal-fired power stations will be built, contributing to an estimated 62-per-cent rise in emissions. Such a 'business as usual' path would be catastrophic, and could see carbon emissions approaching 1,000 ppm by 2100. This would inevitably mean a world on the verge of collapse, with roasting temperatures, catastrophic sea-level rise and wild weather feeding biblical famines, human migration on an unprecedented scale, water wars, mass extinctions and the destruction of entire ecosystems, and widespread social and economic turmoil. In the following sections I will examine in more detail just how hellish a world we will bequeath to our children and their children, if we don't act now.

WHAT SORT OF WORLD WILL DANGEROUS CLIMATE CHANGE BRING?

If we don't take drastic action soon to tackle emissions, it is probable that by the middle of the century it will be increasingly difficult to do so. On the one hand, continued rapid rises in emissions will have triggered rampant and invidious climate change, while on the other, radical and intrusive carbon reduction measures will have been introduced in a desperate attempt to prevent the situation getting even worse. On top of this, an energy crisis arising from the combination of rapidly depleting hydrocarbon reserves and derisory investment in renewable sources could make life that much more difficult. What follows may provide a glimpse of the sort of day our children may wake up to in the UK in August 2050.

As the sky lightens in the east, the city of London remains plunged in stifling darkness. Power shortages and the need to stick to the UK's rigid carbon emissions cap have ensured that towns and cities are no longer lit up like Christmas trees every night. August Bank Holiday dawns, and temperatures are already above 30°C, with a forecast high of 44°C – rather cool compared to the last few summers. The roads are surprisingly free of traffic, with astronomical fuel costs, personal carbon allocations and private usage restricted to three days a week slashing numbers of vehicles on the road. As the suburbs are bathed in blazing sunlight, evidence of a city in decline becomes apparent. Four years of extreme drought has turned gardens into deserts. Swingeing water rationing has now been in force for 28 months, with massive fines and jail the penalty for law-breakers and traffickers. Hose pipes can no longer be purchased, cars cleaned or golf courses watered. On many streets, derelict houses slowly decay, their owners having headed northwards to escape the terrible summer heat. No-one will buy property in southern England now. Parliament has headed north too, retreating to Edinburgh from May to October; partly to avoid the heat but also to get away from the awful smell of the raw sewage flushed into the Thames during the flash floods that come with the near-daily afternoon electric storms, but do nothing to alleviate the drought conditions. To the east, the Thames Gateway has been largely abandoned, never having recovered from the awful storm surge six years earlier when the sea finally overcame the coastal defences to inundate tens of thousands of homes and businesses.

Beyond the city limits, the countryside is transformed, with vast swathes of four-metre-high elephant grass, which supplies the small district power stations, rubbing shoulders with great stretches of indigenous willow and Asian miscanthus that are grown for biofuels. Here and there, derelict vineyards and citrus groves provide testimony to the severe drought and lack of water for irrigation. The economy, too, is crumbling. Caps on aviation emissions and the arrival of a personal mileage limit on air travel have brought the global tourist industry to its knees. Power and fuel costs have sent business costs sky-high and the combination of the two has seen bars and restaurants closing in droves. All but the most privileged now spend the majority of their leisure time at home, glued to their holo-tvs (when the power is on). These days, however, the screens have little to offer in the way of comfort. Across the world, the battles for access to potable water continue, with horrific scenes of international conflict. In the USA, Miami and New Orleans lie abandoned and in ruins after one too many direct hits from the ever-strengthening Atlantic hurricanes. And even along the UK's south coast, trouble is brewing as the inhabitants of the self-governing enclaves established to house migrants from the expanding Mediterranean deserts agitate for more living space and better conditions.

HOW HOT WILL IT GET?

Knowing exactly how hot it will get by 2100 and beyond is impossible. Climate model predictions are ambiguous, and the final outcome will depend on what action – if any – we take in the intervening decades to cut back emissions. The IPCC Fourth Assessment Report forecasts, however, that by 2100, temperatures could be up by 6.4°C, and even higher temperature hikes are not ruled out. Without drastic action now, the world of 2100 is very likely to be one of lethal heat waves, raging wildfires, desiccating droughts, melting road surfaces, buckling rails, and very, very sticky nights.

Just how hot will it get, and how quickly? There is no easy answer. Predictions keep changing as we learn more about the complex interactions and feedbacks of our planet's climate. In its 2007 Fourth Assessment Report, the IPCC predicts that, depending upon how profligate we are with our greenhouse gases, the global average temperature could climb as much as 6.4°C by the century's end. This would elevate the average temperature of our planet from 14.8°C prior to the start of the Industrial Revolution to 21.2°C just 300 years or so later – a staggering rate of increase. There is even a good chance that the rise could be far greater. If the soot particles, chemical aerosols, and other grime in our atmosphere is really masking the true level of warming, then as tighter pollution controls and a switch to gas and renewables begin to make an impression, temperatures can be expected to accelerate, perhaps increasing by as much as 7–10°C by 2100.

Furthermore, examination of past climates reveals that carbon dioxide is even more sensitive to temperature than previously thought, with warmer conditions driving the release of ever more carbon through various feedback mechanisms. The alarming results of a study published in March 2008 by Peter Cox of the UK's University of Exeter, and his colleagues, forecasts that a 4°C temperature rise this century would, on its own, increase carbon dioxide levels in the atmosphere by at least 160 parts per million, accelerating global warming to more than 50 per cent above current, mainstream predictions, and pushing us into unknown territory.

With carbon dioxide levels as low as 450 ppm potentially capable of driving up temperatures by as much as 4°C, and given the snail's-pace progress towards tackling emissions, it is very likely that our descendents will be living in a world at least 3°C warmer than today and possibly much more. In the UK, a sweltering summer like that of 2003 will be considered normal by 2040, and 20 years later the same thing will be regarded as cool. It should come as no surprise that by 2100, heat waves in Europe and the USA will be far more common, more intense, and more prolonged. In Paris, which was badly hit in 2003 by extended periods with temperatures in excess of 40°C, the number of heat waves will increase by one third and they will last close to twice as along. The nights will be even more unbearably sticky too. On 11 and 12 August 2003, night-time temperatures fell to just 25.5°C in Paris, doubling the death rate. By 2100, minimum night-time temperatures during the hottest events may climb several degrees higher than even this. Increasingly roasting summers will also start to become the norm in US cities such as Chicago, where a severe heat wave in 1995 took more than 500 lives in just five days. Bearing in mind that the 2003 European heat wave took at least 35,000 lives, by the end of the century, many hundreds of thousands across the world can be expected to succumb every year.

Extreme temperatures also go hand-in-hand with many other problems, not least increased drought and water shortages, transport difficulties – associated with melting road surfaces, buckled rails, and overheated vehicles – crop failures and wildfires. All this adds up to a huge drain on national economies. The 2003 heat wave cost the French around ten billion Euros, and the Portuguese and Spanish economies suffered almost as much due to hundreds of individual wildfires that raged across the countryside. As woods, forests, bush and scrub become tinder dry, the towering smoke columns of huge wildfires will become an increasingly common sight across much of the world, with North America, Australia and southern Europe suffering particularly badly. Even now, wildfires are causing massive problems, devouring the vegetation across a quarter of Portugal in 2003 and beleaguering communities in California and Australia on an almost yearly basis. It can only be a matter of time before a densely populated area is over-run and many lives are lost.

At present, many – if not most – of us unashamedly search out warmer climes in which to toast our bodies at vacation time. By the end of the century, however, it is doubtful if we will still be flocking to our favourite destinations in the Mediterranean, North Africa, the Canary Islands and Florida, because they will simply be far too hot. In fact, a recent study has suggested that by then people will be heading to the UK for their beach holidays, along with other cooler countries such as Russia and Canada. But this rise in tourism for a few parts of the world cannot begin to make up for the unpleasant living conditions and huge disruption that climate change will bring elsewhere.

If we want to avoid the worst then we must start to turn away from using fossil fuels now. The bottom line is that if we burn all the oil and gas reserves that remain untouched, the concentration of greenhouse gases in the atmosphere will be higher than it has been for 50 million years, with global average temperatures up to 13°C higher than before the Industrial Revolution. This is likely to take several centuries, but when it does come it will mean an environment blighted beyond recognition.

COULD SOME PARTS OF THE WORLD GET COOLER?

With the Atlantic Thermohaline Circulation – the Gulf Stream and associated currents – behaving rather erratically, the probability of a dramatic slowdown, or even shutdown, is not impossible. In fact, a significant slowdown is predicted over the course of the twenty-first century, with potential ramifications not only for the climate of the North Atlantic region, but also for the Amazon Rainforest and the Indian monsoon. A sudden shutdown soon, which admittedly is not likely, would see UK winter temperatures fall frequently below -10°C, snow on the ground for months on end, and chaos in a country where a single snowflake seems to bring everything grinding to a halt.

Earlier, I looked at the current state of the Atlantic Thermohaline Circulation (ATHC) – the Gulf Stream and associated currents – and the possibility that it could slow dramatically or even shut down. Is such a scenario really likely if emissions continue to rise unabated, and what impact would it have on the climate and weather of the UK, Europe and the rest of the world?

Certainly there are changes afoot in the North Atlantic. For example, the Arctic Ocean has been getting less salty over the past 50 years – due to a huge increase in rainfall in the area and faster melting of sea ice and glaciers. Together, between 1965 and 1995, increased rainfall and river outflow dumped an extra 20,000 cubic kilometres of freshwater into the ocean – equivalent to 40 years' flow from the Mississippi river. Melting ice contributed a further 15,000 cubic kilometres, and glaciers, 2,000 cubic kilometres more. Changes in patterns of atmospheric pressure over the North Atlantic, known as the North Atlantic Oscillation or NAO, appear to have speeded up the transfer of moisture from low to high latitudes, and the effect is expected to intensify, raising concerns about the impact of this on the ATHC.

A 30-per-cent slowdown in the ATHC, if it happens soon, could result in a 1°C regional temperature fall within a decade or so. This does not sound like much, but it could bring conditions similar to those that gripped Europe in the Little Ice Age, between the fifteenth and nineteenth centuries, which saw sea ice in the English Channel, frost fairs on the River Thames, and skating on the Dutch canals. If the situation were to worsen so that the entire circulation shut down, then the picture would be bleak indeed. Within 20 years, temperatures across Europe and eastern North America would be 4°C or so lower, bringing chillier summers and appalling winters. UK Met Office simulations suggest that within five or six years of shutdown winter temperatures would regularly fall far below -10°C. In a country ill-equipped to deal with extremes of temperature, such a situation would bring massive disruption and upheaval, with agriculture, health, energy supply and travel worst affected. Winters as bad as or worse than those of 1946–47 and 1962–63 would be the norm, with snow on the ground for months at a time, ice storms and blizzards ubiquitous and ports frozen in by pack ice.

But just how likely is this most extreme scenario? Given a 3°C temperature rise this century, Mike Schlesinger from the University of Illinois puts at evens the probability that the Atlantic Thermohaline Circulation will shut down, but also points out that some models predict that this could happen with a rise as low as 2°C. Other climate scientists think the chances of a shutdown are smaller, although many – if not most – expect the ATHC to slow down to some degree this century. In a recent elicitation exercise, twelve leading climate scientists were quizzed about the ATHC and its future behaviour. All of them foresaw a weakening of the circulation as greenhouse gas concentrations in the atmosphere climbed, and eight assessed the probability of shutdown as significantly higher than zero, should temperatures climb by 4°C by 2100 – which they may well do. Three even suggested that the probability of a shutdown, given such a temperature rise, could be higher than one in three. All the scientists questioned predicted that such an event would trigger dramatic changes across the North Atlantic region, including in temperature, precipitation and sea level.

The ramifications of complete shutdown would, however, stretch far wider than the North Atlantic, with predicted effects farther afield including a weakening of the Indian monsoon and a halving of rainfall in parts of Central and South America. This could slash agricultural productivity and place what remains of the Amazon Rainforest in peril. Another potentially devastating consequence is the predicted fall by one fifth of the global population of phytoplankton – the tiny marine creatures that soak up much of the carbon dioxide that we are pumping into the atmosphere. Combined with rainforest loss this would result in a big leap in the rate at which the greenhouse gases accumulate in the atmosphere, accelerating the warming process even further.

According to the IPCC Fourth Assessment report, the ATHC is very likely to slow down this century, but very unlikely to grind suddenly to a complete halt. How much such a slowdown will affect the climate of the UK and Europe will depend upon how soon it happens, and how much it slows.

WILL EXTREME WEATHER BE THE ORDER OF THE DAY?

The number of weather-related disasters is already climbing relentlessly; a trend that is expected to continue as climate change bites ever harder, bringing more heat waves, torrential rain, and stronger winds. Since 1980, wild weather has led to 600,000 deaths and caused damage totalling US$1.3 trillion, and is now responsible for the average loss of more than 33,000 lives a year. The future could bring gigantic hurricanes and typhoons half the size of the USA, along with bigger tornadoes and more powerful storms battering the UK and Europe.

The number of weather-related disasters is heading relentlessly upwards. Since 1980, around 12,000 events have caused more than 600,000 fatalities, and cost a staggering US$1.3 trillion. On average, extreme weather now takes more than 33,000 lives a year across the world, a figure up by two-thirds since the 1980s. The IPCC Fourth Assessment Report predicts that it is 'very likely' that 'hot extremes, heat waves and heavy precipitation events' will become more frequent. While still the focus of the hottest debate, the IPCC also notes that it is likely that hurricanes and typhoons will become more intense, with more powerful winds and heavier associated rainfall. As I am addressing heat, drought and flood elsewhere, I will concentrate here on the windier aspects of future wild weather, and in particular whether or not we should expect to see a continuation of the trend towards more powerful tropical storms.

The minimum sea-surface temperature needed in order for a tropical cyclone to form is 26°C, but global warming is likely to take averages far higher than that. Already, average surface temperatures in the Atlantic have climbed by 0.7°C over the last century, contributing to a recent 40-per-cent rise in hurricane activity, while in 2005, bath-water sea temperatures of around 30°C in the Gulf of Mexico spurred on Hurricane Katrina towards New Orleans. Over the next quarter of a century, and beyond, sea-surface temperatures will be driven ever higher by climate change. The big worry is that this will spawn increasing numbers of so-called super-cyclones on the scale of 1979's Typhoon Tip, the largest and most intense tropical cyclone ever. While still at sea, winds of 305 kilometres per hour raged around this gigantic storm – at more than 2,200 kilometeres across, half the size of the United States and twice as big as the next largest tropical cyclone. Fortunately, the extreme winds had dissipated to little more than common-or-garden storm force when the typhoon struck Japan. In decades to come, however, warmer seas may well mean more storms on the scale of Tip, roaming the seas looking for a coastline to batter. Should such storms hit shore at maximum intensity then the level of devastation and loss of life would make Hurricane Katrina seem like a gentle zephyr.

Just as for tropical cyclones, there is a continuing – although less acrimonious – debate about what climate change will mean for future storminess in the UK and Europe. And, broadly speaking, the developing consensus seems to be similar – namely that, while we may not experience more storms overall, we can expect to see an increased frequency of the more powerful, and therefore more destructive, variety. One model for UK storminess predicts that we may eventually see a 20-per-cent increase. Following in the footsteps of the great storm of October 1987 and the Burns Night storm of January 1990, any increase in more powerful storms is likely to be confined to the autumn and winter months. While sustained wind speeds are lower, the 'footprints' of UK and European windstorms are generally much larger than the average tropical cyclone. As a result, the area affected is often far greater, with damage and loss of life spread across several countries. Winter storm Kyril, for example, affected 24 European countries in January 2007, taking 44 lives. Bigger storms inevitably mean higher storm surges, increasing the potential for coastal flooding around the UK, France, the Low Countries and elsewhere, together with accelerating erosion around these shores.

The IPCC Fourth Assessment Report says little about tornadoes, and as yet there is no evidence that climate change might be spawning more of these spinning vortices of solid air. Nevertheless, it would seem reasonable that a warmer and more energetic atmosphere might well have some influence on the size and/or number of these storms, which are capable of sustaining wind speeds high enough to embed lengths of straw in solid wood. In the USA, the home of killer tornadoes, the twisters form when cold, dry, air from the north and east collides with warm, moist air from the Gulf of Mexico. Massive thunderstorms are triggered that spin off tornadoes, often in swarms. In 1974, 148 tornadoes rampaged across a dozen south-eastern states, killing more than 300 people and injuring over 5,000. While the impact of climate change on the number and power of tornadoes is not yet obvious, warmer temperatures and more thunderstorms are likely to lead to more frequent powerful tornadoes – the so-called F4s and F5s that can tear the heart out of a target community. As the century unfolds, we may also see more destructive tornadoes in other parts of the world. Surprisingly, the Netherlands has the most tornadoes for its size, and they may become increasingly common during summer storms across Europe. A few decades from now, a tornado slicing through the suburbs of Birmingham, as happened in July 2005, might hardly make the news headlines.

WHERE WILL THE WORST FLOODING OCCUR?

More frequent, and bigger, floods are a sure consequence of climate change. Densely populated, low-lying flood plains and deltas, like those of Bangladesh, Egypt and China, which face the dual threat of increased river flooding and rising sea levels, will be worst hit. South Asia will also be at the mercy of the monsoon – which is expected to be wetter and more unpredictable in the future. In the industrialised West, hurricanes will bring more flooding to coastal US cities, while wetter European winters will lead to frequent flood mayhem. With 3.6 million homes in the UK forecast to be at high risk of flooding, the annual cost of flood damage could climb as high as £22 billion.

In its Fourth Assessment Report, the IPCC highlights changes in precipitation as one of the biggest consequences of anthropogenic climate change. The regions forecast to receive more rain include North America, Europe, and tropical East and South East Asia: all areas with high population densities and large wealth concentrations. Run-off in these regions is predicted to rise by up to 40 per cent by 2050, providing the potential for a huge increase in flooding. By the 2080s, the IPCC reports, up to a fifth of the world's population will live in areas where river flood potential has increased. This is to say nothing of the billions, in developed and developing countries alike, who will be facing a severe and increasing coastal flood threat from accelerating sea-level rise.

In many developing countries, more frequent river flooding – driven by climate change and exacerbated by human activities such as deforestation – will make farming on floodplains increasingly difficult, leading to food shortages and, in the worst cases, famine. The fertile, highly populated and sometimes highly urbanised deltas of the world's great rivers will face a particular threat from the twin pincers of increased river flooding and rising sea levels driving bigger storm surges. At the heart of the explosively rapid growth of the Chinese economy, the Yangtze Delta is especially vulnerable. The region, sometimes known as the 'Golden Triangle of the Yangtze', is home to an economy valued at around US$2 trillion. This is comparable to that of a medium-sized developed country, and amounts to around one fifth of the national economy. The region is home to 90 million people, more than half of them living in urban centres including the great cities of Shanghai, Nanjing and Hangzhou.

The Ganges-Brahmaputra delta is also especially at risk, as it will experience increased river flooding brought about by the melting of the Himalayan glaciers. To make matters worse, in the Bangladeshi part of the delta, just a 50-centimetre rise in sea level will mean enough permanent inundation and flooding to drive six million people from their homes. With flood plains making up 80 per cent of the land area of the country, Bangladesh is probably the most flood-prone nation on the planet. It also has one of the world's highest birth rates, and a population expected to double within 30 years. Virtually all the new arrivals will reside within the flood plains of the great Brahmaputra, Ganges and Meghna rivers, which provide fertile farmland but also bring the risk of death and destruction through massive flooding. As if this isn't enough, a predicted 11-per-cent rise in monsoon-related precipitation by 2030 is forecast to make a further 15 per cent of the country extremely vulnerable to floods.

The Asian monsoon is also intimately tied up with the future flood threat to South Asia. More than half of the world's population depends upon the monsoon rains, and any changes to the pattern can mean the difference between life and death to hundreds of millions of people in Pakistan, India, Bangladesh, China and other countries across the region. Too little rain leads to drought and famine; too much and crops, livelihoods and lives are lost to the raging floodwaters. With most climate models predicting a wetter monsoon in the future, it is likely that the record rains of 2005, and the catastrophic floods that affected 45 million people across India in 2007, are representative of what the region will face in the future. Some climate scientists, however, have predicted that the monsoon will become more erratic, certainly bringing major flooding, but also episodes of drought that could see huge numbers facing famine.

The Western world will not be spared the threat of increased flooding as the world warms. By 2030, Atlantic hurricanes are expected to be 20 per cent wetter, so that US coastal cities will face a two-pronged assault, with water from the skies adding to the problem of seas surging inland. In Europe, meanwhile, winters are predicted to be up to ten per cent wetter within a few decades, leading to saturated soils, increased run-off and bigger, more damaging floods. At the same time, torrential summer cloud bursts, fuelled by higher temperatures, will spawn flash floods and mudslides similar to those seen in several parts of Switzerland in October 2000. Since 1990, floods on the continent have cost 58 billion Euros, and the region already experiences twice as many major flood events as the United States.

There seems little doubt that frequent flooding will be a part of the UK's future, with the annual cost of flood damage predicted to climb as high as £22 billion – 15 times higher than it is now. Incredibly, in spite of this, 350,000 residential properties have been built on floodplains in the last two decades, including more than 20,000 in the last three years. Now, 120,000 more are planned for the low-lying land to the east of the capital and adjacent to the Thames estuary – surely a preposterous action given increasingly dire warnings about future sea levels.

WHICH PARTS OF THE WORLD WILL DROUGHT HIT HARDEST?

Hothouse Earth will bring more of the same for those nations and regions that are already severely water-stressed – Australia, California, southern Europe and much of Africa. Blistering temperatures, insufficient water resources and encroaching deserts will play havoc with the Mediterranean tourist industry, while in Africa drought-induced water and food shortages are predicted to fuel more and bigger conflicts. By the end of the century, London will have a climate comparable to that of Portugal today, while increasingly parched summers will have us saying farewell to the golf course, the traditional village green and the English country garden.

Not surprisingly, a warmer world will make matters far worse for those places where drought is already a serious problem, including Australia, California, the southern Mediterranean, much of Africa, and even the southeastern UK. Southern Europe will struggle to reconcile a rapidly growing tourist industry with ever-dwindling supplies of water. With the

200 or so golf courses around the Mediterranean together guzzling as much water as a city of 2.5 million people, it may be that these are the first to suffer, along with the countless swimming pools that visitors and ex-pats use to keep cool. It won't do the tourist industry much good, but the region is liable to become far too hot for many visitors in any case. 2006 brought a glimpse of the typical southern European summer of the decades to come, with temperatures in the high 30s to 40s Celsius across the region, wildfires raging in Greece, and severe droughts in southern Spain, Italy and France. The pressure of nearly 140 million visitors a year on the arid coastlines of Spain, Greece, Cyprus, Turkey, Tunisia and Morocco is already placing an intolerable burden on water resources, and the WWF recently called for tourists to boycott pools and golf courses to bring some relief. With ever-hotter summers on the way, and the 427 million people living around the shores of the Mediterranean due to be joined by another 96 million by 2025, the pressure on water resources is likely to reach a critical point sooner rather than later, particularly with a 4°C temperature rise predicted to halve freshwater availability across the region.

Africa has come to accept drought, famine and ever-expanding deserts as a part of everyday life, but climate change brings the prospect of worse to come. Few Africans live in the deserts or rainforests, with most inhabiting the land in between where agriculture is possible. Here, however, the slightest variation in rainfall can mean the difference between a bountiful year and a biblical famine – and the difference between a peaceful life and bitter conflict. According to the UN Environment Programme, the current civil war and humanitarian catastrophe in the Darfur region of Sudan is being exacerbated by drought and food insecurity, both of which climate change is predicted to worsen. In northern Sudan, rainfall is down by almost one third in the last 40 years, over which time the sands of the Sahara have advanced southwards by close to 100 kilometres. Looking ahead, temperatures are expected to be up to 1.5°C higher by 2050, with crop yields down by as much as 70 per cent. Both the Sahel region and southern Africa are forecast to get up to 30 per cent drier in the next several decades, placing 250 million or more people at risk of drought and starvation. The situation in southern Africa is predicted to be especially bad, with a drop in rainfall great enough to slash the flow of the region's rivers by half, and cut the availability of freshwater by up to 50 per cent.

Across India, Pakistan and Bangladesh, whether climate change will bring drought or deluge depends very much on the monsoon and how it responds to a warming world. If predictions prove to be correct, then climate change will bring a 20-per-cent rise in the summer monsoon rainfall, making floods more likely than drought. At the same time, it looks as if this might be accompanied by less rainfall further west, leading to the threat of more droughts in Indonesia and southern Australia. Such are the complex interactions of the world's atmosphere and oceans, however, that an alternative scenario is possible. Recent research shows that whenever the Atlantic Thermohaline Circulation has been weak in the past, Asian monsoon rainfall has been significantly reduced. If, therefore, climate change does result in pronounced slowdown in the ATHC, then its ramifications could include increased drought in South Asia.

Things are certain to get a lot drier in the UK, although perhaps not enough to see our capital vanishing beneath giant sand dunes. In 70 or 80 years' time, average UK temperatures will be 3–5°C higher and London will have a climate comparable to that of the Portuguese town of Vila Real, famous (or infamous) for its Mateus Rose wine, today. With baking summer temperatures, and much less summer rainfall, soil moisture in the UK could be up to 40 per cent lower than it is today, with far-ranging consequences. Water will be far more expensive, and could double in price in just 30 years, leading to big hikes in the prices of food staples such as meat, bread, milk, cheese and vegetables. Golf courses could disappear and parks fall into dereliction as they become too expensive to maintain. The traditional village green may go the same way, perhaps replaced by an Italian-style piazza, while the English country garden will give way to a Mediterranean concoction of pungent herbs, olive trees and vines. Worst of all for the Welsh, the hotter, drier conditions are likely to see the last daffodil pushing up daisies – as it were – well before 2050.

WILL DROUGHT MAKE THE WORLD'S DESERTS EXPAND?

As the driest places get even drier, we are faced with the prospect of more and bigger deserts, and the desertification of semi-arid regions that today have too much rainfall to qualify as true deserts. On the northern and southern shores of the Mediterranean, climate change may transform to desert an area that is larger than the UK and home to 16 million people. Southern Africa is destined to succumb to rampant desertification, while the Chinese capital, Beijing, is already under attack from raging sandstorms and encroaching dunes.

The UN has warned that, in just the next ten years, 50 million people may be driven from their homes by expanding deserts – a number that will only increase as the climate gets hotter. The strict definition of a desert is a region that receives less than 250 millimetres (ten inches) of rain a year. This is less than half of London's annual rainfall and about a quarter of New York's. Currently, about one fifth of the Earth's surface is occupied by desert, and although some parts of the planet will become wetter as climate change takes a tighter grip, it should not be a surprise that higher temperatures will bring desert conditions to places that at the moment have just sufficient rainfall to keep the sand at bay.

It is rather timely, therefore, that the United Nations proclaimed 2006 the International Year of Deserts and Desertification. The reason for this focus of attention was the growing concern that both livelihoods and ecosystems will suffer enormously as rising temperatures cause existing deserts to expand and new ones to develop. With land degradation already affecting one third of the planet's surface, the likelihood of huge swathes of dry and semi-arid terrain deteriorating into full desert is high. This has the potential to affect a billion people in 100 countries, with those in Africa being particularly vulnerable. Two thirds of the continent is already either desert or dry-lands, and nearly three quarters of the latter is severely degraded by agriculture, making it highly susceptible to desertification.

On top of this, the situation is being exacerbated by the loss, each year, of an area of vegetation the size of the Netherlands, and by erratic rainfall that will become even more so as climate change takes hold. It is doubtful, given the predicted dramatic loss of river flow, that southern Africa can get away with anything – as the century progresses – other than rampant desertification. Further north, a slight increase in rainfall is expected to prevent the Sahara encroaching much further southwards, but a predicted fall in precipitation in the north is leading to worries for those countries bordering the southern shores of the Mediterranean, and also for southern Italy and Spain. Heat waves have become more commonplace and the region may become up to 40 per cent drier over the course of the next 100 years. Already, desertification in Tunisia and Spain is costing $100 million and $200 million respectively, and these amounts are set to climb. Water is now scarce in Egypt, Libya, Tunisia and Morocco, while climate change and increasing demand – much of it driven by tourism – will place increasing stress on resources in Italy, Greece and Spain. Crete looks as if it will be particularly vulnerable to creeping desertification as within a decade the island could face serious water shortages in five years out of six. Meanwhile, 75 per cent of Tunisia is under threat of desertification, with more communities vanishing beneath the marching sand dunes every year.

A combination of pollution and saltwater penetration of aquifers will impact upon water supplies, and as crops fail and livestock are lost, the Sahara will creep north, first to the Mediterranean shore and then across into Sicily, southern Spain and Greece. One of the most attractive regions on the planet will be devastated, the tourism industry that brings much-needed income and employment will be lost, and valued ecosystems wiped out. A 3–4°C rise would destroy 85 per cent of the extraordinarily diverse wetlands of southern Europe, alongside rich fisheries and a watery environment that hosts seven per cent of the planet's marine species. In all, some 300,000 square kilometres of southern Europe – an area larger than the UK and home to 16 million people, is set to be transformed by climate change into a dead world of dust and rock, where farming of any kind is no longer viable.

Huge tracts of Latin America and Asia, where – in both cases – almost three quarters of all land is degraded by agriculture, are also under threat. In China, gigantic sandstorms are driving the deserts into new areas, choking rivers and burying precious farmland. Massive tree-planting campaigns have been undertaken in an attempt to tie down the blowing sands, with over 30 billion trees planted in the last two decades, but more than 2,500 square kilometres of land is still devoured by the desert every year. Already, more than a quarter of China is made up of desert, and its growing encroachment affects around 110 million people and costs up to $3 billion a year through its impact on farming and transport links. As climate change makes water for irrigation ever scarcer and farming becomes more and more difficult, the sands of the Gobi desert will continue to encroach upon the Chinese capital. The nearest dunes are now just 70 kilometres away from Beijing, and they are creeping several kilometres closer every year, feeding raging sandstorms that frequently shroud the city for days at a time. In the immediate future, this has the potential to disrupt the 2008 Olympics; not long after that, the dunes will be at the gates and the long-term viability of the city will be seriously tested.

WILL THE GREAT FORESTS SURVIVE?

The world's great forests play a crucial role in removing carbon dioxide from the atmosphere and helping to keep the Earth's temperature at a level amenable to life. Now they are vanishing at an astonishing rate, mainly due to illegal logging, the scrabble for cattle grazing land, and the opening up of palm oil and soya-bean plantations to supply the growing demand for biofuels. Deforestation is now responsible for at least one fifth of all greenhouse gas emissions – more than cars, ships and planes together. If the fight to save the great forests is lost, then so is the battle to prevent dangerous climate change.

Along with the tiny plankton that swarm in our oceans, the world's great forests have always acted as our planet's lungs, sucking carbon dioxide out of the atmosphere and slowing down climate change. Now, slash-and-burn policies are driving massive deforestation across the planet, contributing one fifth of all greenhouse gas emissions – more than all the world's cars, ships and planes put together. In fact, over the last 200 years, destruction of the forests has been responsible for almost a third of the rise in atmospheric carbon dioxide levels due to human activities.

Considering their critical role, the scant regard we pay to our forests is astonishing. In the Congo, the world's second largest rainforest is under attack for its timber from US and European loggers, while across South East Asia, in Papua New Guinea, Indonesia and Burma, millions of ancient trees are hacked down and burnt to provide space for farming or to feed the lucrative tropical hardwood trade. In Papua New Guinea, the forest that covers four fifths of the country could be gone by 2020, while in Indonesia little pristine rainforest is expected to remain a decade later.

What is happening in Asia, however, pales into insignificance next to the situation in the great Amazonian rainforest. This unique ecosystem covers seven million square kilometres – an area about the size of Australia – and spreads across seven South American nations. With other smaller broadleaf rainforest ecosystems succumbing to axe, chainsaw and fire, the Amazon now represents more than half of the entire planet's rainforest inventory. But it is vanishing at a staggering rate. A fifth of the original rainforest has already been destroyed, mostly since the 1970s, and in the last decade of the twentieth century, an area twice the size of Portugal was lost. The decaying vegetation left behind by loggers releases carbon dioxide into the atmosphere to complement that no longer absorbed by the extracted trees. As a consequence, Brazil is one of the biggest emitters of greenhouse gases on the planet, with its logging practices accounting for 70 per cent of the 300 million tonnes of carbon dioxide the country produces every year.

Ironically, the newest threat to the Amazon arises from the push for 'green energy' and the desire to move away from hydrocarbons. The prices of palm- and soya oil have been inflated thanks to their use in biofuels, providing further incentive to grub up forests in favour of managed plantations. In the Amazon, freeing up land for soya-bean plantations is now the greatest single cause of rainforest destruction. The Amazonian soya trade is also being fostered by massive demand from the Chinese, whose increasingly animal-protein-rich diet requires more and more soya feed to fatten up poultry and pigs. South East Asia, too, is suffering from the biofuel craze, with the growth in palm-oil plantations driving further obliteration of the rainforests, particularly in Borneo, where the practice is threatening the already-beleaguered orang-utan population.

While not facing the wholesale clearing afflicting their cousins in the tropics, forests elsewhere are also suffering at the hands of climate change. Scorching summers are making life difficult for Germany's great oak trees – half are already sick and there are concerns that within the next 20 years they could disappear entirely. Hotter, drier summers look as if they will also sound the death knell for the beech woods of southern England, perhaps as early as 2030, and in the following decades, oak, ash and Scots pine are likely to suffer too. Rising temperatures are also taking a massive toll on the temperate forests of Siberia, the largest in the world, where the number of wildfires has risen tenfold in the last couple of decades. During the sweltering summer of 2003, an area almost the size of the UK was destroyed by fires – some natural, others started by illegal loggers seeking to satisfy China's ever-growing appetite for resources. Coastal mangrove forests are also on the wane, mainly as a result of increasing urbanisation and tourism. As mangroves seem to be especially good at sucking carbon dioxide from the atmosphere and squirreling it away in the oceans, their disappearance means still more of the gas stays in the atmosphere.

Prospects for all the world's forests in coming decades are depressing, to say the least. Unfortunately, the more forests we lose, the worse things get for those that remain. Carbon dioxide levels in the atmosphere will rise progressively thanks to slash-and-burn practices as well as the fall in the number of trees. This in turn will accelerate climate change, placing extra pressure on any remaining forests. The Amazon region, for example, is forecast to get drier and hotter, leading to a large-scale die-back as the climate becomes more suitable for supporting grassland than trees. The region saw its worst drought for more than 100 years in 2005, and this is highly likely to be the forerunner of many more. Long before 2100, there could well be virtually nothing left of this natural wonder of the world and the estimated 2.5 million plant and animal species that reside within. If the fight to save the great forests is lost, then so is the battle to prevent dangerous climate change.

WHAT ABOUT WILDFIRES?

Wildfires and climate change go hand in hand, with increased warming providing the conditions for more fires and the carbon emissions released by fires contributing to higher temperatures. In a single week the California wildfires of 2007 released as much carbon as all fossil fuel burning in the state over a comparable period. More worrying, however, is the increase in tundra wildfires, and the huge peatland fires in Indonesia and elsewhere in South East Asia. Here, the half a billion tonnes of carbon released by peatland degradation and fires every year really puts into perspective the Kyoto Protocol's aim of cutting global emissions by a shade under 200 million tonnes.

Wildfires, whether natural or intentional, are intimately bound up with climate change, and across increasingly parched areas of the planet they are certain to pose an ever-growing threat to infrastructure and agriculture. Of greater concern, however, is the fact that fires – especially those associated with deforestation and other land clearance, contribute enormously to carbon dioxide concentrations in the atmosphere.

2007 was an appalling year for wildfires. With summer temperatures exceeding 40°C, and vegetation parched by drought, southern Europe, and particularly Greece, was badly affected. Here, fires burnt across more than 2,700 square kilometres, destroyed thousands of buildings and took 68 lives. Later in the year, California was the target. Los Angeles experienced its driest year on record, with just 87 millimetres of rain, while across the state, October fires sparked by tinder-box conditions and hot Santa Ana winds reduced more than 2,000 square kilometres of brush and 1,500 homes to ashes, and took 14 lives. Wildfires are beginning to be a perennial problem in California, and as the Earth warms, climate models predict more of the same, only worse, for southern Europe too.

Another future flashpoint will be Australia, where major bushfires already present a growing threat to Sydney and other large cities. In December 2001 and January 2002, the so-called Black Christmas bushfires raged across 3,000 square kilometres of New South Wales, destroying 200 homes and necessitating the evacuation of 10,000 people. Drought conditions have continued to hold sway across Australia ever since. Even the UK is now at risk from wildfires like those of July 2006, which were particularly damaging to the moorlands of the Peak District in the north of England and the heathland of Surrey in the south. Such was the level of fire risk that public access was suspended across many upland areas.

In a self-perpetuating cycle that constitutes yet another positive feedback system, the warmer the world gets, the more wildfires there are, and the more wildfires there are, the more carbon dioxide is released into the atmosphere, and so on. The California fires of 2007, for example, pumped out 7.9 million tonnes of carbon dioxide in a single week – the same amount that is produced from all fossil fuel burning in the state over a similar period. A comparable situation is to be found in the high Arctic tundra, where increasing temperatures are drying out the scrubby vegetation and making it more susceptible to ignition from lightning. In 2007, for example, a huge tundra fire destroyed around 900 square kilometres of land on Alaska's North Slope. In addition to the massive amounts of carbon dioxide that this would have released into the atmosphere, the resulting blackened tundra absorbs heat from the sun more effectively, resulting in warming and thawing of the permafrost beneath, and the release of the methane to drive further warming.

While tundra fires present a serious problem, they are insignificant when set against the intentional fires set for land clearance and logging. The destruction of tropical forests clearly makes a massive contribution to carbon dioxide levels, but even worse is the burning of the logged and drained peatlands, whose concentrated masses of decayed vegetation contain huge quantities of carbon. This is often accidental, with fires ignited for land clearance burning out of control, but the consequences are dire. Average annual carbon emissions from peatland fires range from 400 million to more than one billion tonnes – and in 1997 this reached two and a half billion tonnes. Around one third of the global peat inventory is in the tropics, with 60 per cent located in Indonesia, the primary peat-burning culprit. Peatlands that have been drained also emit carbon as they oxidise, with the breakdown of South East Asian peatlands, alone, producing up to 238 million tonnes of carbon every year, nearly all of it from Indonesia. In total, South East Asia's carbon emissions from peat fires and peat oxidation amount to more than half a billion tonnes a year. Compare this with the Kyoto Protocol's aim of reducing global carbon emissions by around 200 million tonnes by 2012, and the scale of the problem becomes apparent.

Even in the UK, peat is proving to be a problem, with gamekeepers burning moorland at an unprecedented rate in order to encourage the growth of heather for grouse. This promotes the decomposition and oxidation of the underlying peat, threatening to release the 20 billion tonnes of carbon locked up in UK peat bogs – about the equivalent of the last 150 years' worth of UK fossil fuel emissions. No wonder that Adrian Yallop of Cranfield University has called the moors 'Britain's rainforests'.

Global peat deposits hold about 550 billion tonnes of carbon– so unless the follow-up to Kyoto can come up with a mechanism for slowing or stopping peatland deforestation and draining in South East Asia, the resulting carbon outpourings will negate any emissions savings elsewhere.

WILL THE POLAR ICE CAPS DISAPPEAR?

Within decades, it is likely that the Earth will warm enough to cause irreversible melting of the Greenland Ice Sheet. An additional global temperature rise of as little as 1°C may be sufficient to trigger ice-sheet collapse, which could occur over a period of just 300 years, or even less. Already, one Greenland glacier is sliding seaward at 15 kilometres a year, sometimes surging five kilometres in as little as 90 minutes. At the other end of the world, the picture is not much better, and the chances are that if we lose the Greenland Ice Sheet, the West Antarctic Ice Sheet will go the same way.

The poles are heating up more rapidly than anywhere else. In July 2006, an Arctic high of 22°C was recorded, some 14°C above normal for the time of year, with temperatures at least 7°C higher than normal measured on several occasions during the same month. Not surprisingly, this exceptionally hot summer coincided with record low levels of Arctic sea ice, and predictions that it could all be gone within perhaps five years. Clearly, something very disturbing is happening at high latitudes, and particularly so when you consider that so far, global average temperatures have climbed just 0.74°C since the Industrial Revolution. What, then, will be the fate of the polar ice sheets should temperatures climb another 2°C or more? Some climate scientists I have spoken to are convinced that we are already too late to save either the Greenland Ice Sheet or the West Antarctic Ice Sheet, and probably both, committing us to an eventual sea-level rise in excess of ten metres. If we haven't already crossed the tipping point, then we will certainly do so within a decade or two unless we make drastic cuts in emissions.

As leading climate scientist Jim Hansen points out, 'building an ice sheet takes a long time, but destroying it can be explosively rapid'. There is a very good chance that we are already seeing the early stages of this explosive collapse of the Greenland Ice Sheet. Satellite observations show that the area of ice melting during the summer has risen from 450,000 square kilometres in 1979, an area equal to the size of Sweden, to more than 600,000 square kilometres in 2002, an area greater than that of France. Notwithstanding the progressive ramping up of temperatures at high latitudes, the ice-melting process is itself a self-perpetuating positive feedback mechanism. Summer melting of the pale-coloured surface snow exposes darker ice beneath, which absorbs more heat, leading to more rapid melting. As more and more ice is lost, so the surface is progressively eroded down to lower altitudes where the air is warmer, further accelerating melting.

This type of behaviour has already led to the complete melting of a large ice sheet in Glacier Bay, Alaska, where an ice mass with a volume of 3,000 cubic kilometres (and up to 1.5 kilometres thick in places) has completely disappeared in less than 200 years. What is happening now to the Ilulissat Glacier, on the west coast of Greenland, makes it easy to see why many climate scientists are concerned about the future of the Greenland Ice Sheet. In recent years, the glacier's surface has become pock-marked with moulins – huge holes up to 15 metres across formed by melting – down which torrents of meltwater are pouring. This water is lubricating the base of the glacier to such an extent that it is now moving towards the sea at a rate of around 15 kilometres a year. On occasion, however, the glacier experiences spectacular surges, one of which involved the ice moving an astonishing five kilometres in just an hour and a half – hardly what we understand as a glacial pace.

On average, the Arctic has so far warmed by a little more than 1°C, although this varies from place to place across the region, with temperatures in Alaska and Siberia up by 2–3°C. If climate change drives up global temperatures by a couple more degrees, much of the Arctic, including Greenland, could end up being 5°C warmer. This kind of rise would result in summer melting expanding across the entire ice sheet, and lasting for much longer. With a local temperature rise of 2.7°C thought to be sufficient to trigger the irreversible collapse of the Greenland Ice Sheet, prospects are not good. If and when it goes, computer models suggest that it will not re-form for at least another 60,000 years.

But how long will it take to melt an ice sheet almost as large as Mexico and up to three kilometres thick in places? A few years ago, a figure of 3,000 years was being batted about, but this was based upon top-down melting rather than physical break-up. Now, Tim Lenton, a climate scientist at the UK's University of East Anglia, has suggested that the Greenland Ice Sheet could break up within 300 years. Another 1°C rise could be enough to set this in motion, and with an additional 0.6°C temperature rise already in the system, we are now teetering on the edge of losing the ice sheet and committing ourselves to a seven-metre rise in sea level.

If the picture in Greenland is depressing, it is not much better in Antarctica, where the warming waters of the Southern Ocean along with climbing air temperatures are taking their toll on the West Antarctic Ice Sheet. Here, the buttressing ice shelves are being lost, and the glaciers behind them are accelerating – one by as much as 20 per cent in recent decades – and thinning. If continued warming is sufficient to melt the Greenland Ice Sheet, it is very likely that the WAIS will go the same way, and probably over a similar time scale, resulting in a further five-metre sea-level rise.

HOW HIGH WILL SEA LEVEL RISE, AND HOW QUICKLY?

Notwithstanding IPCC Fourth Assessment predictions that sea level will rise no more than 59 centimetres by 2100, many climate scientists are increasingly worried that the physical break-up of the polar ice sheets may lead to a one- to two-metre sea-level rise this century, followed by several metres more in the next. If this sounds like scare-mongering, the last time that the polar regions were 2–3°C warmer than they are now, sea levels were up to six metres higher. Depending on how quickly the global population continues to climb, the 2080s could see more than five billion people living under threat of rising sea levels – perhaps as many as half of all those alive at the time.

If all the water that is currently locked up at the poles melts, sea levels will rise by 75 metres or so. Without a runaway greenhouse effect taking hold and accelerating out of control, this is a scenario that we are never likely to experience. It is, however, worth keeping in mind as the ultimate and terrible outcome of unmitigated and unstoppable global warming. In its 2007 Fourth Assessment Report, the IPCC projected that average sea level would rise by between 18 and 59 centimetres by the end of the century. These forecasts are clearly very conservative – in fact, the lower-end predictions would require the current rate of sea-level rise (three millimetres a year) to actually slow down, at a time when melting of the polar ice sheets is accelerating dramatically.

On the other hand, a number of climate scientists are concerned that we may be faced with extremely rapid sea-level rise. As previously mentioned, NASA's Jim Hansen has voiced the opinion that collapse of the Greenland Ice Sheet could be explosively rapid, leading to sea levels rising 'a couple of metres this century and several more next century', while IPCC climate scientist Michael Oppenheimer is concerned that 'the time-scale for future loss of most of an ice sheet may not be millennia but centuries.' Hansen has noted that if polar ice sheet melting adds a single centimetre to sea level each year for the decade 2005 to 2015, and this doubles each decade until the increasingly unstable West Antarctic Ice Sheet has more or less collapsed in its entirety, this would raise sea level by more than five metres by 2095. In relation to the speed with which this could happen, there is currently no evidence. In Hansen's opinion, however, a 2–3°C rise in global temperatures would make a sea-level rise of this order inevitable. It is worth remembering that the last time the polar regions were 2–3°C warmer than they are now – during the last interglacial 125,000 years ago – sea levels were between four and six metres higher than today. Even worse, in the Pliocene period, three million years ago, when temperatures were again a few degrees higher, and carbon dioxide levels comparable to what we might expect in the next few decades, sea level was a very scary 20 metres or so higher.

Sea level rose by about 20 centimetres during the twentieth century, and the current rate of rise of about three millimetres a year, which translates to about a hand's breadth every three decades, is certain to speed up – perhaps to a centimetre or two a year if Hansen is proved to be correct. Such a rate of rise would result in the sea encroaching onto land at the terrifying rate of 15–30 metres a year, rapidly inundating low-lying terrain, wreaking havoc with coastal defences, contaminating water resources, and committing vulnerable nations, or at least large chunks of them, to a watery grave. Vast numbers of people would be affected: more than 630 million people – over ten per cent of the world's population – live less than ten metres above the current mid-tide sea level, and 1.4 billion people live within the near-coastal zone. This includes more than 250 million inhabitants of 14 of the world's megacities[8]. The highest population densities are encountered below the 20-metre elevation, and are therefore at greatest risk from storm surges and tsunamis, which will have ever more impact as sea levels rise. Depending on how quickly the global population continues to grow, the 2080s could see as many as 5.2 billion people living under threat of rising sea levels: probably more than half of all those alive at the time.

WHICH PARTS OF THE WORLD ARE MOST LIKELY TO VANISH BENEATH THE WAVES?

A catastrophic sea-level rise of several metres would inundate all, or parts, of many of the world's great cities, return to the sea vast areas of low-lying land in Florida, the Netherlands and elsewhere, promote severe erosion of cliffs and beaches worldwide, and contaminate the aquifers of countless coastal cities. Even a one-metre or so rise by the end of the century is forecast to threaten the homes of a billion people and one third of the planet's farmland. A multi-metre rise would see entire cities abandoned or forced into drastic reconfigurations. In Sydney, the opera house would vanish beneath the waves, while in London, Big Ben would be silenced and the Houses of Parliament submerged.

It is possible that by drastically slashing greenhouse gas emissions in the next few decades we could save the Greenland Ice Sheet and hold off – at the last moment – the crumbling of the West Antarctic Ice Sheet.

Given the total lack of progress so far, however, we may soon have to come to terms with the fact that we are committed to a ten-metre or more rise in sea level in the next few centuries. This could mean that many billions of people would eventually suffer as a result of our failure to take action now.

Even a rise of one metre or so by the end of this century will cause massive disruption in developed and developing countries alike. Projections suggest that a rise of this order would threaten the homes of a billion people, and put a third of our farmland at risk. Two hundred million people could find their food source lost, while 50 million could be forced to find new land and livelihoods. The Maldives would be barely habitable, and large swathes of Bangladesh and the great deltas of the Nile, Mekong, Mississippi and Yangtze rivers would be under water. Around 26,000 square kilometres of the USA – an area three quarters of the size of Belgium – would disappear with just a 60-centimetre rise – with low lying areas of Florida and the Gulf coast, and parts of Maryland and Virginia, being particularly susceptible. Cities at risk include Alexandria in Egypt and Long Beach, San Jose, Naples, Miami and New Orleans in the United States.

A 1.5-metre rise would see 58,000 square kilometres of the United States – equivalent to three times the size of Israel – return to the ocean. Again the Gulf Coast and Florida would bear the brunt, along with North Carolina, which has as much land less than one metre above sea level as the Netherlands. More than 8,000 square kilometres of southern Florida would be swamped, destroying the fabulous and fragile Everglades for ever. A two-metre rise would see Lagos in Nigeria and Shanghai in China struggling to avoid complete inundation, and drown farmland that hosts a quarter of the population of Egypt. The Netherlands, meanwhile, would be engaged in a losing battle to keep the North Sea at bay. Its government is already planning to abandon large areas of land to the sea, and by the end of this century much of the country could be beneath the waves. Across the water, large sections of the UK coastline would also begin to submerge and crumble on a massive scale.

While an upgraded Thames Barrier might still hold back the seas from London following a one-metre rise, it is likely that the barrier would need to be raised on 100 or more occasions a year, having a huge impact on the efficient functioning of the Port of London. The defences closer to the estuary, in Essex and Kent, might not be so effective. This mixed-bag of walls, grassy flats and earth embankments could well prove to be the weak link in the coastal defence system, allowing increasingly violent storm surges to carry the sea many kilometres inland. To cope with a rise of several metres, the entire sea defences for London and the Thames Estuary would need to be rethought, and stark choices made – either to spend many billions on new protective structures, such as a barrier across the outer estuary, or to launch a programme of managed retreat that would involve abandoning much of the capital.

Elsewhere in the UK, it will be impossible to defend the coastline against a rise of several metres, and low-lying parts of Essex, Kent, Lincolnshire, Norfolk, Suffolk, coastal Lancashire, Teeside and the South West will inevitably have to be sacrificed to the sea. As well as inundation, there will also be a dramatic increase in the rate of erosion. Over the past 100 years, around 70 per cent of the world's coastlines have been eroding due to rising sea levels, and as an island, the UK has taken its fair share of battering. Far worse is yet to come, however: the National Trust estimates that half its 700 miles of cliffs and beaches, which make up ten per cent of the UK's coastline, will be severely damaged by erosion over the next 100 years.

If sea levels do rise catastrophically in the next few hundred years, prospects for all major coastal cities are dire. A ten-metre rise, or more, would lead to complete abandonment of some cities and the loss of entire districts of others. Managed retreat, accompanied by rebuilding and reconfiguration, will inevitably mean that familiar skylines like those of Sydney and London will look very different in the future, with many of their current landmarks lost.

ARE WE GOING TO SEE A MASS EXTINCTION OF ANIMAL AND PLANT SPECIES?

We are currently living through the sixth great extinction, this time arising not as a result of an asteroid impact or vast lava outpouring, but entirely as a consequence of human activities. Species are now vanishing a thousand times faster than at any time for the last 65 million years, and climate change is certain to accelerate the extinction rate in the coming century. By 2050, a quarter of land plants and animals may be extinct, including the polar bear, which could disappear in the wild within decades, while by 2100, more than a quarter of bird species may be either extinct or critically endangered.

Not only is climate change causing problems for those human beings who are largely blameless of any contribution, it is also threatening just about every species of plant and animal on the planet. All are completely innocent, but nevertheless many will face the ultimate penalty for sharing a world with humankind – extinction. While the Earth has experienced dramatic swings in its climate before, most notably during the ice ages, rarely before has climate change been as rapid and dramatic as we are seeing today. As a consequence, vast numbers of plant and animal species simply have no time to adapt to the new conditions. Due to a combination of human activities and climate change, the world's ecosystems are in a desperate state – and getting worse. According to the 2005 Millennium Ecosystem Assessment, the natural functions of the Earth are under such enormous strain that 'the ability of the planet's ecosystems to sustain future generations can no longer be taken for granted'. A similarly bleak picture is provided by the Living Planet Index, which monitors the state of the world's biodiversity, and reveals that this fell by 40 per cent between 1970 and 2000. Not surprisingly, the Ecological Wellbeing Index, which incorporates an average of 51 environmental indicators, also shows that very few countries can be counted ecologically healthy.

So far, our world has faced five great extinctions in its 4.6-billion-year history, the last of which was some 65 million years ago when a large asteroid or comet impact – perhaps with the help of great outpourings of basalt lava – obliterated the dinosaurs and up to 85 per cent of all species. This, like the other four mass extinctions, was a natural event. Now, however, we are living through a sixth extinction episode that is entirely of our own making. In its 2006 report, the United Nations Environment Programme warned that we are causing the worst mass extinction since the demise of the dinosaurs. Current extinctions are happening at perhaps 1,000 times the natural rate, with 844 known animal and plant species vanishing in the past 500 years alone. While deforestation, our never-ending thirst for resources, and our reckless treatment of the environment as a whole all play a part, climate change is set to be the greatest driver of future extinctions. By the end of the century, the Earth could be warmer than for at least ten million years, leading to conditions comparable to those that prevailed before the majority of species alive today appeared on the scene. Many will not be able to cope, and by 2050 climate change may have driven a quarter of land animals and plants to extinction.

Already more than half of the world's bird species are under threat, and 14 per cent could be gone by 2100, by which time a further 15 per cent might be on the brink of oblivion. More than 40 per cent of European birds are at risk, as are those that migrate over long distances. In addition to destruction of ecosystems, bird numbers can also be decimated by less obvious consequences of the changing climate, such as an increasing mismatch between the hatching of young and an available food supply.

Nearly a quarter of mammal species are in serious decline, and iconic species such as the chimpanzee, orang-utan, polar bear, black rhino and North American reindeer may be gone in the wild by 2050. As the Arctic sea ice melts earlier and earlier each year, it prevents polar bears from reaching the seals that make up most of their diet, and with the Arctic forecast to be ice-free in summer as soon as 2013, the future of the species is bleak indeed. Despite their prowess as tremendously strong swimmers, drowned carcasses are already turning up – testament to lonely and desperate deaths as weakened bears are forced to try and reach their prey via the sea rather than the ice. And as the ice fails in the face of increasing warmth, the ice-dwelling seals may also find themselves on the danger list – even with the demise of their main predator.

Many animal and plant species under threat live in one of a few dozen biodiversity hotspots. These make up just one per cent of the planet, but host 44 per cent of all terrestrial vertebrate species and 35 per cent of plant species. Environments most vulnerable to climate change are those that are geographically limited so there is nowhere for species to retreat to if changed conditions can no longer support them. They include the tropical Andes, the much-neglected Atlantic forests of Brazil, Paraguay and Argentina, South West Australia, and the marvellous Mediterranean ecosystem of South Africa's Cape Floristic. That the world's mightiest land ecosystem – the Amazon Rainforest – is also under threat goes without saying. Deforestation continues to exact an enormous toll, while climate change threatens to end the vital rains that feed the forest, causing it to dry out and die sometime after 2050. Before the new century dawns, 2.5 million insect species, hundreds of thousands of plant types and thousands of bird, mammal, amphibian, reptile and fish species could be gone for ever.

HOW WILL LIFE IN THE OCEANS FARE?

Not only are the oceans warming up, they are also becoming more acid as they are forced to absorb more carbon dioxide from the atmosphere. Warming of the Southern Ocean is threatening whales, seals, penguins and a multitude of smaller organisms. A combination of warm and acid seas is presenting a huge threat to coral reefs: one fifth are effectively dead, and all could be wiped out within 30 years. Even the plankton that help to slow the level of carbon dioxide accumulation in the atmosphere, by absorbing it to build their tiny skeletons, are in trouble. If we do nothing, the seas could soon be more acid than they have been for more than 300 million years.

Life in the oceans is already suffering, partly as a result of heat from the atmosphere penetrating ever deeper, but mainly because of increasing acidity. The oceans absorb nearly 85 per cent of the extra heat generated by global warming, and records of ocean temperatures over the past 40 years show that on average they have warmed 0.5°C at the surface, with significant warming penetrating down to several hundred metres.

The consequences include a reduction in the growth of plankton – which plays a vital role in absorbing carbon dioxide and forms the basis of many marine food chains; the bleaching of coral reefs; and the disruption of fish breeding and feeding patterns. In the Southern Ocean, around the shores of Antarctica, the sea temperature is only just above freezing, and even a small rise will cause immense disruption to the fragile marine ecosystem, which includes whales, seals, penguins and a multitude of smaller organisms. Since the 1950s, though, summer sea temperatures off the Antarctic Peninsula have climbed 1.2°C, reducing the ease with which sea ice forms in the winter and causing the population of krill to plummet by 80 per cent since the 1970s, threatening fish and whales higher up the food chain. The species that live in the Southern Ocean have nowhere to go as the sea warms, because the Antarctic continent stops them swimming to higher latitudes. Instead, they must either adapt or die.

Coral reefs – some of the most bio-diverse environments on Earth – are also suffering as temperatures climb. If the water gets too warm, the corals expel the tiny, symbiotic algae that live within them, leading to bleaching and, ultimately, death. By the end of 2005, according to the Global Coral Reef Monitoring Network, close to a fifth of the planet's coral reefs were effectively dead, in that they had lost 90 per cent or more of their live coral and had little immediate chance of recovery. On top of this, half the world's coral communities have poor long-term prospects for survival, and 95 per cent are projected to die off if global temperatures rise by more than 2°C. With the top ten coral reefs sheltering some 34 per cent of rare and geographically-restricted marine species, this would be a huge blow to the extraordinary inventory of life on Earth.

In fact, all the coral reefs could be lost in just 35 years, because the usually-alkaline oceans are becoming increasingly acid. This is because they have soaked up close to half of all the carbon dioxide released into the atmosphere by human activities, something like half a trillion tonnes since the Industrial Revolution. While this has done us a favour, because otherwise atmospheric levels would already be up at 435 ppm rather than just 384 ppm, marine life is going to pay a high price. The increasingly acid water will start to dissolve the calcium carbonate skeletons and shells of a whole spectrum of marine organisms ranging from plankton to corals. Worst affected will be those organisms, including corals, whose skeletons are made up of the form of calcium carbonate known as aragonite, which is more soluble in acid waters. With a doubling of carbon dioxide levels in the atmosphere, the combination of acidity and higher water temperatures is likely to see very few reefs surviving by 2050.

Carol Turley, Head of the UK's Plymouth Marine Laboratory, calls ocean acidification a 'potentially gigantic' problem, as it has the capability to completely alter the composition of life in the oceans. Of most concern is how acidification will affect the tiny plankton known as coccolithophores, which play a key role in extracting carbon from the atmosphere by using it to build their skeletons, which sink to the bottom on death, forming sediment and ultimately limestone rock. If the plankton go, then carbon dioxide will accumulate in the atmosphere at a much faster rate, driving greater warming and accelerating ocean acidification.

Ken Caldeira of Stanford University's Carnegie Insitution, one of the first scientists to draw attention to the acidification problem, also regards the issue as critical. In a co-authored paper published in the journal *Nature* a few years ago, Caldeira warned that continued absorption of carbon dioxide could make the oceans more acid than they have been for 300 million years, possibly barring a few exceptional catastrophic acidification events. The oceans naturally absorb around 100 million tonnes more carbon a year than they release, but are now being force-fed around two billion extra tonnes annually – 20 times their natural uptake. Making small reductions to emissions is unlikely to result in anything more than a small dent in this figure, and, as Caldeira has pointed out, anything less than slashing emissions to zero will only slow down the relentless process of acidification. Without such drastic action, it looks as if our oceans will soon be more acid than during the Palaeocene–Eocene Thermal Maximum, 55 million years ago, when warm, acid oceans resulted in a mass extinction of marine species and the composition of the sea took a hundred thousand years or so to return to normal.

COULD LIFE TAKE REVENGE?

While climate change is set to wipe out plant and animal species left, right and centre, it looks as though some of them might be preparing to take their revenge. The world's plants and soils hold up to three times more carbon than is present in the atmosphere, but as the world warms microbial activity in soils accelerates the decay of organic matter, causing them to release their carbon. Add in more from the destruction and burning of forests and peatlands and the decay of drought-blighted crops, and the biosphere becomes a carbon source rather than a carbon sink. By 2100, this could result in a calamitous land surface temperature rise of 8°C.

The world's plants and soils may hold up to three times more carbon than is present in the atmosphere, and they are currently absorbing about a quarter of the carbon dioxide emitted by human activities. Things are predicted to get bad enough as they are, but what if the biosphere breaks down and releases its carbon back into the atmosphere? The impact on the rate of warming could be catastrophic. Unfortunately, as the world continues to warm, it looks as though there is a very high chance that this will happen. Originally, it was hoped that increased levels of atmospheric carbon dioxide might mean enhanced vegetation growth and result in more carbon dioxide being sucked from the atmosphere, but this does not seem to be happening. Instead, as temperatures have risen, soils have warmed up, increasing the activity of microbes so that organic matter has decayed more rapidly, releasing more carbon dioxide into the atmosphere. Over the past quarter of a century, UK soils have been losing carbon at a rate of 13 million tonnes a year, and the same thing must also be happening elsewhere, especially at temperate latitudes, where three quarters of the world's soil carbon is locked away.

The transition from soils acting as carbon sinks to becoming carbon sources is expected to accelerate as warming increases, with other elements of the biosphere joining in. As climate change reduces rainfall in forested areas, for example, the trees will dry out and die. On the one hand, this will mean that they can no longer play a role in extracting carbon dioxide from the atmosphere, and on the other that they will become sources of the gas, either through their decay or as a result of being burnt in wildfires. If the Amazon Rainforest dies off, it alone will return as much carbon dioxide to the atmosphere as has been released from all the fossil fuels burnt in the twentieth century. Amazingly, humankind is helping things along, by intentionally or inadvertently triggering massive fires, which are fuelled by drier conditions and higher temperature. In Borneo, for example, the drainage and drying out of peat swamps, in an attempt to convert them into rice plantations, has led to annual fires that are pumping out huge amounts of carbon dioxide. If things continue at the present rate, some 27,000 years' worth of accumulated peat, spread over an area of 200,000 square kilometres, will go up in smoke before the middle of the next century, adding 50 billion tonnes or more of carbon to the atmosphere.

In Europe too, fires are becoming a real issue. The record European heat wave of 2003 resulted in rampant wildfires, parched soils and swathes of shrivelled and decaying crops releasing an estimated half a billion tonnes of carbon into the atmosphere – around twice the amount generated in the region by fossil fuel burning over the same period. It looks as if this might be becoming a general trend too, with baking summers in the northern hemisphere reducing the ability of plants to absorb carbon dioxide during the growing season, so that they become net producers rather than absorbers of the gas. This is yet another nail in the coffin of the hope that more carbon dioxide in the atmosphere would herald a greener world in which warmer summers accelerated plant growth, which would in turn soak up more of the gas. No such luck. It is now perfectly apparent that more atmospheric carbon dioxide means excessive heat that drives the loss of soil carbon, kills vegetation and triggers wildfires, and so pumps even more carbon dioxide into the atmosphere. It looks as if the biosphere is biting back with a vengeance. And there appears to be another sting in the tail too, with a recent study revealing that warmer, wetter conditions are set to encourage European forests to disgorge nitrous oxide, a greenhouse gas that is nearly 300 times more potent than carbon dioxide. Deciduous, rather than coniferous, forests seem to be most effective at doing this, which is a shame as there is currently a big drive to plant more deciduous trees in order to promote biodiversity.

Few of the global climate models address the issue of vegetation and soils switching from carbon sinks to sources, so it is difficult to predict what their ultimate impact will be. Research undertaken at the UK Met Office's Hadley Centre suggests that the switch will occur pretty abruptly when global temperatures are 2°C higher than pre-industrial levels – in other words by 2050. If we do nothing to mitigate greenhouse gas emissions, the concentration of carbon dioxide in the atmosphere is predicted to rise to between 700 and 980 ppm by 2100, but this is without a contribution from the biosphere. By the last quarter of this century, this is likely to have returned to the atmosphere all the carbon generated by human activities that it absorbed over the last century and a half, adding the equivalent of two thirds of the carbon dioxide already there. Even more carbon could be released due to land-use changes and the destruction and burning of forests. The result, by the end of the century, could be a calamitous 8°C rise in land temperatures, with even hotter conditions to follow.

HOW ELSE COULD THE EARTH FIGHT BACK?

It seems that the Earth might have decided that the best way to tackle the climate change problem is to do its utmost to get rid of the species that is causing it. Gigantic belches of methane gas from thawing permafrost could add another half-trillion tonnes of carbon to the atmosphere, while deep-sea clathrate deposits could pump out 10,000 billion tonnes – more than ten times the amount currently in the atmosphere. Even the rocks beneath our feet may rebel, with loading and unloading of the crust due to rising sea levels and melting ice sheets triggering earthquakes, submarine landslides, tsunamis and volcanic eruptions.

Albeit with no conscious intent, perhaps our planet has decided that the best solution to climate change is to get rid of the species that is causing the problem – us. Certainly, the switching of the biosphere to become a source of carbon will not make our lives any easier. In addition, thawing of the vast expanses of permafrost that stretch across the frozen peat bogs of Siberia, Alaska and northern Canada could release sufficient methane to add another half a trillion tonnes or more of carbon to the atmosphere.

Alongside this, there is the disturbing possibility that changes to the Earth's crust may cause further problems. Rapid loss of the major ice sheets will release the crust beneath, causing it to bounce back up – a process known as isostatic rebound. The crust beneath the Greenland Ice Sheet, for example, is depressed by the three-kilometre-thick ice to hundreds of metres below sea level. If and when the ice sheet melts, the crust will slowly return to its normal, ice-free position. This, however, is likely to mean an increased number of earthquakes that may trigger huge submarine sediment slides around the margins of the island – which may, in turn, trigger giant tsunamis. Similar events, known as the Storegga Slides, occurred off the coast of Norway following the end of the last ice age around 8,000 years ago, sending 20-metre-high tsunamis crashing into the Shetland Islands and resulting in waves three or four metres high battering the east coast of Scotland – comparable in height to the devastating tsunami that struck the shores of Sri Lanka and Thailand in 2004. A little further south, in Iceland, melting of the Vatnajökull ice sheet will release the load on the volcanoes below, almost certainly stimulating an increase in activity.

Even away from the poles, catastrophic melting could disturb the equilibrium of the Earth's crust. If sea levels rise by several metres in the next few centuries, the extra load imposed by the huge weight of the additional water could trigger earthquakes and volcanic eruptions along the world's island chains and continental margins. The ability of water loading to trigger earthquakes has been observed during the filling of more than 70 reservoirs around the world, causing earthquakes in China, Greece, South Africa, India and elsewhere. The most famous incident occurred in western India in 1967, when increased seismic activity followed the filling of the Koyna reservoir, culminating in a magnitude 7 quake that took 200 lives and badly damaged the Koyna dam. With the area seismically quiet prior to the construction of the dam and reservoir, the earthquake activity is widely considered to have been triggered by the weight of more than 2.5 billion cubic metres of water on underlying faults.

Study of past changes in sea level, too, shows that eruptions occurred more frequently when there were rapid rises in sea level following glacial periods, and even today, Alaska's Pavlof volcano shows a marked tendency to erupt in the autumn and winter months, when local sea levels rise by just a third of a metre. As well as being potentially destructive in their own right, coastal earthquakes could initiate submarine sediment slides – not only capable of generating tsunamis, but also of releasing methane from clathrate deposits trapped in the sediment. In total, these could contain a staggering 10,000 billion tonnes of carbon – more than ten times the amount that is in the atmosphere at present.

Other unpleasant side-effects of our interference with the Earth's climate include an expansion of the hole in the ozone layer over the Antarctic, threatening Australia, New Zealand and southern Chile and Argentina with more skin cancers and blindness, and perhaps the development of a similar hole over Europe. We could also see more intense and more frequent El Niño events, which warm the eastern Pacific and cause a massive shift in weather patterns, bringing widespread flooding to western South America and California, and drought to Asia and Australia. El Niño events have been more severe over the last 100 years than at any time in the last 130,000, with those of 1982–3 and 1997–8 being the largest on record. It looks like we might have to get used to it, with one study predicting that a doubling of atmospheric carbon dioxide levels by 2050 will lead to El Niño events happening on average every three years instead of every five as at present. Other research suggests that the climate is drifting towards a general El Niño state – which would be very bad news for those regions to which it brings flood or drought.

The Earth has another weapon in its armoury too. As we continue to burn fossil fuels, it seems we are pumping more water vapour into the atmosphere along with the carbon dioxide, with levels rising by six per cent since 1982. Water vapour is the most common component of the Earth's natural greenhouse effect, but has not previously been considered in the context of global warming because its concentration in the atmosphere was thought to be reasonably constant. If water vapour levels are rising rapidly, however, then we can expect things to get even warmer.

WILL WARS BE FOUGHT OVER WATER RESOURCES?

Water is already a precious commodity that many people simply don't have enough of. Soon, our changing climate will make it so scarce that those countries that covet more will turn their attention to their neighbours' supplies. Two thirds of all human water use is devoted to agriculture, and with three billion more mouths to feed by 2100, the problem can only intensify. The UN has identified 158 flash points where wars could be fought over water, including East Africa, South Asia and the Middle East, and already tensions are beginning to run high.

Water is the most precious of all natural resources, and without it our civilisation, and all life on the planet, would fail. Well before 2100, it is likely that the oil will be gone, and in hothouse Earth, water will be the strategic resource over which pacts are made and wars fought. With the world's population set to be half as big again as it is today, there will be around three billion more mouths to feed. Already, close to 40 per cent of our planet's land area is given over to pasture and crops, which suck up more than two thirds of all human water use. By the end of this century, the loss of land to the sea, flood, drought and higher temperatures will place enormous stress on agriculture across the planet, and drive up demands for water as nations struggle to feed their populations.

The problem is that even the most basic of foodstuffs absorb a huge amount of water in their production. Three thousand litres of water go into producing a kilo of sugar, 5,000 litres are needed to get an equivalent weight of rice or cheese to the table and an astonishing 20,000 litres go into the same amount of coffee. A kilo of best Australian beefsteak costs 50–100,000 litres. Every day you may indirectly be gulping down a hundred or more times your own weight in water.

In developed countries, direct use of water is also constantly on the rise, be it to water gardens or golf courses, fill swimming pools, or clean cars. In the south east of England, consumption is rising by about one per cent a year per head, yet the government still plans to build 120,000 new homes in the Thames Gateway, east of London, where there is a potential problem with drinking water provision. London is not alone: cities across the planet will use 150 per cent more water within just 20 years, a rate of increase that can't be maintained to 2100 and beyond. Long before this the first wars will be fought over water resources as countries covet the reserves of their neighbours or interrupt the flow of rivers passing through several countries to supply their ever-growing demands.

Even today, around one third of the world's population lives in countries that are 'water-stressed'. Close to 2.4 billion people lack adequate sanitation and a billion or so have no water in their homes. By the middle of the century up to 2.8 billion water-stressed people could see climate change driving down the availability of water even further, particularly in Europe, the Middle East and central Asia, southern Africa and parts of Central, North and South America. Such a situation is unsustainable and conflicts are certain. In fact, the United Nations has targeted 158 international river basins that may become flash points as governments battle to provide water for their citizens, agriculture and industry. In many places, conflict is likely to arise over the construction of dams designed to hold back water, or generate power, or both.

Already the seeds of future water wars are being sown. In east Africa, for example, Uganda has secretly drained 75 cubic kilometres of water from Lake Victoria since 2003, much to the annoyance of the Egyptians. Further tensions are rising in the region over the Nile Basin Treaty, originally ratified in 1929, which bars any of the eight other countries that the Nile passes through from reducing the flow of the river to Egypt and Sudan. Ethiopia feels particularly hard done by as it accounts for 75 per cent of the waters flowing into the Nile but uses less than one per cent. With drought biting hard, the government wants to make more use of the river waters for irrigation, a move that the Egyptians oppose on the basis that any reduction in flow will affect their agriculture. With Tanzania and Kenya also desperate for more water, it looks as if the Nile Basin Treaty is now teetering on the edge of collapse.

The government and citizens of Bangladesh are not too happy either, at Indian plans for the largest and most expensive water management project ever proposed. Costing up to US$400 billion and taking at least 14 years to complete, the Indian government plans to divert up to one third of the flow of the Brahmaputra, Ganges and other rivers to drought-prone areas in the south of the country at a rate of 173 billion cubic metres of water a year. As these rivers pass through Bangladesh after travelling through India, there is enormous concern that such a scheme will bring water shortages and have a devastating impact on agriculture there. There is a fly in the ointment, however, to the extent that the rapidly vanishing Himalayan glaciers may so starve the rivers of water that the plan is scuppered before it bears fruit.

While argument and posturing continue in East Africa and South Asia, it may well be the Middle East where the first water war starts. As if there are not enough problems in the region, water is becoming increasingly scarce and is a source of constant tension between Israel, Syria, Jordan and the Palestinians. The latter, in particular, have poor access to water and struggle to find sufficient even though they use just a quarter as much as neighbouring Israelis. Within five years, the water scarcity could come to a head – with violent consequences.

HOW WILL THE CHANGING CLIMATE AFFECT DISEASE AND ILLNESS?

Progressively higher temperatures will see the inexorable march of insect-borne killer diseases from the tropics into temperate regions. Malaria kills 1.5 million people a year – including 800,000 children under five – and another 340 million people could be at risk due to climate change. Malarial mosquitoes are likely to breed in the UK and much of Europe and the USA by 2050, also bringing with them dengue fever, yellow fever, Lyme disease, encephalitis and West Nile virus. Even bubonic plague, carried by rodents, is forecast to become more common. Deaths from heatstroke, skin cancer and asthma will all increase, as will cholera, diarrhoea and food poisoning.

There is no doubt that a warmer Earth will prove to be an ideal breeding ground for disease, and – as usual – the most vulnerable sections of the community in the poorest countries will suffer most. According to the World Health Organisation, the first 12 months of the new millennium saw an estimated 150,000 premature deaths as a result of climate change, along with maybe five million illnesses – and this figure is set to rocket, mainly as a result of disease and starvation. A doubling of deaths from malaria, diarrhoeal diseases and malnutrition is projected by 2030, with sub-Saharan Africa and coastal regions of the Pacific and Indian Oceans forecast to be worst hit.

While climate change will bring extinction to many species, the humble malarial mosquito will revel in hothouse Earth, expanding its range from 45 to 60 per cent of the Earth's surface by 2050 and finding millions of new hosts for its eggs. Each year, malaria kills 1.5 million people, including a heartbreaking 800,000 children under five. In many countries, the disease is as ubiquitous as the common cold, and accepted with the same equanimity. In Ghana, for example, 17 million of the country's 20 million inhabitants are infected by malaria every year. The warmer and wetter conditions predicted for some tropical regions will make the disease more common, with a 2°C rise placing up to 275 million more people at risk, and a 3°C rise increasing this figure to perhaps 340 million. As the world warms, malaria will also spread to higher ground in the tropics, where lower temperatures have so far kept the disease at bay, and into more temperate regions. A 2°C rise will see malarial mosquitoes cross into southern Europe from sub-Saharan Africa and head inexorably north as temperatures continue to climb. By the middle of the century, malaria-carrying mosquitoes could be back in the southern UK after an absence of a couple of hundred years. Areas most susceptible are likely to include the Fens, the Thames Estuary, the Somerset Levels, southeast Kent and the Severn Estuary, with temperatures being warm enough by 2100 to foster a four-month breeding season. And where malaria goes, other insect-borne diseases follow – including yellow fever, encephalitis, Lyme disease, dengue fever and West Nile virus, the latter of which has already rampaged across the United States and into Canada since 1999, and which has now been detected in native British birds. Even bubonic plague, carried by rodents, is predicted to be more common on a warmer planet.

With potable water ever more difficult to access, population numbers and social deprivation increasing, and natural catastrophes on the up, cholera and other diarrhoeal diseases will also become far more common, and may increase by five per cent in just 15 years. In some parts of South America, a 1°C rise is predicted to cause an eight per cent increase in cholera and similar diseases, with young children bearing most of this increased burden. Climbing temperatures will drive an increase in food-borne diseases too, with cases of salmonella food poisoning in the UK increasing by 12 per cent for every 1°C rise. Increased numbers of people will also be killed and injured in extreme weather events, such as floods and windstorms, and as a direct result of heat waves.

As the century progresses, the old and infirm will be affected less by cold winters, and more by sweltering summers. The higher temperatures will reduce the incidence of bronchitis and pneumonia, which affect both the old and the very young, but the heat will be just as dangerous, if not more so, to these vulnerable groups. Death during heat waves occurs as a result of hyperthermia or heatstroke, due to the body absorbing more heat than it can get rid of. Normal body temperature is around 37°C, with a rise of just 3°C being life threatening and brain death beginning at 41°C. Every 1°C rise in the planet's temperature will also increase the death rate from respiratory illness by ten per cent, with asthma sufferers being hit hardest through a combination of warm and humid conditions, increased air pollution and a dustier environment. The number of skin cancer victims is also forecast to rise, as climate change weakens the Earth's protective ozone layer, with an extra 5,000 deaths every year in the UK alone. The incidence of cataracts, which in many parts of the world are the main cause of blindness, will climb too, as more ultra-violet radiation finds its way through the diminishing ozone shield.

By 2100, nowhere will be entirely safe from the new health threats, but some regions will fare much worse than others. As ever, developed countries will have it easy compared to Africa, where disease directly attributable to climate change is projected to kill up to 182 million people by the end of this century – with the poor and the innocent paying the ultimate price to maintain the lifestyles of the rich and the guilty.

WHAT WILL HAPPEN TO FOOD SUPPLIES?

Around one in eight people in the world do not have enough food to eat. Climate change, in the form of climbing temperatures, more droughts, torrential rains, hail storms, and an increase in plant pests and invasive weeds, is set to make this situation far worse, causing crop damage and livestock loss around the globe. Water-starved southern Africa may bear the brunt, but just a 3°C rise will see crop yields falling across Africa, Australia, Europe, Russia and the United States, placing 400 million more people at risk of hunger.

Today, an estimated 854 million people don't have enough food to eat on a daily basis – that is around one in eight. Inevitably, climate change will make this situation worse, as crops and livestock suffer from droughts, high temperatures, floods, torrential rain, hail storms and an increase in plant pests and invasive weeds. The fact that the planet's population is set to top nine billion by 2050 will not help either. With a temperature rise of just 3°C, another 400 million people will be at risk of hunger as a warmer world translates into one of failing crops. Forget the idea that higher temperatures bring bumper harvests – they don't. It was hoped at one time that the damage threatened by droughts, wild weather and soaring temperatures might be offset by higher crop yields due to faster photosynthesis driven by higher levels of atmospheric carbon dioxide, but recent experiments have shown that this is not the case.

A 1°C temperature hike would actually benefit agriculture in most developed countries, while causing a slight reduction in crop yields in the tropics. An additional 1°C rise, however, is projected to reduce crop yields in Africa by ten per cent, cause yields to fall for the first time in Europe, the United States and Russia, and place 200 million people at risk of hunger in Africa and Asia. In the tropics, a 3°C rise in temperature could see crop yields down by a third, having a massive effect on the livelihoods of billions, while in Australia, a 4°C increase could render entire regions unusable for agriculture. In the UK, crops such as beet, barley and potatoes will disappear, to be replaced by sunflowers, soya (for biofuels) and four-metre-high elephant grass (to provide a carbon-neutral fuel for power stations). Wheat production is likely to surge, too, especially in the north where rainfall will be more plentiful, and the UK could become Europe's breadbasket as soaring temperatures in the Mediterranean countries make the crop unviable there. Around the world, one estimate suggests, a 3°C rise may result in up to 5.5 billion people living in countries or regions blighted by significant reductions in crop production.

The availability of water will be the key to food production and food security in the next 100 years, and, as mentioned earlier, it will be an increasingly scarce resource. More evaporation, changes in precipitation patterns, reduced flow or loss of glacier-fed rivers, and increased demand for irrigation will all play a role, as will the ever-greater needs of growing megacities, especially in India and China. Even now, 250 cubic kilometres of water is sucked out of India's aquifers for irrigation every year, while only around 100 is replaced – a recipe for future disaster. Together with Pakistan and China, India probably accounts for over half of the planet's total use of underground water for agriculture, but the same hell-for-leather approach to sucking the aquifers dry is being adopted across the world, from Vietnam and Indonesia to Iran and Morocco, Mexico and Argentina, and even the United States. Using up long-term water resources for short-term gain – hardly a sustainable policy – is storing up enormous problems for the future.

India, Bangladesh, Nepal and China are in a particularly precarious position as their rivers, which provide much-needed water for agriculture and to recharge aquifers, are fed by glaciers in the Himalayas. At present, these glaciers pour vast quantities of water into Asia's rivers every year, but as the ice disappears, rivers like the Yangtze, Yellow and Ganges will be increasingly starved of water. Already, China's Yellow River sometimes dries out to such an extent that it fails to reach the sea, and in the future the flow of the Ganges could fall by 70 per cent and other rivers by up to 90 per cent. Such reductions would have a cataclysmic impact on the food security of half a billion people or more, and bring the prospect of famine to South and South East Asia.

The news for Africa is not good either. There is some evidence that parts of the Sahel region – immediately south of the Sahara – may see more rain, which will boost farming and reduce the incidence of hunger and famine, but the jury remains out on this. More convincing is the prediction that climate change will bring a major reduction in rainfall in southern Africa, reducing river flow, and placing 100 million people under threat of a devastated agricultural system and mass starvation. Some rivers, including the Orange River, the fifth largest in Africa, may dry out completely, making agriculture impossible across a large swathe of the south.

By the last few decades of this century, climate change will have ensured a fall in food production across the developing world, which will have a devastating impact worldwide. As usual, the greatest hardship will fall on the poor: subsistence farmers who are struggling to grow just enough food for their families. In less than 20 years, climate change could depress cereal production in Africa by two to three per cent. This sounds like an insignificant amount, but it could be enough to leave 10 million people under growing threat of starvation. Translate this scenario to other parts of the planet, push up temperatures another 2, 3, 4 or even 5°C, and widespread malnourishment, hunger and famine could be spread right across the developing world by 2100.

WILL CLIMATE CHANGE DRIVE MASS MIGRATION?

Climate change could force a staggering one billion people to leave their homes, and 250 million might be permanently displaced within 50 years. Already, there are estimated to be around 30 million environmental refugees, and this number could rise ten-fold or even further as the seas rise and the deserts expand. In South and South East Asia, many millions of people will be forced out of the crowded coastal cities by rising sea levels, while in North Africa and southern Europe, the increasingly dry conditions will push a multitude of people north. In China, the expanding Gobi desert will keep large elements of the population on the move, while the USA will need to find space for millions displaced from southern Florida and the Gulf Coast.

Wars, civil strife and economic and social problems have always kept huge numbers of people on the move, and the UN estimates that there were close to ten million refugees worldwide at the end of 2003 as a result of these causes. Increasingly, however, large numbers are being driven from their homes or their countries for environmental reasons, including scarcity of resources, unequal land distribution, natural and man-made disasters, dam and reservoir construction, environmental degradation and climate change. Estimating the number of environmental refugees is far from an exact science, but there could already be as many as 30 million, and a dramatic rise in numbers is certain as climate change bites harder. Desertification alone threatens the livelihoods of around 135 million people, while sea-level rise in the coming century will mean hundreds of millions more are forced to move elsewhere. Before the end of the century, climate change might have ousted as many as a billion people from their homes, thanks to rising sea levels, drought, natural catastrophes and environmentally-related conflicts, and as many as 250 million could be permanently displaced within 50 years.

There is currently a big debate in progress about where people should go when the sea rises and the deserts expand, and who should bear the responsibility for their future livelihoods and prospects. On one side are those who say that the polluters should pay – after all, most, if not all, of those displaced will have contributed little in the way of additional greenhouse gases to the atmosphere and should be bailed out by those that have. This 'polluter pays' idea argues that the countries responsible for climate change should take environmental refugees in proportion to their profligacy, so – for example – a country like the USA, which is responsible for close to 30 per cent of all global carbon emissions to date, should take the same percentage of exiles. There is a strong counter-argument, however, that is not lodged in racism or xenophobia, which is that all those refugees that find homes in industrialised countries will inevitably embrace their extravagant lifestyles, thereby bumping up carbon emissions far further than if they had maintained their original ways of life. In other words, the last thing that the Earth needs at such a critical time is another 100 million Americans – or western Europeans for that matter.

To be realistic, the 'polluter pays' path is very unlikely to be followed. However much guilt or responsibility they feel, most developed countries are certain to take a more politically expedient route and allow in a trickle of those that climate change displaces, rather than a flood. To do anything more would undoubtedly lead to a voter backlash as well as leading to economies and social structures buckling under the stress of climate change. Furthermore, many environmental refugees will be unlikely or unable to leave their region and head for a new life halfway across the planet. What is more likely is that they will be displaced internally or into neighbouring countries. Inevitably, the bulk of the tens of millions who will eventually be driven from Bangladesh as the sea encroaches will head for India: a society that is comfortingly familiar. Similarly, when the low-lying islands of the South and West Pacific – like Tuvalu – disappear beneath the waves, most of their people will end up in Australia and New Zealand.

Figuring out just how many people will ultimately be displaced by climate change is an exercise in picking a number out of thin air, and totals vary enormously from a few hundred thousand to a few hundred million a year. Most will be pushed out by rising sea levels, which will have the greatest impact along the crowded coastlines of South and South East Asia and parts of Africa. Encroaching desertification and land degradation will hit North Africa and southern Europe hardest, and massive internal migration and resettlement will also occur, for example from southern Florida and the Gulf Coast to other parts of the United States, from the increasingly drought-afflicted interior of Australia to the margins, and anywhere away from the ever-expanding Gobi Desert in China.

One thing is certain, which is that shifting vast numbers of people around the planet will be a far from orderly affair. One estimate suggests that by the middle of the century, climate change will have driven 150 million people into neighbouring areas and across borders, triggering social volatility, racism, resentment and bitterness among indigenous populations that might themselves by suffering food and water shortages.

Biblical migrations on a scale to dwarf anything seen today will undoubtedly bring instability and conflict to many parts of the world, and provide fertile ground for terrorist recruitment – perhaps targeting those industrialised nations whose wasteful and thoughtless activities got them into the mess in the first place.

While the USA will have trouble dealing with the millions who will be internally displaced by rising sea levels and expanding areas of long-term drought, the UK will also have its problems. Severe and growing water problems, along with escalating temperatures, are likely to see a movement of the population northwards, and there will also be increasing pressure for the UK to take environmental refugees – from Commonwealth countries, but more especially from within the EU. Perhaps enclaves will be established on the south coast for migrants from North Africa, Italy, Spain and Greece, while those Dutch who have given up the battle with the North Sea are allocated living space across the water in the parts of East Anglia and Lincolnshire that are still above the waves.

WILL SUMMER SUN AND WINTER SPORTS HOLIDAYS BE THINGS OF THE PAST?

Today's traditional holiday destinations are certain to suffer as baking temperatures, drought, flash floods, hurricanes and the rest make southern Europe, Florida and the Caribbean increasingly unattractive – and with warmer weather at home, future generations are far less likely to head abroad for rest and recuperation. If they do, the new hotspots are more likely to be southern Sweden and the Baltic coast rather than Greece or the Canary Islands. Ski resorts and hothouse Earth simply don't mix, and many will go under as the snow lines rise remorselessly. Within decades less than two thirds of Alpine resorts could have reliably good snow, with reduced business costing US$2 billion in Switzerland alone.

Unlike our generation, our children and grandchildren are likely to be shunning the sun rather than seeking it. Drought, water shortages, creeping desertification, blazingly hot days and sweltering nights, flash floods, wildfires, the possible re-emergence of malaria and the appearance of other mosquito-borne diseases will make traditional holiday destinations like southern Europe and the Canary Islands increasingly unattractive. One recent study suggests, not surprisingly, that in the future far fewer northern Europeans will be flying to the Mediterranean for a summer dose of sun – preferring instead to enjoy more traditional, and slightly cooler, holidays at home. Wales, Ireland and England's south coast are also predicted to prove increasingly attractive to our continental neighbours, particularly those facing blazing weather and acute water shortages at home. The losers in the holiday business, as the world heats up, are expected to be Greece, Italy, Spain, and the Caribbean; their mantles being transferred to southern Sweden, the Baltic coast, the Alps, Ireland, Croatia and southern Britain. Broadly speaking, tourism will shift poleward and uphill, where the sun is less of a demon and where water is not rationed. The travel industries of Germany and the UK, two of the top three most-travelled nations on the planet, will be particularly affected. At present, 72 million Germans head abroad every year, along with 53 million Brits, leaving unreliable weather behind. As the weather at home becomes warmer, however, many of these travellers are expected to soak up the sun at home. This is great for the home economies, but not so good for travel agents or the former destination states, particularly those relying heavily on tourist income.

Staying at home, however, might prove not to be as attractive as it sounds. In the UK, the risk of wildfires placing national parks out of bounds, drought conditions in the southeast, and erosion of tourist beaches and cliff walks due to rising sea levels may lessen the country's appeal – and the same applies to other temperate locations that may hope to benefit from the demise of traditional holiday destinations.

Across the planet, iconic tourist traps are destined to succumb to higher temperatures, encroaching seas and a plethora of associated nuisances. In Florida, beaches will be lost as the ocean rises, and more powerful hurricanes will threaten property, lives and livelihoods, while coral reefs and other coastal ecosystems surrender to higher sea temperatures, seawater inundation and storm surges. The Caribbean will fare equally badly, suffering a similar increase in stronger storms, along with beach erosion and the loss of coral reefs, and water and power shortages. Much of Europe, Florida and the Caribbean could all see the re-emergence of malaria, dengue fever and other tropical diseases. Australia could lose the jewel in its crown, the Great Barrier Reef, while the Maldives, Seychelles, Goa and Kerala are threatened by rising seas, and in the latter two cases by more powerful cyclones and a potentially erratic monsoon.

As a keen skier and Alpine enthusiast, it pains me to say it, but the winter sports industry is also a dead man walking. The 2006 European winter sports season was the warmest in the Alpine region for at least 1,300 years – that is since the Medieval Warm Period, and perhaps longer. Early December temperatures in the city of Grenoble, the self-proclaimed capital of the French Alps, touched 22.4°C, while grass-covered – rather than snow-covered – pistes postponed the season across the region. Unless stalling of the Atlantic Thermohaline Circulation brings far colder winters, we will see more of the same, with rising snow lines and more unpredictable snowfall sounding the death knell for many, if not most, winter sports resorts. In Scotland, the industry is already teetering on the edge of extinction as warmer winters bring more unreliable conditions, and a United Nations Environment Programme (UNEP) report warns of economic hardship and closure for many ski resorts in the European Alps, particularly those at low altitude. As soon as the 2020s, the total amount of snow here could drop by almost one third, and perhaps one half by the 2050s. The UNEP report forecasts that by 2030, or 2050 at the latest, the snow line will have risen by around 300 metres, leaving just over 60 per cent of resorts in the Alps with reliably good skiing, and up to half facing economic hardship or bankruptcy. In addition to the rising snow line, the first snows are predicted to arrive later so that seasons will shorten. Below around 1,200 metres the winter snow cover is unlikely to be continuous. By mid-century, the potential cost of the effects of climate change on the winter sports industry is predicted to be up to US$2 billion in Switzerland alone.

CAN THE GLOBAL ECONOMY SURVIVE?

In 2006, UK economist Nicholas Stern alerted us to the fact that climate change may plunge the world into the equivalent of the Great Depression of the 1930s, or the chaos brought about by the world wars of the twentieth century. He calculated that dangerous climate change can be combated by spending just one per cent of the planet's GDP a year, but the reality is that it may take much more than this, as the latest science shows that atmospheric greenhouse gas concentrations need to be capped at far lower levels than those advocated by Stern. However, if we turn away from this challenge, we could leave the world with no economy at all.

If failing to act on emissions in the next few years means that dangerous climate change becomes a reality later in the century, then it will undoubtedly have a massive impact on the global economy. Inexplicable as it may seem, this is not something that most economists appeared very concerned about until one of their own, Sir Nicholas Stern, former Chief Economist at the World Bank, published his much-hyped tome, *The*

Economics of Climate Change. Stern's review has been praised for bringing the climate change message home to big business – which, although it will pay scant attention to two and a half thousand scientists, apparently bows to the wise words of a single economist. Certainly, the review does its bit in terms of presenting climate change as a serious problem, and highlighting the fact that the global economy will suffer hugely if nothing is done to tackle it. In a nutshell, Stern's message is that, if we start now, we can combat and manage climate change by spending as little as one per cent of the world's GDP a year, which currently works out at US$720 billion. If we choose to do nothing in the next ten or 20 years, however, the global economy could eventually contract by up to five per cent a year 'now and forever', bringing widespread economic and social disruption on a scale to rival the two world wars and the Great Depression.

While they sound disheartening enough, Stern's predictions are almost certainly over-optimistic. This is because his calculations assume that stabilisation of the concentration of greenhouse gases in the atmosphere at somewhere between 500 and 550 ppm (carbon equivalent) is enough to avert dangerous climate change. The science now tells us, however, that this is nowhere near sufficient. Stern also suggests that emission cuts of as little as 25 per cent could stabilise emissions within the range 450–550 ppm, which is not impossible but extremely unlikely. He does admit, however, that the longer-term stabilisation of emissions will require a cut of 80 per cent or more, which is at least in the right ball park. The real problem with the Stern review is that although the author presents us with a 'cost' of one per cent of global GDP annually to stabilise emissions in the 500–550 ppm (carbon equivalent) range, he bottles out of giving a comparable figure for stabilising emissions at 450 ppm – instead fobbing us off with the vague notion that this would be 'very difficult and costly'. Unfortunately, for Stern's calculations and for all of us, it is looking increasingly likely that failure to stabilise emissions at even this figure will mean that dangerous climate change becomes inevitable.

While Stern's findings have captured the limelight since they were published in late 2006, his is not the only report to venture into the economics of climate change. One study, more optimistically than Stern, suggests that even achieving the highly ambitious target of stabilising emissions at 450 ppm would set back the world's GDP just 0.5 per cent by 2100. Another forecasts that through stimulating investment in new energy and transport technologies, tackling emissions could actually increase the global GDP by up to 1.7 per cent over 100 years.

The harsh reality is, I suspect, that preventing dangerous climate change, whether defined as keeping emissions below 350 ppm or 450 ppm, or preventing temperatures climbing more than 2°C above pre-industrial levels, is going to be staggeringly difficult. Given that we have just a few years to change the mindset of close to 200 national governments, whose common grail is ever-greater and ever-faster economic growth, any show of optimism is hard. When it becomes apparent that considerably more than one per cent of GDP a year will be needed to tackle the problem, it is almost certain that many governments will turn away, preferring not to know or hoping that others will act to solve the problem for them. Most of the world's nations, I fear, will be happy to place themselves on a war footing to fight others of their race, but not to battle the greatest environmental threat that our society has ever faced.

If, then, we fail to act in time to prevent catastrophe, what sort of state will the global economy of the late twenty-first century find itself in? In the worst case, given a world in the grip of climate chaos, with insufficient food and water, widespread wars and civil strife, environmental terrorism, and an energy famine driven by plummeting oil and coal reserves, there is a strong argument that an integrated global economy may fail to function at all. While one has to be blind or stupid not to see the darkness that is coming, many will still excuse inaction on climate change on the basis that it costs too much to do anything about it – a strange and illogical argument. Surely to avoid the threatened collapse of modern civilisation we should be paying whatever is needed?

WHAT SORT OF SOCIETY WILL MY CHILDREN AND THEIR CHILDREN INHERIT?

If the world's leaders fail to deliver a realistic and workable solution to the climate change problem when they meet in Copenhagen in 2009, then it will be our children and their descendents who will reap the whirlwind. Without action soon, dangerous climate change will transform the world of 2050 and beyond into one in which disruption, conflict, social breakdown and economic failure are endemic. The lives of our children and their children will be defined by a deteriorating physical environment, the loss of personal freedoms, and a continually depressed economy, with little hope of things getting any better.

Whether or not our offspring and their descendents will lead long, happy, and prosperous lives depends to a considerable degree on the world's response to the climate change threat over the next few years, and in particular in the approach to the crucially important 2009 UN climate conference, when the nations of the world will come together in an attempt to hammer out the most important political agreement ever made. If, in Copenhagen, the world's leaders fail to deliver a realistic and workable solution to the climate change problem, then our children and their children will be left with a world of increasing disorder and confusion, and a future far more uncertain than that handed down to us by our parents.

In 2007, the US Centre for Naval Analyses warned that climate change will have an increasingly destabilising impact on the world, acting as a so-called 'threat multiplier', particularly in countries and regions that are already unstable and volatile. Four years earlier, the Pentagon – hardly a body that is prone to hyperbole – published a study on abrupt climate change that contained a number of descriptors of our future world that are likely to prove pretty accurate. The authors of the report forecast that 'disruption and conflict will be endemic features' of the future and, most chillingly, that 'once again warfare would define human life'. While the Pentagon report is specifically concerned with what would happen if the ATHC shut down, heralding a much colder climate across the North Atlantic region, the type of violent, combative and fragmented society that it foresees could equally well apply to a global society besieged by wholesale dangerous climate change. With rising sea levels, creeping desertification and increasing drought driving environmental migrations on a biblical scale, battles for water raging across the continents, competition for energy and resources promoting wars and civil strife, and a failing economy, it is difficult to be optimistic about our world in the second half of the twenty-first century.

Even in the most developed countries, everyday life will become increasingly difficult. It is perfectly possible that the world's governments may have come to their senses and agreed to slash emissions; too late to prevent dangerous climate change and its manifold ramifications, but with the hope of averting an even worse situation. This would mean the introduction of drastic measures to cut emissions, which would almost certainly impinge seriously on personal freedoms. Individual carbon emission caps could be set, with limits on everything from car use and air miles to energy consumption. Even based upon Stern's optimistic forecasts, the global economy could be sunk in a depression to match that of the 1930s, or even far worse. Looking back to this period in history could provide a glimpse of the sort of world we could be faced with post-2050. Following the stock market crash of 1929, international trade collapsed to just one third of its previous level, and as a consequence profits, prices, tax revenues and personal incomes tumbled. In the UK one in five people were out of work, with up to 70 per cent unemployment in some towns and cities. Millions were destitute, while a quarter of the UK population barely survived on a subsistence diet. At the height of the depression, in 1933, 15 million Americans – a quarter of the workforce – were unemployed. Forty per cent of the US banks that existed in 1929 were gone three years later, tens of thousands of businesses went bankrupt and the US GDP dropped by 30 per cent. Lasting from 1929 to the start of World War II in 1939, the Great Depression was the longest economic collapse in the history of the modern industrial world, and in fact share prices in the USA did not reach the levels of the late 1920s again until 1954.

While many elements of the Great Depression might be replayed in a climate change-driven depression of the future, one big difference remains. Industry and commerce were eventually able to recover in the 1940s and 1950s, thanks to the availability of unlimited energy and resources, and building upon the demands of a global conflict. In our future world, both energy and resources will be at a premium. It is probable that rather than underpinning the global economy as it does today, oil will be a luxury item after 2050. Similarly the demands of a population of nine billion or more will mean that there are simply insufficient material resources to go around. The corollary of this is that the depressed world of the second half of our century will have no obvious salvation. The lives of our children and their children will, as a result, be defined by a deteriorating physical environment, a restriction of personal freedoms, and a continually struggling economy, with very little hope of things getting any better.

PART 3: WHAT CAN I DO?

A recent poll has revealed that many of us now care deeply about climate change and how it might affect our children and grandchildren. Too many of us, however, are turning away or choosing not to look because we feel that there is little we can do as individuals. In actual fact, however, as citizens acting in concert we can do a huge amount. For a start, each and every one of us can reduce our 'carbon footprint' – our personal quota of carbon dioxide production. In the USA and Australia this is, on average, 20.4 tonnes a year and in the UK, 9.8; in Chad, it is just 0.01 tonnes. We need to remember that everything we do and buy has a carbon cost, and if we want to bring this down we need to examine carefully every aspect of our lives, and make changes. Many are obvious – ditch the 4x4, drive less, fly less, cycle more, walk more, dump the patio heater, use low-energy light bulbs, buy 'green' energy; some are less obvious – shop locally, eat seasonally, cut down on meat consumption. All, however, are important if we, personally, are to make a difference.

AM I TO BLAME?

Yes. We all are. Every single thing we consume and every service we make use of generates greenhouse gases, so we must accept collective responsibility for our predicament. Through the way we live our lives, we are consuming our way to catastrophe: we buy a new mobile phone, on average, every 18 months; we dump 1.5 million computers every year, and we throw away our own weight in rubbish every seven weeks. For everyone on the planet to live at the same standard as a UK citizen would require the resources of three planet Earths. Clearly that doesn't add up, so something has to give.

All of us privileged enough to live in the developed world are to blame. As avid consumers of the goods and services whose manufacture and provision generate the greenhouse gas emissions that are changing our climate we have to accept collective responsibility for the mess we are in. Our desperate search for anything new, innovative and trendy that can put us one up on our friends and colleagues reached new heights of insanity in 2007 with the unveiling at Harrods of a gold-and-diamond saucepan, retailing at a cool £100,000. In a world where nearly three billion people are living on less than 50 pence a day, why anyone would wish to make, sell or buy such an item is utterly incomprehensible. The only reason would appear to be that we, in the industrialised West, have become completely disengaged from the rest of the world. Our lives are not defined by the bigger issues of the day, such as global poverty, the destruction of the environment or, unhappily, climate change, but by how much our houses are worth, which new mobile phone model we must have, or how many new outfits we need for the summer holidays. We are consuming our way, unthinkingly, to catastrophe. We dispose of 1.5 million computers every year, most of which work fine, and buy a new mobile phone every 18 months. We get through so much stuff so quickly that we chuck out our own weight in rubbish every seven weeks or so.

As Jonathon Porritt, chairman of the UK government's Sustainable Development Commission, puts it, consumerism has 'created unsustainable equalities and threatened to tear apart the very fabric of our society'. At the heart of consumerism are shops and shopping. Perhaps 1.5 to 2 billion people worldwide are now rich enough to consider what they want in their lives ahead of what they need, driving up demand for things that the other two thirds of the planet's population can barely comprehend – like the world's most expensive cocktail, launched at London's Movida nightclub and costing £35,000, which is enough to feed around 80 of the world's poorest families for an entire year.

The thing about rampant consumerism is that although it underpins the developed world's industrial and commercial infrastructure, and thereby drives both general environmental degradation and climate change, it is not making us any happier. Between 1970 and 2000, average individual prosperity in the UK climbed 80 per cent, while our average Life Satisfaction Index flat-lined. It follows then, that having less does not make us any unhappier – which is just as well, because simple mathematics tells us that the current consumer frenzy cannot continue. According to the New Economic Foundation think-tank, the UK is second only to the USA in terms of the resources we devour. For everyone on the planet to live at the same standard as a UK citizen would require the resources of three planet Earths. And for the teeming billions across the globe to embrace the lifestyle of American citizens, 5.3 Earths would be needed. Clearly, with the Chinese and Indian economies expanding at breakneck pace, the planet's population continuing to climb inexorably, and with resources – oil in particular – becoming increasingly scarce, crunch time is coming. Even if climate change does not stop the global economy in its tracks, the simple fact that we have now outgrown our one and only planet certainly will. We cannot, then, continue to shop until we drop. Despite the fact that the economies of the industrialised countries are built upon the assumption that we, our children, and our children's children will keep on consuming, this is an idea that is ultimately unsustainable on a small and crowded planet with limited resources. As Tony Juniper, Director of Friends of the Earth, points out, 'our consumer culture is completely out of step with the capacity of the planet'.

So what to do, then? Shopping ethically is a start, but shopping less is far better. Forget about fashion – whether in relation to mobile phones, computers, fridges or clothes, fashion is all about built-in obsolescence, and can only survive in the most advanced consumerist societies. Hang on to your electronic appliances and white goods until they stop working, then think carefully about whether or not they actually need replacing (I get on perfectly well without a mobile phone, a Blackberry or a tumble drier). Regarding clothes – invest in well-made, long-lasting garments, and when they start to wear, why not consider make-do and mend? Celebrate 'Buy Nothing Day', and use www.buylesscrap.org to donate money that you don't spend on 'crap' to charity. You might even decide to join the 'compacters': a rapidly expanding movement launched in San Francisco and dedicated to 'cutting clutter and waste in our homes and simplifying our lives'. The hard facts are that climate change has been driven by an epidemic of consumerism, particularly in the last half century. It is a scourge, however, that is on its last legs, so we might as well start getting used to a world where being the first to have the latest mobile phone or new season's frock means less than nothing. Like it or not, the time is coming when we will all be compacters.

WHAT IS MY CARBON FOOTPRINT?

A carbon footprint is a measure of the amount of carbon dioxide an individual consigns to the atmosphere. The average carbon footprint for a UK citizen is just under ten tonnes, compared with just over 20 for an American and 0.01 tonnes for a resident of Chad. If yours is close to the national average, you can do a great deal to make it smaller. Aim initially for eight tonnes, with four tonnes as a longer-term goal. If your carbon footprint is 21 tonnes or more, then you must be Jeremy Clarkson and there is no hope for you.

Pretty much everything we do has a carbon cost that contributes to our personal carbon footprint; a measure of the amount of carbon dioxide we, as individuals, despatch to the atmosphere. Internationally, carbon footprints are hugely variable, and in 2004 ranged from 69.2 tonnes, for a resident of Qatar, down to 0.01 tonnes for a citizen of Chad. This means that it would take nearly 700 Chadians to produce the same amount of carbon dioxide as a single resident of the world's most carbon-profligate state. On average, UK citizens each pump out close to ten tonnes of carbon dioxide every year, and for US citizens that rises to 20 tonnes. Although China overtook the USA, in 2006, as the world's biggest producer of carbon dioxide because of its much larger population, the average carbon footprint per citizen is less than five tonnes a year.

The averages published for different countries hide a considerable variability in footprint size between individuals, dependent on their lifestyles. Someone who flies ten times a year, drives a 4 x 4 and has two homes is likely to have a much larger footprint than a person with no car who flies once a year and lives in a small flat. Whatever your lifestyle, however, there are always ways you can reduce the size of your footprint – and it is possible to achieve a whopping three-quarter reduction without seriously altering the way we live. There are a number of books out there on carbon footprints, including *Carbon Counter* by Mark Lynas, but probably the easiest way to pin down the size of yours is to use one of the numerous carbon calculators available online. Not all carbon calculators are the same, but the Climate Outreach and Information Network (COIN), has checked and rated online calculators both for their overall ease of use and accuracy, and for their accuracy within specific sectors – such as air travel, land travel, home fuel emissions, and so on. The most accurate way to calculate your overall carbon footprint would be to use those calculators rated best within each sector, which can be found on COIN's website: http://coinet.org.uk/materials/carboncalculations. Alternatively, you can go straight to the site of the calculator most highly rated by COIN, Resurgence.org, at http://resurgence.org/energy/index.htm. This detailed and accurate carbon calculator tells you what it is doing and why, and also works out your calculations for you.

Be warned, calculating your carbon footprint properly is not something you can do in a spare five minutes. It needs preparation and time. The nearest thing I can liken it to is filling in a tax return, but please don't let that put you off. Based upon the Resurgence calculator, you will first be asked for information on your electricity consumption, so you'll need to have your bills for the last four quarters in front of you. If you have an electricity meter, you will need to know how much, on average, you put in every week. Next you will be asked for similar information on your gas, oil, coal and wood consumption. Then the focus shifts to transport, requiring, first, information on personal car mileage, then additional journeys by car, along with all those by taxi, bus, trains and aircraft. It is almost certain that you will not have all the information to hand for this, and will have to make some guesstimates – the more accurate the better. The next section addresses fuel-intensive leisure activities, and can be skipped unless you happen to be a fanatical jet-skier or pilot, or spend your spare time puttering about in a motor launch or hurtling around a motor-racing track.

Finally, the difficult bit, estimating how much of the carbon dioxide emitted by UK industry, commerce and agriculture – as it produces or ships in our asparagus, Italian frocks, DVDs, mobile phones, and plasma-screen televisions, and maintains our national infrastructure – actually applies to you. The Resurgence calculator suggests some numbers for this, which you can plug in. Alternatively, you can follow the suggestions of COIN's George Marshall. To paraphrase; if you are a shopaholic, must have the latest of everything, and eat mostly packaged convenience food, add three whole tonnes. If you are thrifty, buy new things when you need them and get most of your food from supermarkets, add two tonnes. If you are already deeply green, grow your own organic food, shop locally, are an avid re-user and recycler, and spurn out-of season produce, add 0.6 tonnes. Now tot everything up. Anything above ten tonnes and you are an over-consumer and could do far better. Anything above 21 and, as climate journalist Mark Lynas recently noted in the *Guardian* newspaper, 'you must be Jeremy Clarkson. Shoot yourself now...'

In the first instance, you should be aiming to reduce your carbon footprint to around eight tonnes, which will be the UK average by 2012 if we meet our Kyoto target. But don't stop there – four tonnes would be a good target to aim at in the longer term. The best way to reduce your footprint quickly is to get to grips with the big emission sources: improve your home energy efficiency and consumption and fly less. But smaller changes in your lifestyle will help too.

CAN I MAKE A DIFFERENCE?

Everything we can do, as individuals, to tackle climate change, is important – from the big things, like making our homes energy efficient, flying and driving less, and perhaps producing our own energy, to the small things, such as thinking about what we buy and eat, and how we dispose of our waste. The important thing to appreciate is that, acting in concert with millions of others, you can make a difference. If all of us in the UK made sure that our appliances were properly switched off when not in use, for example, we could do away – at a stroke – with at least a couple of the ten new nuclear power plants being railroaded through by the current UK government.

With the most recent research suggesting that by 2050, global greenhouse gas emissions will have to be down at least 90 per cent, everything we can do to play our part is important. There are big things we can do, like making sure our homes are energy efficient, flying and driving less, and perhaps making our own energy, but also small things, such as thinking about how and where we shop, what we buy and eat, and how we dispose of our waste. All are important in making a difference. Our everyday lives need to be defined by the mantra 'reduce, re-use, recycle', but we also need to remember that this is the least we must do to help tackle climate change. As COIN's George Marshall rightly points out, a sense of proportion is needed in relation to the personal measures we take to reduce the emissions that are causing climate change. This is borne out by the fact that a return flight from the UK to Australia will have the same impact on the climate as the manufacture of three-quarters of a million single-use plastic carrier bags, or 176,000 overfilled kettles. Marshall's message is that voluntary action alone cannot 'save the planet'. No amount of reducing, re-using and recycling will prevent dangerous climate change, without a revolution in social attitudes, political action and economic behaviour. This does not mean, however, that the small things are unimportant, especially if undertaken by tens or hundreds of millions of people. If all of us in the UK, for example, made sure that our appliances were properly switched off when not in use, we could do away with two, or maybe three, of the new nuclear power plants that are currently in the planning stages. The big things are of course key to tackling climate change, but for there to be any prospect of making a successful transition from our current, consumption-oriented society to an environmentally sustainable one, a new mind-set will be needed that encompasses everything we do in our daily lives.

Recently, a colleague mentioned to me that a somewhat eccentric scientist friend of his had calculated, in a spare minute, that if all the men on the planet grew beards, the amount of energy saved would curb emissions sufficiently to solve the climate change problem. I have not tried to duplicate the calculation, and I have my doubts that a more hirsute race would be sufficient to get us out of our predicament, but the idea does illustrate the point that small changes in behaviour, if undertaken *en masse*, can make a huge difference.

An Ipsos Mori poll, conducted in 2007, suggests that nearly half of the people in the UK believe that climate change is the greatest threat facing mankind. At the same time, however, most of us remain so-called 'fair-weather environmentalists' who tinker with our lifestyles around the edges, but are too attached to our cars and foreign holidays to seriously consider doing without them. If, like increasing numbers of us, you drive a gas-guzzling 4 x 4, people carrier or souped-up saloon, ameliorate your local climate with patio heaters, eat out-of-season asparagus that has travelled half way across the planet, or fly to a holiday retreat in the Loire or Tuscany every other weekend, there is huge scope for reducing the size of your carbon footprint, from extra-large to petite, or even size zero. The same goes for those of us who drive half a mile down the road to pick up a lottery scratch card, pay 50 pence to fly to Spain on Ryanair, and leave the computer, video, television and DVD player on stand-by for years at a go. While some clearly don't give a damn, most of us are not consciously behaving in a manner that is damaging to the environment, it is just that we don't think sufficiently hard – if at all – about the consequences of what we do. It is also a fact that the ramifications of how we live our lives, as individuals, are not made sufficiently clear, and although climate change is at last big news, it still occupies a peripheral position in relation to most people's daily lives.

There is clearly a willingness to change, however, and a *Guardian* poll in 2006 suggested that 90 per cent of its readers recycle as much rubbish as possible, while more than three-quarters had switched off the television instead of leaving it on standby, turned down the central heating, or installed at least some low-energy light bulbs. A quarter of those questioned said that they now used a bike instead of the car for at least one regular journey, or had decided against a holiday that involved flying. If such climate-friendly measures could be extended, just a little, and adopted by all UK households, the impact on the carbon footprints of both families and the country as a whole would be significant, and the same can be said of the populations of other industrialised countries, where profligate and unthinking lifestyles result in emissions out of all proportion to need. What we have to remember is that every single thing we do and buy has a carbon cost, and if we want to bring this cost down we must examine carefully how we lead our lives, and make the required changes. Multiply these changes a million, ten million, or a billion times, and then we really will start to see a difference.

HOW CAN I MAKE MY HOUSE MORE ENERGY EFFICIENT?

The 25 million homes in the UK release 147 million tonnes of carbon dioxide every year, around 28 per cent of the country's emissions, so there is huge scope for improvement. If you don't already have it, start with loft and cavity wall insulation. Think about a wood-pellet boiler or wood-burning stove to heat your rooms and water, make sure all your light bulbs are low energy and that you switch all electronic gadgets off when not in use. Buy the most energy efficient appliances and turn your thermostat down to 21°C or lower; ditch the patio heater and don't be tempted by air conditioning.

Emissions reduction begins at home, where we in the UK conspire to produce 28 per cent of the country's carbon emissions. The UK's 25 million draughty, leaky homes are the least energy efficient in Europe and together release 147 million tonnes of carbon dioxide every year, so there is enormous room for improvement. First and foremost, make sure that you have decent insulation in the loft – at least 27 centimetres thick. The average house loses one third of its heat through the roof, and with the cost of insulation low, government grants available, and the improvement in energy efficiency paying for the cost of insulation in a year or so, there really is no excuse. It will also shrink your household carbon footprint by a little under a tonne, and save you £100 a year in energy costs. If you have cavity walls, get them insulated too: most houses lose another third of their heat through the walls. In addition, you might think about double glazing – either primary or secondary – which will cut heat loss down even more. On average, a central heating system in a UK home will result in 3.6 tonnes of carbon dioxide every year, a figure that will drop when you turn down the thermostat on your cosy, insulated home. Speaking of thermostats, a healthy temperature is between 19 and 21°C, so if yours is set at 26°C, turn it down. Just 1°C will save almost a quarter of a tonne of carbon dioxide a year. You might also consider trading in your boiler for a more efficient one, or – even better – heating your house and water with a carbon-neutral wood-pellet boiler or wood-burning stove.

So much for the house itself, what about fixtures and fittings and all those energy-absorbing white goods and electrical gadgets? With 20 per cent of all electricity generated in the UK used for lighting, switching to low-energy light bulbs is a good place to start. These use a fifth of the energy of conventional bulbs, last 12 times longer, and can reduce the cost of the average family's electricity bill by £240 a year. If everyone followed this route, the putative energy gap that is being used as an excuse to sell nuclear power to the British public would be substantially reduced. If every American did the same, it would have the same effect as taking 7.5 million cars off the road. It looks as though the energy-guzzling types of light bulb are on the way out in any case, with the EU, Australia and the UK all planning to have bans in place within the next four or five years – not really surprising when you consider that only five per cent of the electricity fed into the bulbs actually generates light, while the rest is wasted as heat.

Other simple energy-saving measures include ensuring that mobile phone chargers are not left plugged in with no phone attached, and that TVs, DVD players and video recorders are not left in standby mode. About eight per cent of the electricity supplied to our homes is used up by such 'vampire' appliances and gadgets. This is equivalent to the electricity generated by two gas-fired power stations or more than 1,500 wind turbines, and results in more than 3.5 million tonnes of carbon dioxide being added to the atmosphere. Energy used in the home has doubled in the last 30 years and is projected to climb by a further 12 per cent by 2020. In fact, the Energy Saving Trust has determined that, in the absence of a drastic change in lifestyles, the never-ending stream of new entertainment and consumer electronics in UK households will alone mean that by 2020, the country will need another 14 average-sized power stations.

When replacing appliances, make sure that you choose the most efficient versions. Europe's fridges on their own are responsible for 62 million tonnes of carbon dioxide every year. Add to this the emissions arising from washing machines, dishwashers, tumble dryers, computers, televisions and the rest, and the final figure is huge. By choosing your appliance carefully, however, you can save money as well as energy and emissions. The most efficient fridge-freezer, for example, will only cost you £34 a year to run, whereas the least efficient will set you back £74. The same goes for computers, with the most efficient costing just over £15 a year and the least, a whopping £84. Choosing the most energy-efficient tumble dryer (although using a clothes line or drying rack would be far better for the climate), washing machine, dishwasher and television, along with the aforementioned fridge-freezer and computer, could save you a total of nearly £400 a year, compared with the most energy-profligate types. Remember, saving just 1p of electricity an hour means saving £90 a year.

If you only do one thing, for heaven's sake get rid of the patio heater. With temperatures climbing, the one thing we don't need is a device specifically designed to heat up the outside. In the UK alone, more than 700,000 patio heaters pump out up to 380,000 tonnes of carbon dioxide every year. If you have one, ditch it and put on a pullover. Don't be tempted by air conditioning either. Use blinds instead to keep out the sun during day and open windows at night... or move further north!

CAN I BUY RENEWABLE ENERGY OR MAKE MY OWN?

After making your home as energy efficient as it can be, why not go one step further and buy your electricity from a provider that uses renewable sources? You might also consider installing a solar water heater, a ground source heat pump, solar photovoltaic panels, a wind generator or a combined heat and power boiler, and generate your own heat or power. Ultimately, you may decide to make all your electricity and go 'off-grid'.

Making your house as energy efficient as possible is one of the best ways of reducing the family's carbon footprint and helping in the battle against climate change. You can go even further, however, by purchasing renewable energy and even by generating some of your own. The place to start is on the website www.electricityinfo.org, where you can find out how much of the electricity supplied by your provider comes from a renewable source. For most providers, this is just a few per cent – for example, at the time of writing, British Gas sources 4 per cent of its electricity from renewables, Sainsbury Energy, 3.6 per cent, and Midlands Electricity, 3 per cent. If your provider is this stingy with its renewable energy component, then switch to one that isn't. The top three are Ecotricity, with a 24-per-cent renewable share, Green Energy, with 32 per cent, and Good Energy with an unbeatable 100 per cent. Switching to Good Energy online (www.good-energy.co.uk) takes just minutes, and although it will cost a few pounds more every month, it will reduce your household's carbon footprint by a full two tonnes.

Switching supplier so that all, or much, of your energy comes from renewable sources will make you feel a bit smug, and rightly so, but why not go further? Centrally-generated power is incredibly inefficient, with more than two thirds of the energy lost before it even gets to your property. On-site micro-generation, on the other hand, using solar panels, small wind generators or ground heat pumps, does not suffer from this problem, and is therefore far more efficient. On top of this, its potential is massive. The UK government estimates that micro-generation could supply a quarter of the country's electricity by 2050, while the Energy Saving Trust thinks that the figure could be as high as 40 per cent, at the same time cutting emissions by up to 15 per cent. The UK Conservative party is proposing to make decentralised power generation an important part of a future energy mix; suggesting that as early as 2020, a million homes and businesses could be producing 2 GW of electricity – equivalent to one fifth of the country's current nuclear capacity. Micro-generation has application across the world, in developing and developed countries alike, and has a far brighter future than nuclear power. Combined with a big energy efficiency push, it has the potential to transform energy production and at the same time make a very large dent in emissions.

There are a number of different ways to generate your own energy, of which solar power is the most common in the UK. Alternatives are small wind turbines and combined heat and power (CHP) – high-tech domestic boilers that produce electricity as they heat water, feeding unused power into the national grid when not needed by you. You can also opt for systems that, instead of producing electricity, heat your water and feed the central heating system so that you don't need to buy in power for heating. Solar water heating is the most popular of these, but ground source heat pumps, which utilise the Earth's heat, are also growing in popularity.

With small wind generators proving to be pretty unreliable in urban areas, most people who have gone for the energy-generating option have plumped for solar photovoltaic panels – the kind that generate electricity rather than just heating water. While there is enormous potential, the growth of domestic solar electricity, and indeed all forms of micro-generation, in the UK has been crippled by poor government support. Extraordinarily, despite being massively oversubscribed, the government first suspended its system of grants for home micro-generation projects, and then reintroduced it with the level of maximum grants slashed. In summer 2007, the Low Carbon Buildings Programme (LCBP) had close to £19 million in its coffers to support domestic micro-generation. The money available per household, however, has been cut from £15,000 to just £2,500, resulting in many homeowners abandoning their plans to embrace micro-generation. Currently, the LCBP provides up to 30 per cent of the cost of installing a wind generator or ground source heat pump, and £2,000 for each kilowatt generated by solar photovoltaic. The good news is that if you go ahead, some energy providers will actually pay you for any electricity you feed back into the grid.

While the UK government drags its feet on micro-generation, Germany is showing just what can be done. In the last three years, government incentives have led to the installation of more than 300,000 solar energy systems, and micro-generation now provides 12 per cent of the country's electricity. The huge popularity of home-power generation in Germany is being driven by a feed-in tariff, which requires electricity suppliers to buy home-generated power at prices substantially above market rates – allowing households to get up to a ten per cent return on investment by selling electricity back to the grid. Such schemes are also operating in Denmark and Spain, but the UK government refuses to follow this excellent way of promoting the uptake of micro-generation and renewable technologies.

The ultimate goal of every micro-generator is to supply all their domestic electricity using homespun technologies, and go 'off-grid'. If you get this far, Good Energy – bless their hearts – will pay you 4.5 pence for every unit of electricity you generate, even though you use it all yourself. How can you resist?

ARE RECYCLING AND COMPOSTING WORTH THE EFFORT?

The UK is the worst recycler in Europe, recycling less than 20 per cent of its waste. The government is hoping that by 2020, we will be recycling or composting half of our domestic waste, but this is going to take some doing. After 2010 local authorities will be penalised for sending excessive amounts of waste to landfill, and it is likely that they will pass on this cost to households who don't pull their weight. This means we need avoid excessive packaging, think about everything we throw away, and compost anything we can.

While reducing and reusing are certainly best, recycling still has a huge impact on our energy usage, and therefore on our greenhouse gas emissions. There are also other environmental benefits, including conserving increasingly scarce natural resources, cutting down on landfill waste and incineration, and reducing environmental contamination. Yet we in the UK are appallingly bad at recycling. Every hour we throw away enough rubbish to fill the Albert Hall, with more than 80 per cent of this consigned to landfill sites or incinerators. Compare this with the Netherlands, where three quarters of waste is already recycled or composted, and with Germany, Austria and Belgium, where the figure is well over half. Clearly it is possible for the UK to improve hugely on the current figure of 18 per cent of waste recycled or composted, because some local authorities are already doing rather well. In St Edmundsbury, Suffolk, for example, more than half of waste is recycled or composted, while South Cambridgeshire and Lichfield in Staffordshire are doing almost as well. The trouble is, this is balanced by the hopeless record of places like the London borough of Newham, where the figure is just over six per cent, or Liverpool, where it is not much higher. Broadly speaking, the further north you go in the UK, the worse we seem to be at doing something useful with our domestic waste. Discounting London, where a pathetic 17 per cent of waste is recycled, more than a quarter of waste in the south and east is recycled, while in the north and west, this figure falls to below 20 per cent. If the pattern is looked at in more detail, it appears that it is those parts of the country that are most urbanised, and host the major cities, that are the worst at recycling – a big problem as these are the very regions that produce the most waste. Even with our current poor level of recycling, we are already reducing emissions equivalent to taking three and a half million cars off the roads. Just think what we could do if we really tried.

Every year, UK homes create up to 30 million tonnes of rubbish, or about half a tonne per person, more than two thirds of which could be recycled or composted. Between 40 and 60 per cent of household waste, including paper, is biodegradable and can be turned into compost, while a further eight per cent, including metals and glass, can be recycled indefinitely. Why then is the national average for recycling and composting so low? The answer is partly down to us not thinking about how we dispose of our rubbish and partly down to inadequate encouragement from many local authorities. This is changing, however, with the government imposing, from 2010, swingeing financial penalties on local authorities who persist in sending most of their waste to the country's overflowing landfill sites. Certainly there need to be big changes if the government is to meet its very ambitious target of recycling half of all the country's domestic rubbish by 2020. These are likely to include rewards, perhaps in the form of council tax rebates, to households who recycle more and throw away less. The government is also pressing for reductions in packaging, junk-mail and plastic carrier bags, but with no legislation planned it is difficult to foresee any big changes soon. With packaging making up half of all domestic rubbish, it is quite extraordinary that there is no major effort to see this dramatically reduced.

The evidence is that the majority of us want to recycle, with nearly two thirds of people in England now committed recyclers – up from less than a half just two years ago. There are still far too many people, however, who are needlessly and thoughtlessly just throwing everything in their dustbins, including an astonishing one third of all the food they buy. Yet another target is to increase the energy produced from the gases generated by food waste decomposition. This, of course, will require food waste to be collected separately, and for us to dispose of it in the right bin. Better still for the climate would be for us not to waste so much food in the first place. Recent research has shown that a lot of food is disposed of because many consumers simply cannot manage their food properly. They don't check the contents of cupboards, fail to make shopping lists, don't understand sell-by and use-by dates, have their fridges at too high a temperature, cook too much for each meal, and throw away leftovers.

While using more food waste as an energy source, as the government plans, is admirable, why not make use of it yourself? Invest in a compost bin, which will transform much of your waste food into good, fertile compost for the vegetable patch. Many councils now provide subsidised bins; alternatively invest in one of SmartSoil's Swedish composters, which can transform pretty much all waste food, including cooked meat and fish, into high-quality compost in just a few weeks. Not only will this benefit your garden enormously, but it will save emissions by cutting down on the load that the refuse lorry will have to carry, and also reduce the methane emissions that would inevitably result from your cast-off food rotting anaerobically (without oxygen) in a putrid landfill site.

SHOULD I THINK ABOUT HOW I SHOP?

Recycling is good, but reducing and re-using are better. Small changes to the way you shop can have a real impact: shop locally, spurn plastic carrier bags, avoid excessive packaging, and just buy less. Make fewer trips to superstores, or switch to home delivery, and sign up for an organic vegetable box. Leave excess packaging behind at the till – it almost certainly won't be recycled, but you will be making the point that enough is enough. Better still, shop at that nice little grocer down the road, where everything is wrapped up in brown paper bags that you can use for your sandwiches... and then compost.

Recycling is an important part of cutting down on waste and reducing our greenhouse gas emissions. The more we re-use what we have, however, and reduce what we buy, and therefore what we eventually throw away, the less waste we actually generate in the first place. How we shop and what we buy can make a big difference to our individual and household carbon footprints. Patronising independent shops, farm shops and others that supply local produce, for example, can help reduce those emissions generated by the aircraft that fly goods in from foreign parts and the

HGVs that trundle around the country carrying nearly half of all the food on sale in the UK. Everyone has to go to the supermarket sometimes, but make a list beforehand – and stick to it. With the huge range of products cramming the shelves, there is enormous temptation to buy all sorts of things that you don't actually need, and which end up uneaten, unused, and binned. Going to the supermarket less, and visiting shops with a perfectly adequate, but less gargantuan, range of products is a good way to cut down on buying stuff that you can easily do without.

If the service is available, having your supermarket shopping delivered is another way of doing this, as product lists on a computer screen offer far less temptation than the real thing, enticingly presented on the shelves. Home delivery also has the added bonus of replacing your journey to the supermarket, and that of a few dozen others, with a single trip by the delivery van. If you do make use of home delivery, don't forget to choose a 'green' delivery slot, which will mean taking advantage of a delivery van that is already due to be in your area. This may not be the quickest option, but it is the most climate-friendly. On the subject of home delivery, you can also do a lot worse than having an organic, locally-sourced vegetable box delivered, rather than going for supermarket vegetables, the provenance of which is frequently impossible to check, and often far from local. Other things you can do are to buy services rather than stuff, for example by downloading your music rather than buying plastic-boxed CDs, or rent tools, appliances and electronic hardware that you won't often use.

Thinking about how you shop can start even before you leave the house. Take re-usable shopping bags or a shopping carrier, so that you are not tempted to make use of plastic carrier bags. Every year in the UK, we use more than 13 billion plastic carrier bags, each of which has an active, useful, lifespan of less than an hour before it is consigned first to a bin, and then to a landfill site. Fortunately, the plastic carrier bag seems to be on its way out. In 2002, the Irish government put a 15 per cent tax on single-use plastic bags, which reduced usage by 90 per cent. At a stroke, bag use dropped from 328 per customer every year, to just

21. Sadly, the UK government is dragging its feet – as it is on many environmental issues – and has refused, as yet, to legislate to solve the problem. Central government's sluggish measures may well be overtaken by events, however, with the London boroughs considering either an outright ban or a bag tax, and 80 small towns in the UK having already introduced voluntary bag bans or planning to do so. Elsewhere, too, the plastic carrier bag is under attack, with at least 40 countries, states or big cities imposing bans or considering doing so. With between 500 billion and one trillion plastic carrier bags distributed every year, growing action to get rid of the problem hasn't come a moment too soon. And this is not just about reducing emissions, either. Bangladesh banned carrier bags in 2002, when they were identified as one of the main causes of serious flooding – through blocking drains.

Equally important is reducing the amount of packaging you bring home, partly because more packaging means more emissions and partly because it will form half, by volume, of everything you throw away, much of which will end up in landfill. If, like me, you spend half of Christmas Day using bolt-cutters to extricate children's toys from dozens of wire ties and apparently welded-on plastic cocoons, you have probably uttered several expletives against the current trend in packaging, whose aim appears to be to make it impossible to actually get at your purchase. Manufacturers and the big retail chains say they are serious about cutting back on packaging, but when you see cucumbers individually heat-sealed in plastic, it is obvious that they have a very long way to go indeed. Disgracefully, one sixth of the money we spend on food every year goes on packaging. This is one area where the consumer can make a difference, by simply leaving excess packaging behind at the till. It almost certainly won't be recycled, but if enough people make the point the message will eventually get through. Better still, shop in that nice little grocer down the road, where everything is wrapped up in brown paper bags that you can use for your sandwiches and then compost.

DOES WHAT I EAT AND DRINK MAKE A DIFFERENCE?

What you eat and drink, and how much, can have a big impact on the size of your carbon footprint. If you are obese, slim down – you will be doing the climate, as well as yourself, a favour. If you are more svelte, take some time to think about where the food you buy comes from, and how far it has travelled. Eat locally, seasonally and organically as far as possible, and shun the apples or asparagus flown in from half a world away. Give frozen foods and ready meals the elbow and avoid like the plague mineral waters shipped in from Fiji, or jollied up with multi-vitamins.

According to Ian Roberts, a professor of public health at the London School of Hygiene and Tropical Medicine, obesity is making climate change worse. Just think about it. Why is the country with the most obese population on the planet also, until China forged ahead in 2006, the biggest emitter of greenhouse gases? Obese people eat about 40 per cent more calories than their more svelte counterparts, so with food production accounting for around one fifth of greenhouse gas emissions, they have significantly larger carbon footprints. According to Roberts, the more sedentary lifestyles of the obese are also likely to involve driving more, especially over short distances, spending more time at home in front of the TV, and being kept cool in summer by air conditioning. With the number of obese adults worldwide quadrupling to 300 million in the last quarter of a century, things can only get worse.

Even for those of us who are a little less bulky, taking time to think about what we eat can make a huge difference to our carbon footprint. Start by checking where food has come from – it may add a few minutes to your shop but it is well worth it. A study undertaken five years ago by Sustain, a UK-based alliance for better food and farming, reported that a sample shopping basket of organic food contained 26 food items that had travelled 250,000 kilometres, the equivalent of a journey to the moon, leading to the release of 80 kilos of carbon dioxide in the process. Even within the UK, food is constantly whizzing about from farm to warehouse to distribution centre to supermarket, to homes, and food now accounts for one quarter of all HGV miles.

The solution, generally, is to eat seasonally and locally: don't touch those New Zealand apples when you can buy perfectly good ones grown just down the road. Avoid asparagus flown in from California, and wait for the home-grown equivalent, which may have emitted nine hundred times less carbon dioxide to reach the store. Unfortunately, the situation is not always quite so simple. UK tomatoes grown in energy-intensive greenhouses, for example, will generate three times more carbon dioxide that those shipped by road from Spain. At the same time, ship-borne fruit from abroad, which does not need too much refrigeration – such as bananas – does less damage to the climate, while easily perishable foreign fruit, which requires low temperature refrigeration and transport by air, will result in significantly higher emissions. Frozen food should be avoided, as storage at low temperatures uses energy. Organic is generally better for the climate, as the energy expended in the making of fertilisers and pesticides is saved. As yields are typically lower, however, energy associated with cultivating and harvesting tends to be higher. All in all, though, switching to an organic diet can reduce your food footprint by nearly one quarter, provided it is UK sourced.

Being careful about what food you buy can slash your food-related emissions by a huge 90 per cent. Even better, rent an allotment and grow your own. Not only will this reduce your carbon footprint, but it will make you fit, healthy and relatively guilt-free. Avoid ready meals: they are cooked twice before they reach the table, which is energy wasteful; they have probably been stored for months, requiring more energy; and they are often buried in a mass of unnecessary packaging.

I must admit that I am occasionally partial to a nice New Zealand pinot noir, but while it helps me to relax, it does nothing but harm to the climate, so it's best to keep indulgences like this for special occasions. Even booze from closer to home can be extremely far-travelled, with the average bottle of beer exported to the UK from Germany clocking up as many as 38,000 kilometres as it shuttles about between brewery, warehouse and supermarket – almost equivalent to a round trip to New Zealand.

While beer and wine are clearly essential to any balanced diet – well, in my book, anyway – the same cannot be said of bottled water. In the UK we consume three billion litres of the stuff a year, much of it shipped from abroad. One supermarket even sells water that has travelled 10,000 miles across the planet from Fiji. Furthermore, it takes seven litres of water and 162 grams of oil to make every plastic bottle designed to hold – you guessed it – one litre of mineral water. The UK bottled-water market is already worth £2 billion a year, but it is still coming up with gimmicks to sell more. Now you can buy water with added 'regenerative' or 'protective' vitamins, surely one of the most idiotic concepts ever invented. If you want to drink water when you are out, carry a flask-full with you or, if you are in a restaurant, ask for tap water – you will save a fortune too. On top of this, some bottled waters have been found to be contaminated, on occasion, with benzene, antimony and naphthalene, all potentially dangerous chemicals, while others contain enough sodium to cause concern for those with high blood pressure or heart problems. In addition, carbon emissions are produced by the aircraft, ships and HGVs used to lug the water around, while more emissions – and other very unpleasant chemicals – are produced when billions of the empty plastic bottles are incinerated rather than recycled.

SHOULD I BECOME A VEGETARIAN?

Worldwide, the meat industry is responsible for around 12 per cent of all greenhouse gas emissions – not far behind those produced by cars, trains, boats and planes put together. While the average UK citizen only eats the equivalent of a lamb chop or chicken breast a day, reducing your meat consumption or cutting it out altogether can make a significant dent in your carbon footprint. Even if vegetarianism doesn't appeal, try to cut down to just two meat-based meals a week, and choose poultry, pork, lamb or mutton – which are generally less energy-intensive than beef. Buy organic meat that is produced in the UK, or, even better, locally sourced, rather than shipped across the world.

Evangelical vegetarians are prone to make the point that 'meat is murder'. Well this is certainly true in relation to the climate, because meat-eating is responsible for a substantial proportion of greenhouse gas emissions. Overall, the meat industry conspires to generate an astonishing 12 per cent of global emissions; compared, for example, to the 3.5 per cent currently arising from commercial aviation, and almost as much as all cars, trains, boats and planes put together. Even worse for the climate is the fact that chickens, sheep, goats, pigs and, especially, cows, and the agricultural infrastructure required to support them, generate some of the most harmful greenhouse gases of all: nitrous oxide, which is 296 times more potent than carbon dioxide, and methane, which is just 23 times as bad.

In the UK, the meat and dairy industries are responsible for eight per cent of the country's emissions. Compared with other developed nations, such as the USA, the level of meat consumption of the average Brit is pretty low: about the equivalent of one lamb chop or piece of chicken breast a day. Nevertheless, we now eat half as much meat again as we did 40 years ago. Against this, increasing numbers of us are recognising that meat eating is not really that good an idea: the number of vegans in the UK has increased tenfold in just the last decade, and is now reported to stand at one million – that is one in 60 of us. Globally, however, as more wealth drives dietary change in developing countries, meat consumption is predicted to climb rapidly and to be twice as high by the middle of the century as it is today.

Of all meats, beef is by far the least climate friendly. According to www.openthefuture.com, for example, as much greenhouse gas, in the form of methane, is generated by a burping, farting cow during its lifetime as from all the energy used to fabricate, feed, or raise the components of a cheeseburger. Another study, by Japan's National Institute of Livestock and Grassland Science, has gleaned that producing one kilogram of beef results in more emissions than driving 250 kilometres while leaving all the lights on at home, and this is without including the cost of transporting the meat. More than two thirds of the energy involved in beef production is utilised in making and transporting the animals' feed. On top of this, the production of the animal feed itself is a serious and growing threat to climate change, with the industrial-scale production of soya now overtaking timber as the main force behind Amazon deforestation. Following a Greenpeace investigation, which implicated large-scale soya farming financed by US-based commodity multinationals in the illegal destruction of the rainforest, some of the biggest European food manufacturers and supermarkets, and fast-food retailers like McDonalds and KFC, have agreed not to use illegally grown Amazon soya. While this is undoubtedly a very positive move, the worry is that the illegal soya will find other markets, most notably in China. If you cannot give up the beef, at least stick to organic meat fed on grass rather than on soya feed, which involves the emission of 40 per cent less greenhouse gas and the use of 85 per cent less energy.

Taking the plunge and avoiding meat altogether would only reduce your food and drink footprint by around six per cent. This is because milk and cheese, which make up an important part of a vegetarian diet, are also a product of burping, farting cows, and therefore a major source of greenhouse gas emissions. Further greenhouse gases also result from the energy expenditure required to process and store dairy products. Becoming vegan will make a bigger dent in your footprint, but then again, you can never be quite sure where that replacement soya has come from. Still, an organically-produced nut roast with accompanying vegetables, washed down with a bottle of local organic beer, will only add around 200g of carbon dioxide to the atmosphere. At the other end of the spectrum, a New Zealand lamb chop with vegetables sourced in South Africa, finished off with a Chilean Chardonnay, will result in the addition to the atmosphere of a climate-busting ten kilogrammes – 50 times as much.

If you can't face cutting out meat altogether, then try to cut down to just two meat-based meals a week, and choose poultry, pork, lamb or mutton – which are generally less energy intensive – rather than beef. Also choose organic meat that is produced in the UK, or even better, locally sourced, rather than shipped in from the far side of the world. Whatever you do to reduce your meat consumption, the important thing to remember is that on its own it is not going to drastically shrink your carbon footprint. To be honest, cutting out meat altogether, while still flying eight times a year, driving a couple of gas guzzlers, and having an energy inefficient home, is hardly worth the bother.

HOW CAN I CUT MY DRIVING-RELATED EMISSIONS?

So infatuated are we with our cars that between 2003 and 2004, only 1.8 per cent of journeys between two and five miles in the UK were made by bicycle, against 78 per cent by car. In the USA, where nearly 100 million people are clinically obese, a routine involving its citizens walking five kilometres or cycling 20 kilometres a day would reduce carbon emissions by a huge 11 per cent. In the UK, driving accounts for 40 per cent of the average person's greenhouse gas emissions, so there are plenty of opportunities for big savings: drive more energy efficiently; replace the gas-guzzler with a hybrid; join a car club; embrace public transport more; get on that bike.

It goes without saying that walking and cycling more and driving less is a good thing – both for the waistline and the climate: while driving a car uses up 58 calories an hour, cycling at a moderate pace uses up 400 or more calories. Unfortunately, the reality is that people are walking and cycling less and driving more. Between 2003 and 2004, only 1.8 per cent of journeys of between two miles (3.2 km) and five miles (8 km) in the

UK were made by bike, compared to 78 per cent by car. In the USA, where nearly 100 million people are clinically obese, a routine involving its citizens walking five kilometres or cycling 20 kilometres a day would reduce the country's carbon emissions by a huge 11 per cent, and result in a far thinner population. This in turn would save another $117 billion on health care, sufficient to reduce US emissions by a whopping 33 per cent. Driving less can make a huge difference to an individual's carbon footprint, and taking the train instead of using a medium-sized hatchback for a 30-kilometre round trip will save 1.5 tonnes of greenhouse gas emissions a year – or double this for an SUV. An average car emits its own weight in carbon dioxide for every 10,000 kilometres or so, as well as resulting in 15 tonnes of waste during production.

In the UK, driving a car accounts for 40 per cent of the average person's greenhouse gas emissions, so there are plenty of opportunities for big savings. If you have an SUV then get rid of it. In the present circumstances, there is simply no justification for driving a vehicle that releases up to 12 tonnes of carbon dioxide every year and has a fuel efficiency lower than a motor vehicle that was all the rage almost a century ago. Travelling just a few kilometres an hour below the speed limit can also help, and slowing down just a little on a short daily commute can result in a quarter of a tonne saving annually on emissions. Even correct tyre pressures can make a significant difference, by chopping ten per cent off fuel costs, while avoiding idling can cut emissions by up to 13 per cent. More tips on how to drive greener can be found at: www.ecodrive.org. You might also give biofuels a thought, but as I will discuss later, these have their own disadvantages.

A good way to start is to opt for a lower emissions car, of which there is a growing choice. The Toyota Prius petrol-electric hybrid is probably the best known, and emits just 105 grams of carbon dioxide per kilometre, compared with 170–200 grams per kilometre for most cars on UK roads. Even better, for urban driving, you could go for the all-electric Nice Mega City or the Reva G-Wiz. Designed in California and built in India, the latter is the world's best-selling electric car – not really surprising given that it does the equivalent of 600 mpg and costs just £50 a year to run. Or, if you are terminally addicted to speed, why not put your name down for a Tesla Roadster? Admittedly it costs around £50,000, but it does do 0–60 mph in four seconds, has a maximum speed of 130 mph (210 km/h) and, most importantly, is all electric. The Tesla can do 400 kilometres on one charge – that's almost London to Newcastle – and the cost works out at just half a penny per mile. Even though the electricity the cars use is largely, in the UK at least, produced by the burning of fossil fuels, the result is still a 40 per cent reduction in greenhouse gases compared with petrol engines. Find out everything you need to know about green cars at www.whatgreencar.com.

Alternatively you can think about joining a car club. This excellent idea is spreading fast, and involves sharing a local fleet of cars on a pay-as-you drive basis. In the UK, car clubs can be found in London, Bristol, Brighton, Edinburgh, Norwich and elsewhere, and they are also increasingly common in the USA and Europe. To find out more check out City Car Club at www.citycarclub.co.uk. Worldwide, organised car-share schemes now have one third of a million members, still a drop in a tea-cup, but you have to start somewhere. The most recent initiative was launched by the London Borough of Islington, who, to tackle the problem of a chronic shortage of parking space, are dangling the carrot of car-share membership in front of residents, in return for them giving up their cars.

Of course, the best way to cut your transport emissions is simply to drive less, and to walk, cycle or use public transport more. A recent study by Cycling England calculated that a 20-per-cent rise in UK bicycle journeys would save the taxpayer more than half a billion pounds, reduce congestion and healthcare demands, and – of course – help bring down the country's greenhouse gas emissions. According to the report, government investment in cycling initiatives of just £70 million could reduce carbon dioxide emissions by 35,000 tonnes and cut as many as 54 million car journeys a year by 2012. Even more ambitiously, plans were recently announced to pump £400 million into the development of a dozen cycle 'super-highways' in London, in an attempt to get people out of their cars.

IS IT OK TO FLY?

The UK is in the grip of a 'binge flying' epidemic. In 2006 Brits took a staggering 234 million flights; around four for every UK citizen. We in the UK now produce more carbon emissions from air travel, per head of the population, than any other country. Both UK and European aviation emissions will double by 2020 and, if no action is taken, 15 per cent of all global carbon emissions will come from flying by 2050. In the UK, the government's response is to build more runways to cope with demand – a ludicrous way forward when it claims to be serious about slashing emissions by up to 80 per cent. If the government won't act then the people must.

British flyers are the most polluting on the planet, on average pumping out 1.6 tonnes of carbon dioxide every year – more than double that of the average American. In 2006, Brits took a staggering 234 million flights, pushing up UK aircraft emissions to 5.5 per cent of the country's total, and driving them up faster than any other source. Between 2004 and 2005 alone, UK aviation emissions shot up by more than seven per cent; and since 1990 they have doubled. Looking ahead, they are predicted to almost double again by 2020, while by 2050, on present trends, they will have climbed high enough to cancel out a very large chunk of the government's planned emissions savings. The rapid hike in aircraft emissions is taking place across the planet, with EU emissions forecast to double by 2020, and global emissions, currently just 3.5 per cent of the world total, expected to climb to 15 per cent by mid-century.

This relentless rise in aviation emissions is a serious obstacle to tackling climate change. Not only does it negate measures taken in other sectors to reduce emissions, but it also has an impact on warming that is substantially higher than that caused by emissions at ground level. As well as pumping out carbon dioxide, aircraft also produce other greenhouse gases, in particular nitrous oxides, which are especially potent at high altitude. In addition, the contrails produced by high-flying aircraft have a tendency to transform themselves into wispy cirrus clouds, which may also have a warming effect. In all, the impact of aircraft releasing greenhouse gases at high altitude is thought to be between two and four times what it would be if those gases were released at ground level.

There are plenty of good reasons why we need to fly, but we must make an effort to fly less if we want to prevent aircraft emissions from going through the roof. With the world's climate going to pot, it is simply selfish to take several flights a year. Flying to Sydney and back will add nearly five tonnes of carbon dioxide, or around 50 per cent, to the annual carbon footprint of a UK citizen, while even a trip to Malaga will tag on nearly 0.4 of a tonne. A return flight from the UK to Florida's Disney World will pump out the same amount of carbon dioxide as an entire year's driving, while a quick jaunt from London to Glasgow emits six times as much by air as on the train. Even with the best will in the world, the chances are that most people will continue to fly as much as they do now, or even more, unless and until the cost goes up. So far the UK government's only action has been to double the aircraft duty, from £5 to £10 for short flights, and from £40 to £80 for long-haul journeys, in an effort to cut emissions, or at least slow the rate of increase. While the government claims that this will save the equivalent of 750,000 tonnes of carbon every year by 2011, many think that the impact on the number of people flying will be minimal. On top of this, what is especially galling for passengers is that there is absolutely no guarantee that the money raised by the levy will be used to help tackle climate change.

At the same time as claiming to be reducing passenger numbers through taxation, the UK government is inexplicably using predicted increases in passenger numbers as an excuse for pushing through airport expansion plans. Without action, the number of airline passengers in 2020 could be up to three times higher – at 460 million – than at present; that would be up ten times on 1970. The UK is now the world hub for air traffic, with one in five international passengers passing through a UK airport. A third runway at London Heathrow and a second at London Stansted, not to mention the development of other airports, will push this figure up even higher in coming decades. It is completely nonsensical to allow this to happen at a time when the country needs to slash emissions as quickly as possible. Other countries recognise this, and France, for example, has ruled out any airport expansion.

In recent years the flying bug has been chivvied along by the appearance and astonishingly rapid growth of low-cost airlines like EasyJet and Ryanair. While having little, if any, regard for the damage their growing emissions cause, such companies attempt to justify their existence in terms of their rock-bottom fares allowing the less well off to travel by air. In reality, however, the low-cost airlines are being kept afloat mainly by the comfortably well off flying more often.

Stopping flying on its own will not prevent the climate changing, but we must substantially rein in aircraft emissions if dangerous climate change is to be avoided. As individuals, we must make an effort to use ferries and trains wherever possible, and fly only if an alternative form of transport is not available. As things stand at the moment, we are doing the opposite: In 2005, air travel accounted for 81 per cent of all UK overseas trips, up from 60 per cent in 1981, while sea travel fell from 42 per cent to 12 per cent. We need to reverse this trend. Europe – in particular – now has a growing high-speed rail network connecting most major cities. Let's make the most of it.

ARE 'GREEN' HOLIDAYS REALLY POSSIBLE?

In relation to its impact on climate change, it is impossible for any holiday involving flying to be defined as 'green'. The greenest holidays are those that produce minimal carbon emissions; in other words, those that involve walking, cycling, sailing or riding and where travel is by train or boat. If your rest and recuperation has to involve flying long-haul, then at least holiday in a low- to medium-income country, where your spending will do more good, and aim to limit the size of your carbon footprint while there. Personally, though, I think staying in a cosy yurt on the edge of Bodmin Moor would be far more fun.

In addition to attacking the UK's 'binge flying' epidemic, Mark Ellingham, of *Rough Guides* fame, has also labelled world travel 'the new tobacco': a product that is equally dangerous and just as addictive. Although you might imagine that Ellingham would be the last person to bite the hand that feeds him, after 25 years of trying to get people up off their backsides and onto the nearest plane, train or ship, he has come to the conclusion that there is simply no such thing as an 'ethical' or 'responsible' holiday, and he is right. In particular, any holiday that involves flying leaves its fingerprints all over the environment and, in particular, on the climate. The whole idea of a so-called eco-friendly holiday that involves travelling to the other side of the planet is an oxymoron.

Not only do such trips drive up the atmospheric concentration of greenhouse gases simply getting there and back, but many 'eco-holidays' are also threatening to damage or destroy the very things they are trying to promote. Whether to the rainforests of Borneo, Australia's Great Barrier Reef or the unique fauna of the Galapagos Islands, bringing in more and more tourists, whose increasing demands inevitably require more supporting infrastructure, is bound to have a detrimental impact. Flying halfway across the world to stay in a grass hut in near-pristine rainforest is simply not green. The most eco-friendly holiday you can have is a cycling or walking holiday in your own country – no emissions, no danger of damaging a fragile environment, and absolutely no guilt at all. The trouble is that as in every other aspect of our consumerist lives, we have learned to want and expect more of our vacation than a couple of brisk weeks behind a windbreak on Skegness beach, or ten days camping in a muddy field in the English Lake District. In the developed world at least, many of us can afford to spend two weeks in Thailand or Tahiti, and a weekend in Vilnius or Lisbon, so that's just what we do.

As increasing hordes of sightseers are shipped out or flown to ever-more-exotic locations, such as Antarctica and Svalbard, concerns are growing that such vulnerable places will be changed for the worse and for ever if tight restrictions are not placed soon on the numbers of visitors. Accomplishing this fairly would be tricky and unpopular, but one UK think-tank, the Centre for Future Studies, claims that the answer lies in a global lottery in which the prizes are permits to visit the world's iconic tourist destinations. Not only would this protect our planet's most sensitive environments by limiting visitors, but it could also raise much-needed funds to enable a more proactive approach to preserving the best of what our natural world has to offer.

Unless or until such an admirable scheme is up-and-running, however, we will have to take the decision ourselves to be responsible tourists.

That doesn't have to mean a muddy Lake District or windblown Skegness every year, but it does mean limiting foreign trips, visiting countries that, wherever possible, can be reached by train or boat rather than plane, and cutting right back on long-haul trips to the ends of the Earth. Those of us in the UK have no excuses, because we are now blessed with a superb and burgeoning fast European rail network that can take us from London to the Swiss Alps in a little over seven hours or to the south of France in a shade under. No hanging about for hours in packed and stuffy airport terminal buildings, far more comfortable seats, and reasonable prices too. The greater distances involved and the rudimentary rail network reduce such opportunities in North America, but even travelling by car with a full passenger load will generally result in less emissions than travelling by air.

Instead of Thailand or Tahiti then, you could try walking in the Pyrenees or Swiss Alps or cycling in France or the Low Countries, and if these don't have you reaching for your hiking boots or bike helmet, check the Web for sites packed with ideas for sustainable, climate-friendly holidays. Be very careful, though, of the many impostor sites, such as the not-so-responsible www.responsibletravel.com, which claims to be driven by the green ideal while offering luxury, carbon-footprint busting holidays to watch orang-utan in Borneo or to enjoy the peace and tranquillity of rural Vietnam – all by air. If you feel that you have to travel thousands of kilometres for rest and recuperation, at least travel to a low- or medium-income destination, where your spending will have greater benefits for the local economy than it would have in Sydney or New York, and try as much as possible to reduce your carbon footprint while there. But why not instead stay in a cosy yurt on the edge of Bodmin Moor (www.yurtworks.co.uk/holidays/index.htm), cruise the spectacular Dalmatian coast in a traditional wooden schooner (www.dalmatiancoast.com), or take a train to the Swiss Alps and walk the high alpine route from the Eiger to the Matterhorn, (www.andiamoadventours.com/aa_swiss_eiger_zermatt.html). These are just a few ideas, but there are many more ways to have a fantastic holiday that don't involve ending up with an oversized carbon footprint.

WHAT ABOUT CARBON OFFSETTING?

Don't worry about the impact on the climate of your next flight to Florida, your excessive driving, or heating your poorly insulated home, you can assuage your guilt by getting someone else to plant some trees in Indonesia. This is how carbon offsetting is supposed to work, but does it really? Trees may not survive, and may actually be responsible for increased warming if planted outside the tropics, while other offsetting schemes that purport to invest your money in climate-friendly schemes in developing countries sometimes have dodgy credentials. The only real solution, of course, is to fly less, drive less and make your home more energy efficient.

It has been the fashion for some time for those who purport to have greenish credentials, those who like to feel guilt-free, or those who think it is simply trendy, to 'offset' their carbon emissions. This translates, as George Monbiot of the *Guardian* so perceptively puts it, into 'buying a clean conscience by paying someone else to undo the harm you are causing'. In other words, if you feel you have to fly to Australia, you can compensate for the greenhouse gases pumped into the atmosphere in order to get you there by paying for a tree to be planted, which – so the theory goes – will ultimately absorb this and more carbon dioxide from the atmosphere. Alternatively, the money could go to a company that invests in green energy, such as solar or wind power. While contributing to renewable power schemes certainly can't do any harm, the best solution would be not to fly to Australia at all.

The problem with carbon offset schemes is that they make people think they can carry on as usual provided they pay someone else for the pleasure. It doesn't, however, take a rocket scientist to realise that if everyone on the planet offset their carbon emissions, we might have more trees and more investment in green energy, but we would still be using up fossil fuels at an ever-increasing rate. And in any case, all those trees might not help much at all. Not only is there evidence that trees trap dust which, if it were allowed to get into the atmosphere, would block the sun's rays and help keep temperature down, but research published in 2007 suggests that planting trees anywhere outside the tropics actually warms the planet rather than cooling it down. As well as absorbing carbon dioxide, trees also trap heat from the sunlight that falls on them, so pushing up temperatures more than if they hadn't been planted. Anywhere outside a narrow band around the equator, it seems that this warming effect more than compensates for any cooling achieved by the trees removing carbon dioxide from the atmosphere. Above 50 degrees north, for example across the Siberian tundra, planting forest is an even bigger no-no, as it presents a darker surface that is more effective at absorbing the sun's heat.

Tree-planting to neutralise carbon emissions is, nevertheless, a burgeoning global business worth more than £60 million in 2007; a figure predicted to top £300 million by 2010. From a carbon-offsetting point of view, however, the trees planted in your name may well not help in the fight against climate change. Firstly, they might not survive, succumbing to disease, drought or fire before reaching maturity. Secondly, even if they do reach maturity, they will eventually die and decay, releasing their carbon dioxide back into the atmosphere. On top of all this, personal carbon offsetting schemes are currently unregulated, and a UK parliamentary enquiry in 2007 highlighted serious problems with some schemes, especially those involving tree planting. One way in which offsetters can dupe unsuspecting customers is by taking money to pay for tree planting, or other 'green' schemes, that would happen anyway, in which case there is absolutely no benefit to the climate at all.

As an alternative to tree planting, you can also assuage the guilt arising from your five – or fifteen – flights a year by supporting a climate-change-friendly project in the developing world; perhaps a biomass energy scheme in Indonesia or a wind farm in India. Again, however, there are problems, the main one being the principle underpinning the whole idea, which is that we in the developed world can carry on as normal while asking someone else to do the work. On top of this, many schemes, particularly in India, which is the favoured host of offsetting projects, are poorly validated, if at all, and have highly dubious credentials in relation to helping cut emissions.

Despite its questionable benefits, personal carbon offsetting does not look like going away, at least not yet. Offsetting schemes are now even moving beyond the airline sector, with insurance companies, oil companies and energy suppliers all providing services that respectively offset car mileage, petrol consumption and electricity and gas usage. Rather than sign up to these, however, the real answer is to drive less and make your home more energy efficient. If you really have to fly, and everyone does sometime, then offset using the accredited Gold Standard scheme supported by organisations like Friends of the Earth and the WWF, which guarantees that your money will be invested in worthwhile, sustainable and validated projects that actually benefit the climate. You can do this online at www.cdmgoldstandard.org.

ARE THERE HELPFUL GADGETS THAT CAN MAKE HOME-LIFE GREENER?

Generally, gadgets and climate change don't mix, but there are now some out there that can help reduce emissions. Standby busters make sure that your computer, hi-fi, TV and DVD player are all switched off properly, and intelligent plugs close down peripherals once you turn off your computer. Smart energy monitors tell you just how much electricity you are using in real-time, green kettles boil just enough water for your needs, and solar, wind-powered and wind-up chargers keep your mobile phones, PDAs and MP3 players on the go. There is even a steam washer that uses less energy and reduces ironing, and a GPS system that finds you the most fuel-efficient route.

It has taken surprisingly little time for innovators and entrepreneurs to spot the lucrative niche for clever, trendy – and useful – gadgets that can help to reduce our personal energy emissions. Not surprisingly, a number of these target the distinctly climate-hostile standby mode on computers, hi-fi systems, televisions and the like: most of us seem loath to turn these off when we have finished working, listening or watching, but now you can buy a piece of electronic jiggery-pokery that will do it for you. By plugging your TV or computer into the Standby Buster, you can switch it off standby mode just by pressing a button on a wireless remote. With Bye Bye Standby, it is as easy as switching off a light. Just plug your appliances into the smart adaptor, put the wireless control switch on the wall, and flick it off when leaving the house or going to bed; saving on average £40 a year with minimum effort. You can also buy an Intelliplug, which switches off any peripherals, like printers or speakers, when the master switch on the computer or hi-fi is flicked.

It seems intuitive that if we could actually see how our home energy usage was draining our bank accounts, then we would take measures to cut down, and research has shown that this is the case. As a consequence, the number of 'smart' meters, which show us exactly how much energy we are using at any time, can now be bought. One, known as the Wattson, is clipped to your electricity meter (no electrician needed), and shows your electricity usage in real-time – and tells you how much money you are spending. To encourage you to cut back, the display turns blue when energy usage is low, and red when high. Another is the Owl wireless energy monitor, which costs less than £50 to buy and can even be rented. In trials, users of the Owl cut their electricity usage by up to a quarter once they were able to see just how much they were spending. You can also buy plug-in energy monitors, which will tell you how much energy particular devices or appliances are using. In addition to monitoring energy expenditure, there are also gadgets that can help reduce the amount of energy used. When attached to a fridge, for example, the SavaPlug reduces the electrical current when the coolant motor is idling, saving up to one fifth in running costs.

If, like me, you inevitably fill the kettle with too much water, even for a single cup, then one of the most useful energy- (and water-) saving gadgets is the Eco Kettle. This ingenious device stores water in a separate compartment, and – at the touch of a button – releases the exact amount of water to be boiled for the number of cups you want – anything from one to eight. It also uses almost a third less energy than a normal kettle.

One of the reasons why our home power usage has gone up so quickly is because of the ever-expanding range of must-have personal gadgets – everything from mobile phones, digital cameras, MP3 players, and PDAs to electric toothbrushes and even – heaven forbid – electric pan scourers. You could give the national grid a break and use the sun or the wind outside your back door to recharge your gadgets, rather than a nuclear power station hundreds of kilometres away. Put the HYmini portable wind-power generator in a fresh breeze for a few hours and it will store enough energy for you to recharge your mobile phone, or electric pan scourer, at will. Or you can harness the power of the sun by using a Solio solar power charger. With the Solio you don't even have to venture outside, as it will work if placed close to a window. It will also remain charged for months, and can be topped up – if need be – from the mains, as can the HYmini. Alternatively, if you have a strong arm, a wind-up charger might be just the thing. A couple of minutes' cranking will provide five or six minutes of talk time on a mobile, or an hour of stand-by time. The latest wind-up chargers will also work with Blackberries and iPods.

Another energy saver worth thinking about is the Steam Direct Drive washing machine. This utilises steam as well as water to wash more efficiently, using a third less water and a fifth less energy. On top of this, your washing comes out crease free, saving more energy by cutting down on ironing. And if you really have to drive, the Novogo S700 GPS system can at least help to make your trip greener by having an option that shows you the most fuel-efficient route. You may not get to your destination as quickly, but you will feel less guilty.

There are lots more gadgets out there that can help reduce energy consumption – from wind-up radios and torches to solar-powered door chimes and headphone radios – all of which can lend a hand in keeping power usage down. This of course will be a complete waste of time if you have not insulated the loft, or made sure that heat is not being lost through ill-fitting doors and windows. While the little things can help, it is the big things that will really drive your home energy usage down.

WHAT CAN I DO TO REDUCE EMISSIONS AT WORK?

Embracing climate-friendly measures at home is well and good, but your efforts can be cancelled out if your workplace is energy inefficient or doesn't recycle. If this is the case, cajole and harass your colleagues and your boss until things improve. Get the thermostat turned down, push for a 'smart' heating system, and suggest your company switches to a green energy provider. Make sure the lighting is low energy and that lights and computers are switched off at night. Promote a car-share scheme and request decent facilities for cyclists. Argue for train not plane wherever possible, or, better still, video conferencing.

It's one thing being climate-friendly at home, but your sterling efforts can be completely cancelled out by poor environmental practices and energy-inefficiency in your workplace. Clearly it is more difficult to make changes in an environment where you are not the boss, and making a significant difference will depend on your powers of persuasion and the receptiveness of your colleagues. This said, however, an impressive 85 per cent of UK employees polled indicated that they were keen to help tackle climate change by cutting their energy emissions at work.

A good place to start is with the lifts – using the stairs takes less energy and boosts your fitness. More important, however, is temperature control. When my wife worked in Florida, she used to take a pullover to work because the air conditioning made it so chilly in the office – completely crazy when the temperature outside was often more than 30°C. In the UK, offices and public buildings are invariably far too hot. At University College London, where I work, the temperatures in some parts of the building are so high – I would guess in excess of 35°C – that it is actually difficult to breathe. A pleasant working temperature is recognised to be between 19°C and 21°C. If the thermostat in your workplace is set any higher, attempt to get it turned down, ideally to the lower figure. Anyone who claims to be cold can wear a pullover, although given an outside temperature of 19°C, most of us would be in T-shirts. Find out if there is an automatic seasonal heating plan that switches on whatever the weather, and if there is, lobby to get it changed. You might also draw attention to the fact that 'smart' heating schemes are now available, which adapt to external temperatures and can be turned down low at night and at weekends. Also try to find out about insulation, and if it does not come up to scratch, push for something to be done about it. Energy-saving measures are hardly worth bothering with if the heat that is generated is disappearing through the roof. Best of all, get your company or workplace to switch to a green energy supplier that gets all, or a high proportion, of its energy from renewable sources. Inevitably, as summers get hotter, there is going to be an increasing clamour for the installation of energy-intensive air conditioning. A better way forward, however, is to install blinds to keep the sun out, and allow staff to dress down to better cope with the hotter conditions.

Needless to say, lighting is something that you could help to tackle too. Larger workplaces already use lower energy fluorescent lighting, but if this is not the case, push for high-energy incandescent bulbs to be replaced by low-energy alternatives. Campaigning for lights to be switched off in empty rooms and when they are not needed can also have a significant impact on energy usage, slashing up to 15 per cent off the lighting bill. At the same time, get people into the habit of turning off their computers and peripherals properly when not in use.

Recycling is just as important at work as it is at home, and the amount of waste produced may well be far higher. Make sure, firstly, that waste is being recycled, and if not, push for this to happen. Small things are important too – recycle printer cartridges, dispose of batteries properly, and use both sides of the paper when note-taking or printing.

You might also want to encourage greener travelling to and from work. Good ways to do this are through making sure that there are facilities for cyclists, for example a secure bicycle rack and a shower, and by limiting parking or getting rid of it altogether. Promoting a car-share scheme is also an easy but effective way to cut back on transport-related emissions or, if your company is big enough, it might even be possible to negotiate having your workplace serviced by public transport. Increasing flexible working can also help, as employees who do some of their work at home will travel less. If your company has a large throughput of materials and finished products, you might be able to request a rethink of transport logistics, including making more use of the rail network, and increasing greener road trips, wherein deliveries and pick-ups are made in the same areas.

If you work for a big company with offices around the world, flying is going to be a big issue. While not ideal, offsetting using the Gold Standard scheme is better than nothing; alternatively, encourage the use of rail where available. Best of all, however, is to make more use of telephone- and video conferencing. With over six billion passenger miles flown in the UK every year, many – if not most – by business travellers, and with almost half of all European flights travelling under 300 miles, the widespread use of video conferencing could make a huge dent in aviation emissions. Conferencing studios cost just a few hundred pounds an hour, so it would seem to be imprudent not to make more use of them. Last but not least, get your company to seek advice from the Carbon Trust (www.thecarbontrust.co.uk), the publicly funded body set up to offer free advice to companies looking to put in place energy-reduction plans.

IS THERE MORE I CAN DO?

Ensuring that you and your family live more sustainable and climate-friendly lives is an excellent start, but there is so much more that can be done, from growing your own food to starting up or getting involved in community-wide initiatives. This is where big changes can really be accomplished. In the UK, more than 50 villages, towns and cities are developing plans to ban plastic shopping bags, while others are looking to become low-carbon, or even carbon-neutral, communities. Spread the climate change message to local schools, invest in climate-friendly companies, have a green wedding, and think before you start a family. And when it is time to go, unembalmed in a biodegradable coffin would be a nice touch.

Changes in personal lifestyle, multiplied a million-fold or a billion-fold, can make a serious contribution to tackling climate change, but there is also much more we can do as individuals, households and communities. Some things are obvious, like growing more of your own food. Aside from the beneficial impact on emissions, growing your own fruit and vegetables and keeping bees or chickens is fun and healthy. In London allotments alone, 16,000 tonnes of vegetables are grown every year, while up to 200,000 households across the nation keep chickens.

Get out and about in the community too. Don't be afraid to shout about climate change from the rooftops; organise climate change awareness seminars and talks; get climate scientists to come along or even think about speaking on the subject yourself. If you need help and support, COIN (www.coinet.org.uk) provides training courses on speaking about climate change. One of the best ways of getting the climate change message across to those who have little awareness of the issue is through their children. Make sure that your kids and their classmates are being taught at school about our changing climate, and what we can and should be doing about it. Again, you could help to get speakers along or talk yourself. There are also several good websites that help to get children interested in the environment, including www.ecofriendlykids.co.uk, www.eco-schools.org and www.sustainablelearning.info.

You might also think about getting your street, council ward, village or town involved in a green initiative that contributes towards cutting emissions. This may sound a daunting task, but it can be and is being done. In early 2007, wildlife camerawoman Rebecca Hosking managed to persuade shopkeepers in the English town of Modbury, Devon to eschew plastic carrier bags. Now more than 50 UK towns, villages and cities are planning to follow suit, including London. Other communities are going even further. The Oxfordshire village of Wolvercote, home to climate-change activist and writer Mark Lynas, is taking up the challenge of making itself a low-carbon community, which involves a raft of initiatives, from improving awareness of climate change to encouraging the growing of fruit and vegetables, car sharing, and raising money for solar panels for the village school and village hall. The Cheshire village of Ashton Hayes is going even further, and attempting to become the UK's first carbon-neutral community by embracing solar panels and small wind generators, and with plans for a biofuel- or woodchip-powered micro-energy grid.

Mindful of the fact that the price of oil has now topped US$115 a barrel for the first time, and will almost certainly continue to climb, you could push for your community to consider life without oil. After all, the black stuff is not only very bad for the climate, it is also running out, and may become scarce and prohibitively expensive sooner than you think. To get ready for the post-oil era, so-called 'transition towns' in the UK, including Totnes in Devon and Stroud in Gloucestershire, as well as some London boroughs, like Brixton, are already taking measures, such as introducing community 'currencies' that can only be spent in local shops, increasing self-sufficiency, and undertaking oil-vulnerability audits, to help their populations cope when it comes to the crunch. In the USA, too, some communities are looking ahead to a world without oil: Austin, Texas wants to source all the energy for city buildings from renewables by 2012, and Woodstock, New York is planning to leave no carbon trace within ten years.

On the bigger stage, if the state or national government is not coming up to scratch on climate change, then pester, cajole or harass your MP, congressman or other representative. If this has no effect, then vote them, and their party, out of office next time round. You can also make a contribution to the greening of the business community by investing in the growing number of companies with climate-friendly credentials – and make money at the same time. Shares in California-based Clipper Windpower, for example, tripled in value between 2006 and 2007. Remember, though, that the value of company shares can go down as well as up, so a safer bet could be to invest in funds such as HSBC's Climate Change Fund, which buys into companies that are involved in tackling climate change.

As far as those big personal milestones are concerned, keep your wedding – if you are planning one – small, and local. The average UK wedding pumps out 14.5 tonnes of carbon dioxide; to get this down check out www.eco-weddings.com. Everyone likes babies, but there are just too many of them. Each child born in the UK will consign nearly 1,000 tonnes of carbon dioxide to the atmosphere in its lifetime, and each new US citizen twice as much, so it makes sense to consider the climate when planning a family. And when you finally shuffle off the mortal coil, go for a natural burial, unembalmed and in a biodegradable coffin, rather than a gas-powered and highly polluting cremation. Find out more at the Natural Death Centre (www.naturaldeath.org.uk).

WHAT SHOULD OTHERS BE DOING?

As individuals, consumers and voters, we are far from powerless. To have even the faintest chance of avoiding dangerous climate change, however, requires a global accord that is also inclusive of national governments, international agencies, the business community, economists, scientists, technologists, and many more. Achieving a 90-per-cent cut in greenhouse gas emissions is not something that any one nation or trading block or ideology can accomplish on its own – it's all or nothing. It would be encouraging to know that such a global accord was already coming together and that we were on the brink of a clean, sustainable revolution, but this remains far from the reality. True, awareness of climate change, its causes and its potential and manifold ramifications is now at an all-time high, but our efforts at tackling the problem are – despite Kyoto – patchy, poorly coordinated and simply not yet sufficient to even make a dent in rising greenhouse gas emissions.

Few countries are on target to achieve emissions cuts commensurate with their Kyoto obligations, while the rampant economic growth of some not required by Kyoto to cut emissions – in particular China and India – threatens to drive a coach and horses through any future climate-change agreement. The tropical forests of Brazil and Indonesia are still giving up their carbon in ever-larger doses as they are slashed and burned, while the number of cars on our roads and planes criss-crossing the skies above our heads keeps climbing. But there are plusses as well as minuses. Both the USA and China are waking up to the seriousness of the problem, while the EU is at last showing signs of acting tough, both with its own member states and on the global stage. Carbon is at last a commodity that can be taxed and traded, renewable energy is taking off in a big way – at least in some countries – and in so-called Contraction & Convergence, about which more later, there is now a wholly fair and equitable mechanism for cutting global emissions.

Crop-based biofuels, which appeared so promising just a couple of years ago, now look like a bad idea, but scientific advances offer the promise of vehicles fuelled by hydrogen or even more exotic substances. The capturing and storing of carbon may have a useful role to play, and seems the only way of dealing with China's current obsession with coal. Reviving the nuclear power industry seems to be missing the point, however, as do various scary geo-engineering schemes designed to stop global warming in its tracks. In early 2008, emissions are still very much on the rise and global temperatures remain on an upward trend, but increasing numbers of climate-friendly initiatives do provide room for the very tiniest amount of optimism.

IS THE UK A WORLD LEADER IN TACKLING CLIMATE CHANGE?

While hassling the rest of the world about the importance of tackling climate change, the UK government is dragging its feet at home. It will meet its Kyoto emissions target more by luck than judgement, but miss Blair's goal of a 20-per-cent cut in carbon dioxide emissions by 2010. And if consumption, rather than production, of carbon dioxide is measured, UK emissions are actually up 19 per cent rather than down 15 per cent on 1990 levels. The government wants emissions to be cut by at least 60 per cent by 2050, but exactly how they intend to accomplish this is unclear.

For a decade or more now, successive UK governments have talked a lot about climate change, but performed consistently badly. Despite hectoring the rest of the world about the critical importance of tackling the problem, the UK is at best lagging badly behind and at worst actually going backwards. Just a few years ago, the Blair government not only guaranteed that it would meet its Kyoto obligation of cutting emissions of a 'basket' of greenhouse gases, including carbon dioxide and methane, by 12.5 per cent below 1990 levels by 2012, but also that it would ensure that carbon dioxide emissions were down a whopping 20 per cent by 2010. Things don't seem to be going to plan, however, and although a big switch from coal-burning to gas-fired power stations meant that emissions fell significantly in the early 1990s, carbon dioxide emissions actually rose in half the years between 1996 and 2006. It is still likely that the required 12.5 per cent cut will be achieved on time, mainly due to a steep fall in landfill methane emissions driven by more recycling. Certainly, a 20-per-cent reduction in carbon dioxide emissions by 2010 will not happen, and the government has now revised its figures down to 15–18 per cent. In any case, this is all fairly irrelevant, as our Kyoto commitment does not cover emissions from aeroplanes or ships entering and leaving the country. Mainly thanks to the huge increase in cheap flights, our true emissions are actually significantly higher now than they were in 1990. Furthermore, if you choose to look at the UK's consumption of carbon dioxide, rather than its production – that is, if you include all the energy used in manufacturing goods for the UK market that happens in China, and all that consumed by British people while abroad – the UK's carbon footprint balloons, with current total greenhouse gas emissions shooting up from 15 per cent below 1990 levels to 19 per cent above.

Looking ahead, the Gordon Brown government has announced grandiose plans to cut emissions by 60 per cent by 2050 and is even toying with a figure of 80 per cent. Of course, neither is inclusive of aviation and shipping emissions or total carbon consumption. Even so, the figures still look wildly optimistic, especially when you consider that this is a government that has given the go-ahead to 150 road-building projects, is allowing the construction of a huge new coal-fired power station, and is bullishly committed to a major expansion of UK airports, including a third runway at London's Heathrow. At the same time, climate-friendly light rail schemes proposed for the cities of Portsmouth, Leeds and Liverpool have been abandoned because they are supposedly too expensive.

While countries such as Germany have pushed ahead and developed renewable technologies at great speed, progress in the UK has been slow.

In Germany, the feed-in tariff, which guarantees an excellent rate for renewable energy, has proved so popular that 12 per cent of the country's electricity now comes from renewable sources. In the UK, the figure is a measly 4.6 per cent. Germany now has 250 times the solar-power capacity of the UK, and – although the UK is far windier – ten times the wind-power capacity.

The EU has made a firm commitment that by 2020 a fifth of the energy of its member states will come from renewable sources. The UK, however, seems to have absolutely no chance of getting anywhere near this target. Although Gordon Brown has indicated that the UK will meet its obligations, many suspect that this will be accomplished by wheeling and dealing that will allow the UK to wriggle out of the commitment, rather than by any real boost to the country's renewables industry. The Secretary of State for Business, John Hutton, recently announced plans to increase the UK's offshore wind power capability by 33 times over the next 12 years, but experts have ridiculed the target, pointing out that there is just not enough capacity in the market to build this many wind turbines so quickly. Germany, meanwhile, has a target of 27 per cent for electricity from renewables by 2020, and other European countries, such as Spain and Denmark, are also far ahead of the UK.

The UK government does have plans to recycle or compost up to 50 per cent of domestic waste by 2020, wants all homes built from 2016 to produce no carbon at all, and seems to be supporting a local authority initiative that requires builders to ensure that new developments have on-site renewables that generate at least ten per cent of their energy. There is also talk of a tidal barrage across the Severn estuary, capable of producing six per cent of the country's electricity, while a recent initiative requires that the true economic cost of climate change is factored into all policy and investment decisions covering planning, energy, transport, housing and construction. Together, however, all this adds up to far less than many other nations are doing. With renewable energy resources, in the form of wind, waves and tides, that are the envy of the world, the UK has still somehow contrived to miss the boat.

CAN THE USA REALLY BE AS BAD AS IT'S PAINTED?

Successive administrations have turned their backs on international agreements to tackle climate change, denying until recently that any problem existed. At city and state level, however, there has been a revolution, with close to 800 cities and more than 30 states signing up to significant cuts. California governor Arnold Schwarzenegger is playing a leading role by promoting solar energy and hydrogen power, and fighting central government in a bid to slash state car emissions. This is all fine, as far as it goes, but the USA remains one of the world's biggest polluters, and produces half its electricity from coal, with just 0.8 per cent coming from renewable sources.

The USA has long been the bad boy of global warming, and until 2006 was the biggest polluter on the planet. That dubious distinction now goes to China, although per person, of course, the USA is still streets ahead: the average American is responsible for over 20 tonnes of carbon dioxide a year, around four times that of the average Chinese citizen. By 2006, US emissions had jumped 16 per cent on 1990 levels, and show no signs of a consistent fall, although mild weather contributed to a 1.4 per cent drop in that year. Americans make up just four per cent of the world's population, but pump out more than a fifth of all greenhouse gases. Extraordinarily, the 19 million residents of New York State have a bigger combined carbon footprint than the 766 million people living in the world's 50 poorest countries, and if the US states were independent nations, 25 of them would feature in a list of the 60 biggest greenhouse gas polluters. Nevertheless, successive governments have opposed any serious proposals to tackle climate change. The overwhelming weight of scientific evidence has now forced the country to accept that climate change is real, and can only be tackled through deep cuts in emissions, but the Bali climate conference showed that when it comes down to the nitty-gritty of putting measures in place, the USA remains as sceptical as ever.

Notwithstanding the federal government's snail-like progress, much has been happening elsewhere in the USA. In the last couple of years, awareness has bloomed across the country, and 85 per cent of Americans now believe that climate change is happening. In addition, a third of US citizens polled in 2007 regard it as the greatest environmental threat, while seven out of ten want central government to do more about it. More surprisingly, despite the negative stance of the Bush administration on mandatory targets, another national poll found that more than two thirds of Americans would support the USA signing up to an international treaty that required a 90-per-cent emissions cut by 2050.

Much of the credit for this new awareness must go to Nobel Laureate Al Gore and his widely acclaimed film *An Inconvenient Truth*, which squeezed a vast pile of climate change data into a succinct, glossy, and broadly accurate blockbuster aimed at the average American. Three other individuals have also played critical roles in forcing both administration and citizens to take climate change more seriously. Jim Hansen, NASA's vociferous senior scientist, fought back against government-orchestrated attempts to shut him up, and continued to highlight concerns over tipping points, the potential for catastrophically rising sea levels, and the need to act now to avoid the worst effects of a changing climate. On the day that the Kyoto Protocol came into force, 16 February 2005, Mayor Greg Nickels of Seattle launched the US Mayors Climate Protection Agreement, aimed at getting participating cities to strive to 'meet or beat' a seven-per-cent emissions cut (below 1990 levels) – the suggested Kyoto target for the USA. By early 2008, the mayors of 780 cities, representing almost 80 million people, had signed up. Nickel's call-to-arms has also galvanised the nation's states, half of which have now launched plans to cut emissions. Well ahead of the bunch, of course, is California. Here, despite a lifestyle that encompasses driving a six-litre Hummer that does as little as 15 miles to the gallon, governor Arnold Schwarzenegger has placed climate change at the heart of state policy. Among other measures, he has called for an 80-per-cent emissions cut by 2050, is requiring state utilities to produce at least 20 per cent of their electricity from renewables by 2010, and has strongly promoted both solar energy and hydrogen power. He is also pushing through measures to ensure that the state has a million solar-powered homes by 2015, and to build a Hydrogen Highway network, with filling stations to support increasing numbers of vehicles powered by this innovative fuel. He is even suing central government for refusing to allow the state to place tough limits on car emissions, which contribute 40 per cent of California's greenhouse gases. Elsewhere, 31 states, mainly in the north-east and mid-west, are also looking to make significant emissions cuts, placing nearly half of the US population in areas where serious measures are being taken to tackle climate change.

Centrally too, things are changing, with several senate bills in 2007 addressing some aspect of climate change. Most astonishingly, in late 2007, George Bush signed into law an energy bill that set statutory targets for fuel economy in new cars, low-energy light bulb use, and more efficient white goods. While pretty small beer when measured against the scale of the problem, these initiatives do mark a change in the administration's thinking. Clearly, though, there is still a very long way to go. The country remains the world's number two polluter, renewable energy accounts for just 0.8 per cent of electricity nationally, and half of the country's energy is still produced from coal.

WILL CHINESE GROWTH MAKE ALL OUR EFFORTS A WASTE OF TIME?

China, now the biggest emitter of greenhouse gases on the planet, is taking climate change seriously – but not seriously enough. Despite aiming to generate 15 per cent of its energy from renewable sources by 2020, it is opening a new coal-fired power plant, on average, every four days. China's soaring emissions are a result of an explosively expanding economy, driven to a large degree by Western consumerism, and we, therefore, must share the blame. Nevertheless, China has to be made to see that dramatic cuts in its emissions are in everyone's best interests.

China's staggering rate of growth makes it extremely difficult to be optimistic about our chances of preventing dangerous climate change. In 2006, Chinese emissions surged upwards by nine per cent, while those of the USA fell by 1.4 per cent, leaving China at the number-one spot in the polluting stakes for the first time. The Chinese government quite reasonably points out that, per head of population, emissions are very modest: at around five tonnes, just one quarter of US per-capita emissions and just over half of those of the UK. Nevertheless, the Chinese population is 1.3

billion, and en masse, in 2006, they flooded the atmosphere with 6.2 billion tonnes of carbon dioxide. With China's emissions up a colossal 73 per cent since 1990, and the economy forging ahead, it is difficult to see how we can hope to keep concentrations of greenhouse gases in the atmosphere below the threshold that will trigger dangerous climate change. To fuel its explosively-expanding economy, China is planning the construction of 550 coal-burning power stations by 2030, driving an expansion of coal's contribution to global energy consumption, which is expected to double by just 2015, and causing emissions to head even higher.

The Chinese economy is now the fourth biggest on the planet, and closing fast on Germany in third place. On average, the Chinese economy grew at a rate of 8.7 per cent a year over the last ten years, and recently hit an astonishing 11.2 per cent. As Lester Brown points out in his book *Plan B 2.0: Rescuing a Planet Under Stress and a Civilisation in Trouble*, if this continues, by around 2030, China's income per person would equal that of the USA, but for consumption to also be equal would require that two thirds of the world's grain harvest went to China, along with the bulk of all other resources. If four cars for every three people were to become the norm, as in the USA, then 1.1 billion of them would clog the roads, and the area needed for parking would be as great as that currently used for growing rice. Ninety-nine million barrels of oil would be needed every day, but the world only produces around 82 million barrels today, and this figure is expected to fall significantly. Plainly, this can't happen: there are simply insufficient resources on the planet to support unfettered growth in China and, come to that, India, Brazil and other developing countries that are currently seeing breakneck growth.

While the continuing rapid rise in Chinese emissions can't be denied, it is worth considering, once again, the underlying cause: economic growth in China is being driven by consumerism in the industrialised nations, which demand the manufacture of more and more goods using the country's cheap labour. One way to slow the Chinese economy, and as a result its emissions, is to think about what we buy and where it comes from. This will have the added benefit of saving on shipping and aviation emissions too.

As a country, China stands to be severely affected by climate change, in particular through flooding, more powerful typhoons, drought and desertification, and its leaders are fully conscious of this. As a consequence they are trying to reconcile growth with the development of a greener economy that encompasses the construction of carbon-neutral eco-cities, an expansion of renewable energy from a commendable eight per cent today to 15 per cent by 2020, the closure of around 1,000 of the most inefficient power plants, and a drive to make industry 20 per cent more energy efficient within five years. In addition, a massive tree-planting campaign has been launched with the aim of covering a fifth of the country with forest, although – as mentioned earlier – this may not be particularly climate-friendly. Admirable as these initiatives might be, they do not include any targets for the reduction of greenhouse gases, and at the moment the country is not bound by any international treaty either. Seventy per cent of China's energy comes from burning coal – the biggest source of greenhouse gases – and a new coal-fired power station currently opens, on average, every four days. It is this that is predicted to lead to a tripling of China's emissions by 2050, given a business-as-usual scenario. For there to be any chance of preventing dangerous climate change, this can't be allowed to happen: China must be bound into whatever international climate agreement comes out of Copenhagen in 2009.

Somehow, China needs to be made to see that nothing less than draconian measures will allow us to cut global emissions by the 90-per-cent minimum needed by 2050 – and that, if we fail, China will suffer more than most, with predictions suggesting that productivity of the nation's three staple foods – maize, rice and wheat – could fall almost 40 per cent, bringing the prospect of widespread food shortage and famine. Clearly, economic growth will slow as resources, especially oil, become increasingly scarce and consumer demand falls away as a result – and this in itself may have a dramatic impact on emissions. Pro-actively, however, much needs to be done, particularly through improving energy efficiency, embracing renewables on a bigger scale and capturing and storing the carbon produced by the almost countless coal-fired power plants.

HOW ARE OTHER COUNTRIES DOING?

With greenhouse gas emissions a quarter higher than in 1990, and rising rapidly, it's clear that the global community as a whole is not doing very well. India's burgeoning economy has seen its emissions climb by 83 per cent in the last thirty-five years, while Australia's profligacy has earned it the label of worst per-capita polluter of all the major nations. Japan's emissions are still on the up, while Brazil and especially Indonesia have seen continued deforestation supporting rapid rises in emissions. Even the EU, widely recognised as the world leader in terms of pushing emissions cuts, is in danger of failing to meet its Kyoto target, despite Germany's enormous efforts.

With global greenhouse gas emissions climbing by more than 25 per cent since 1990, and now rising by around 2.5 per cent a year, it is easy to see that countries other than China, the USA and the UK have also failed to pull their weight. India, another of the world's most rapidly expanding economies, has even out-done China and seen its emissions climb by a huge 83 per cent since 1990. But while the sub-continent's emissions grew by a full five per cent in 2006, at only about half a tonne of carbon dioxide a year per head of population, they are still far below those of a US or UK citizen. As with China, though, it is the total amount emitted that is important, and with a population of more than 1.1 billion, half a tonne per head adds up to quite a bit. As a result, India is now the world's fourth highest greenhouse gas emitter, after China, the USA and Russia. Not bound to any reduction target by Kyoto, India is sticking – in public anyway – to the idea that, as a developing nation, the climate change problem is nothing to do with them and that they should not, therefore, have to be part of the solution. Unfettered economic growth across the sub-continent would, however, make it impossible to keep temperatures from rising above the 2°C mark, which means that India has to be a part of any future international climate change agreement.

In fourth place, Russia, with a falling population and plans to expand natural gas and nuclear energy, seems to be quite well placed to reduce its emissions. The same can't be said of fifth-placed Japan, however, where emissions have climbed by 14 per cent since 1990, against a Kyoto target of cutting emissions by six per cent. If deforestation is taken into account, then the emissions rankings change, with Indonesia and Brazil shooting up to third and fourth places respectively. With the biofuel craze driving the destruction of ever more forest to make space for palm oil and soya, the impact that these two developing nations have on the climate is already massive.

For the last 11 years, Australia has, in John Howard, had a premier at least as sceptical of climate change and international measures to combat it as George W Bush. Notwithstanding claims that by not cutting down as many trees, Australia has actually reduced its emissions, the reality is that emissions have climbed by eight per cent since 1990. Now the country is the worst polluter of all the industrialised nations, releasing more than 27 tonnes of carbon dioxide (equivalent) into the atmosphere for every citizen. There is hope, however: newly-elected Prime Minister Kevin Rudd signed the Kyoto Protocol on his first day in office and promises a much more climate-friendly approach in the future.

Like the UK, the European Union is vociferous about climate change, but has problems practicing what it preaches. Kyoto requires the 15 pre-2004 members of the EU to cut their emissions by an average of eight per cent by 2012; so far, though, they have managed just two per cent. While Germany (obviously), France, Finland, the UK, and others are meeting or exceeding their individual Kyoto emissions targets, Austria, Portugal and, in particular, Spain, are sticking spokes in the works. Spain is permitted, under Kyoto, to allow its emissions to rise by 15 per cent, but by 2005 they had increased by more than 50 per cent, driven by a rapidly expanding economy, a huge building boom in the south, and a growing population that has increased from 40 to 45 million since 2000. The good news is that Spain is aiming to source 12 per cent of its electricity from renewables by 2012, and all new homes must now have their own solar panels. The bad news is that the country will fail miserably to meet its Kyoto target, so making it increasingly difficult for the EU as a whole to honour its obligation.

Looking ahead, the enlarged EU was praised, at the Bali climate conference, for seeking an ambitious global target of 25 to 40 per cent lower greenhouse gas emissions by 2020. This was spiked by the USA, but will hopefully be revisited in future negotiations. More disappointingly, the EU's own blueprint for tackling climate change, published just before we go to press, calls for a lower emissions reduction target of just 20 per cent by 2020, with the caveat that this will rise to 30 per cent if the rest of the world joins in. Over the same period, the contribution of renewable energy is set to climb to 20 per cent.

There is no doubt that, at the moment, Germany is the driving force behind EU climate change initiatives, and is, to a large degree, making up for the poor performances of other states that are unable or unwilling to do their bit. Germany is so far ahead of other countries in the application of emission-reduction technologies that it is aiming for a 40-per-cent cut by 2020. Without a sea-change in policy, on the other hand, the UK will be lucky just to reach the 16-per-cent greenhouse gas reduction target that it has been allocated in the new EU plan.

IS THE CORPORATE WORLD PULLING ITS WEIGHT?

In a consumer world, business and industry must respond to their customers' wants and needs or risk failure. Consumers are already driving rapid growth in organic produce and ethical products, and have the power to force corporations to reduce packaging and introduce other climate-friendly measures. With customers apparently ready to boycott companies that don't pull their weight, the message is getting through to the likes of Wal-Mart, Toyota, HSBC, M&S and the Co-op. For many businesses, however, 'green-wash' is the name of the game: jumping onto the climate-change bandwagon while doing next to nothing to keep it moving.

In our consumer-driven society, the corporate world responds to our needs – it has to in order to prosper. Excessive consumerism keeps the wheels of industry turning, which in turn drives climate change, but as consumers we have the power to force the commercial world to change its behaviour. Look no further than the massive growth in organic and fair-trade products in recent years for evidence that this can happen. And if the results of a recent UK poll, conducted by one of the world's biggest advertising agencies, are to be believed, companies should be worried:

nearly all of those questioned said they were concerned or very concerned about the impact of their purchasing decisions on the climate, while almost three in four UK families said they would boycott a company that did not reduce its environmental impact. Making companies change the behaviour of centuries, however, particularly when it is likely to mean slower growth and smaller profits, will undoubtedly involve a tough battle.

The fact that many major companies still really don't care about the impact of their operations on the climate is demonstrated by the fact that less than half of the FTSE100 – the 100 biggest companies on the London Stock Market – have published plans to cut back on emissions. This is astonishing when one considers that they are likely to have to shell out more than £16 billion to 'trade' away their emissions under the EU's Emissions Trading Scheme, which could add up to almost ten per cent of pre-tax profits on average. Being high-carbon in an increasingly low-carbon world costs money, but the message has yet to reach the board rooms of many of the world's biggest corporations.

The greenhouse gas emissions produced by the world's worst polluters are truly extraordinary. Topping the list, to no-one's great surprise, is ExxonMobil, which is responsible for as much carbon dioxide as the whole of the United Arab Emirates. Taken together, the world's top ten biggest emitters, which also include Shell, BP, Wal-Mart, General Motors and Toyota, release as much carbon dioxide into the atmosphere as the UK. While those that have a European base will find their emissions increasingly curtailed by the ETS, any possibility of the giant US corporations seriously cutting back on emissions must await a change of government and the introduction of a comparable cap-and-trade mechanism on the other side of the pond.

Changes are afoot, however, as consumers, shareholders and poor publicity conspire to get some companies to change their spots – or at least to think about doing so. Having taken considerable stick in relation to its weak green credentials, Wal-Mart, for example, has committed itself to reducing emissions by one fifth by 2015, sourcing all of its energy from renewable sources, while also cutting back on waste and stocking greener lines – initiatives that, given the company's huge size, could have an important influence on consumption habits across the globe. Japanese car-maker Toyota is aiming at a 20-per-cent emissions cut by just 2010, while US General Motors is looking to an eight per cent cut by the same date. In the UK, Marks & Spencer have an ongoing £200-million project that encompasses selling more locally sourced food, abandoning sending waste to landfill sites and even recycling clothes hangers. Through its Climate Partnership, global banking group HSBC has donated £100 million to climate-friendly charities, while pushing to become carbon neutral itself. The most plaudits must, however, go to the UK's Co-operative Group, which in 2005 sourced 98 per cent of its electricity from good-quality renewable resources, making it one of the planet's biggest users of green power. The group is also building wind farms on its own land, using solar panels and wind turbines on its buildings, aiming to cut electricity use by a quarter by 2012, and has slashed its carbon dioxide emissions by almost half in just four years.

While the Co-op shows just what can be accomplished, it remains something of a beacon among the UK's corporate community. A strong smell of green-wash still hangs around many companies, where being green, or being perceived to be green, is seen primarily as an opportunity for good PR and to increase business share – the job of Public Relations and Corporate Social Responsibility departments, and nothing to do with core business. Oil companies are especially good at this, presenting a green face while presiding over one of the most polluting industries on the planet.

With UK business responsible for about 40 per cent of the country's carbon dioxide emissions, the Confederation of British Industry (CBI) could certainly be taking a far stronger lead. Despite pledging to 'do what it takes' to meet the UK's greenhouse gas reduction targets, the confederation has so far only come up with the proposal that companies will work towards cutting collective emissions of 370 million tonnes by one million tonnes over the next three years. Big deal!

DOES TAXING CARBON HAVE A ROLE TO PLAY?

Carbon taxes are already with us in the form of fuel duty, air passenger duty and the climate change levy on business energy use. There is, however, scope for a great deal more. Proposals include taxing energy-inefficient appliances such as patio heaters and plasma-screen televisions, charging the owners of the biggest gas-guzzlers for the privilege of clogging up our streets and polluting the planet, and offering tax rebates for green home improvements. Windfall taxes on oil company profits, to be spent on renewable energy, are popular with some, while cutting income tax and instead piling duty onto goods and services according to their climate impact could be a vote winner.

Although they are abhorred by many, taxes provide one of the most successful means of driving wholesale changes in behaviour. Carbon taxes already exist and are likely to become more common as the need to change the way we live and work becomes progressively more urgent. They are invariably based upon the 'polluter pays' principle, targeting everyone from the company that produces carbon emissions to those who buy that company's products. For example, duty on fuel, air passenger duty and the climate change levy – a tax that adds around 15 per cent to energy bills – are all taxes on businesses, but the cost is invariably passed on down the line to the consumer. To date, so-called green or climate-friendly taxes are not generally set at high enough levels to cause much of a change in behaviour, either by businesses or by consumers, but this could and should change. As concern over climate change grows, people are becoming more accepting of green taxes, but only if they feel that the cash raised is actually being used to help tackle the problem. The fact that UK air passenger duty is not ring-fenced in this way is one reason why both airlines and passengers are annoyed about the tax. You might expect that with climate change now such a huge issue, green taxes might be higher now than ever. At least in the UK, however, this does not seem to be the case. A freeze on petrol tax following the 1999 fuel blockades meant that in 2006 they stood at 2.9 per cent of the country's GDP, compared to 3.6 per cent seven years earlier.

In coming years and decades, tax is likely to be used far more widely in order to help achieve the huge cuts in emissions needed by 2050. In its Fourth Assessment Report, the IPCC highlights the importance of taxing everything that causes greenhouse gas emissions, from food to flying and light bulbs to lignite. Only by ensuring that the 'polluter pays' principle applies to all goods and services will there be any possibility of preventing dangerous climate change. This principle was reiterated by Paul Ekins, a co-director of the UK Energy Research Centre, who has called for the government to introduce tough regulations and taxes on energy-inefficient appliances such as plasma televisions and patio heaters. This also chimes with tax proposals put forward by the UK's Liberal Democrat party, which wants owners of the country's biggest gas-guzzlers to fork out close to £2,000 a year for the right to drive them, and would like to see airlines taxed on the basis of their emissions. Others, such as the WWF and the UK's New Economics Foundation, have zeroed in on the oil business, demanding a windfall tax on profits to pay for the setting up of an oil legacy fund that can help towards expanding the renewable energy sector. Such a fund was established by the Norwegian government in the late 1990s and now totals more than £110 billion, and the idea of a UK version was given a boost by Royal Dutch Shell's announcement, early in 2008, of record annual profits touching close to £14 billion. In addition to the stick of higher taxes, the carrot of lower taxes could also have an important role to play, for example through council tax or stamp duty rebates for those who make their homes more energy efficient, and the reduction of VAT on climate-friendly home improvements.

One radical move, suggested by HSBC's director of economics, Stephen King, might be to change the balance of taxation so that the bulk is raised on the basis of what we spend on goods and services rather than on what we earn. At the moment, the vast bulk of the UK government's tax receipts come from income tax, National Insurance contributions, VAT and corporation tax, whose alteration probably will not make our behaviour that much more climate friendly. Prior to Pitt the Younger introducing income tax to the UK in 1799 to pay for the war with Napoleon, however, most government revenue was raised by tariffs. Maybe it is once again time for a major readjustment of the way in which the state raises its cash – perhaps through cutting income tax while piling duty onto the most polluting goods and services.

Such realignment in revenue raising could even be managed via a scheme along the lines of that proposed by Richard Starkey and Kevin Anderson at Manchester University's Tyndall Centre for Climate Change Research, within which every citizen has their carbon emissions rationed in order to satisfy a national carbon budget. Each household would be allocated an amount of greenhouse gas it can emit, based upon the number of adults it contains. Emissions would be tracked via a 'carbon card', which would need to be handed over when purchasing petrol, paying a gas or electricity bill, or buying an air ticket. Trading would be possible, allowing, for example, individuals or households with a penchant for 4 x 4s and patio heaters to buy additional 'carbon units' from more altruistic citizens or low-carbon families. A brave new world indeed.

WILL THE CARBON MARKET SAVE THE WORLD?

Carbon can now be traded like any other commodity, although it is one that everyone wants to get rid of rather than covet. The aim in a carbon market is to be responsible for less of it, either by emitting less, or by paying someone to take any excess off your hands. In 2007, the official global carbon market was worth nearly US$60 billion, with most of the trading taking place within the framework of the EU's Emission Trading Scheme. The ETS, however, has so far failed to drive significant emissions reductions, and even if it ultimately helps to cut EU emissions by 20 per cent by 2020, there is a feeling that this could be too little, too late.

For thousands of years, markets have been where we have bought and sold stuff that we like and want. Now, there is an international market for carbon, but with one huge and fundamental difference: carbon is something that we don't like and don't want, so the international carbon market is based on the seemingly odd premise that you pay someone to take it off your hands. The big question is, will the growing carbon trade, which totalled nearly US$60 billion in 2007, make a worthwhile dent in emissions quickly enough?

Before a carbon market can exist, there has to be a system in place that allows carbon to be priced and traded. As mentioned earlier, there are now two trading mechanisms: the UN's Kyoto Clean Development Mechanism (CDM) allows industrialised countries and individual companies to outsource their emissions savings to developed countries; while the EU's Emission Trading Scheme (ETS) facilitates carbon trading between Europe's 12,000 or so biggest industrial plants, which together are responsible for more than 40 per cent of EU emissions. The UK is also about to launch another, the Carbon Reduction Commitment, designed to encourage supermarkets, hotel chains and other big energy users to cut their emissions. On top of these 'mandatory' markets, there are much smaller voluntary ones, where businesses and even individuals can offset emissions, either via established trading mechanisms such as the Chicago Climate Exchange, or over the counter. While the USA does not yet have a national mandatory carbon market in place, there are now a number of regional markets operating amongst north-eastern states and amongst some western states and Canadian provinces.

Neither the ETS nor the CDM got off to a particularly good start, and so far neither has made much of an impact on emissions, either within Europe or worldwide. For this to happen, carbon has to command a high price, so that polluters have a real incentive to produce less of it, and low-carbon, renewable energy sources get a boost. The higher the price of carbon goes, therefore, the more attractive becomes electricity from wind, wave, tidal and nuclear sources, and the less appealing are coal, oil and gas power stations.

The ETS got things completely wrong when it launched its first phase in 2005, by allowing so many emissions 'permits' that they ended up being dished out free by member states to the big, energy-intensive installations, such as power stations and petrochemical plants, that are obliged to be part of the scheme. As with any commodity, too much of a good thing, or in this case too little of a bad thing, sends the price down. As a consequence, there was no need to trade permits, no reason to cut emissions, and the price of carbon collapsed to almost nothing.

Phase two of the mechanism, which started on 1 January 2008, and which runs until 2012, has been tightened up somewhat, so that there are fewer permits around and increased demand for these has kept the price of carbon up at about 19 Euros a tonne (early February 2008). However, despite calls from environmental groups and others that permits should be auctioned to the highest bidders, the majority are still given out free. Because they can be sold on by installations that don't use up their allocations, this means that some companies still stand to make whopping windfalls. In addition, phase two also allows nearly 80 per cent of carbon savings to be made by 'offsetting', with companies investing in 'green' projects in developing countries rather than cutting emissions. Not only does this raise the risk of involvement with poorly validated emissions reduction schemes in far-flung places, it also discourages investment in renewables and other green initiatives at home.

An even tighter ETS phase three will run from 2013 until 2020, with the scheme covering installations responsible for half of all EU emissions, and with emissions permits cut back year on year to achieve a 21-per-cent cut on 2005 levels by 2020. Permits will be centrally allocated from Brussels, rather than via member governments as at present, a significant proportion of them will be auctioned, and energy companies will have to buy all their permits at auction. For the first time, the aviation industry will be obliged to join up, although they will not have to buy all their permits at auction until the final year of the scheme. There still, however, seems to be a lack of urgency, a dragging of feet and too many loopholes and get-out clauses in the detail. At its conclusion, phase three is designed to deliver a 20-per-cent cut in EU emissions (on 1990 levels) – or even a 30-per-cent cut if other major polluters such as China and the USA also agree to cap emissions, which they may well do. With global emissions needing to fall by at least 90 per cent by 2050, however, the ETS could be delivering too little, too late. A carbon market can clearly make a huge difference to emissions levels, but with so little time left, it must be managed far more tightly so as to deliver the sorts of savings that we need, when we need them.

WHAT IS THE FAIREST WAY TO CONTROL EMISSIONS?

Contraction & Convergence is based upon the simple and fair principle that everyone on the planet has the right to emit the same amount of carbon dioxide. Progressively lower ceilings for global emissions would be defined, with each country's emissions quota eventually proportional to the size of its population. Any country unable to use its allocation could trade entitlements to emit with a nation that needed more. A well-publicised goal of C&C is the convergence of emissions so that each human emits about one third of a tonne of carbon dioxide every year, stabilising greenhouse gases at around 450 ppm in 2100.

There is a way of cutting global greenhouse gas emissions that is equitable, sensible and workable. Contraction & Convergence, or C&C, is the brainchild of South African musician Aubrey Meyer, founder of the London-based Global Commons Institute. Meyer, one of the most extraordinary characters on the climate change activist scene, grasped the urgency of finding a viable solution to climate change before most of us realised there was a problem, and almost 20 years ago he gave up a career playing with the London Philharmonic Orchestra and writing for the Royal Ballet to focus on the issue. Through the vehicle of the grand-sounding Global Commons Institute, which was actually launched in Meyer's bedroom and is still close to a one-man band, the C&C concept has been forced onto the world stage by Meyer's unstinting enthusiasm and incredible work rate. So successful has the lobbying process been that C&C is now a serious contender for forming the basis of the post-Kyoto climate agreement.

So what is it all about? The underlying principles are simple: first, that greenhouse gas emissions must be reduced to ensure 'safe and stable' concentrations in the Earth's atmosphere; second, that the mechanism used to accomplish this must be fair to all, and should therefore be based on the idea that every man, woman and child on the planet has the right to emit an equal amount of greenhouse gas. First of all, nations would agree upon a stable atmospheric concentration of carbon dioxide in the atmosphere. Next, a global emissions 'contraction' budget would see emissions progressively brought down in line with the concentration considered to be safe, and perhaps reviewed annually in order to take account of new science. This global 'carbon cake' would then be shared out regionally, for example to the EU, African Union, and the USA, in the form of tradable entitlements, with individual countries negotiating their own quotas within these bigger 'slices'. As the global carbon budget is progressively contracted, so the allocation of emissions entitlements would converge, by a specified date, towards individual country quotas proportional to national populations. The advantages of this are manifold. It is scrupulously fair, complicated negotiations are not needed, every country would have a target, and the agreed levels for overall emissions can be linked to scientific criteria for preventing dangerous climate change. The mechanism also permits emissions trading so that developing countries unable to use up all their entitlements can sell them to industrialised countries desperate for more.

A suggested working goal is the stabilisation of the carbon dioxide concentration in the atmosphere at 450 ppm by the end of the century, which would require an average annual emissions target for every man, woman and child on the planet of about one third of a tonne. The scale of this challenge is immense, but with increasing scientific evidence that only a zero-carbon world, or something approaching it, will have any chance of thwarting dangerous climate change, even this tiny carbon footprint may actually be too big. Just how much emissions in the industrial countries are going to have to come down can be seen from the fact that even one third of a tonne of carbon dioxide is almost 60 times less than the average American or Australian emits now. On the other hand, it is 15 times higher than the carbon produced in a year by a citizen of Chad. Clearly, the big losers under C&C will be the richest countries and most wasteful emitters, while the winners will be poorer nations and those that embrace clean technologies and low-carbon lifestyles.

Although C&C was originally dismissed by some as thinly disguised communism, almost every day now brings further high-powered support. As long ago as 1995, the Indian government signed up to the framework, and two years later it was adopted by the Africa Group of Nations. Most surprising of all, just before walking out of the Kyoto climate negotiations in 1997, the US delegation conceded that C&C contained 'elements for the next agreement that we might ultimately all seek to engage in': good news, perhaps, for Copenhagen in 2009. Other supporters include China, the European Parliament, the UN Environment Programme, and even the World Council of Churches. Most recently, and perhaps most significantly, the German chancellor, Angela Merkel, also publicly backed C&C. In the UK, the government has been lukewarm, to say the least, but there is plenty of support elsewhere, including from the Royal Commission on Environmental Pollution and from 180 MPs who supported C&C in an early-day motion in parliament.

Whether or not C&C will form the basis of any post-Kyoto climate agreement remains to be seen, but there is certainly nothing else on the table that can hold a candle to it in terms of simplicity, elegance and downright even-handedness. And I am sure that adoption of C&C by the international community would prove to be an almighty relief to Aubrey Meyer, who commented, in a recent *Guardian* interview, that he 'did not realise that it would take quite so long to change the world'.

CAN SCIENCE AND TECHNOLOGY GET US OUT OF OUR FIX?

The wise and judicious application of science and technology are vital if we are to have any chance of successfully short-circuiting dangerous climate change. Not the whacky planetary engineering schemes that play fast and loose with the future of our race and our planet, but the new applications, cutting-edge research and truly innovative ideas that could bear fruit, such as super-efficient wind turbines based upon spinning sycamore seeds; huge, rechargeable batteries for storing solar and wind energy; powdered metal fuels for cars; petrochemical products from grass or algae; hydrogen from artificial photosynthesis, and even electricity produced by squeezing water along arrays of tiny tubes.

Without science and technology our chance of preventing dangerous climate change is less than zero. What we need, however, is science and technology used wisely and judiciously to facilitate big cuts in emissions and to ease the switch from a profit-driven global economy to one where sustainability is the key measure of success. What we don't need is the gung-ho application of wild and whacky schemes with the potential to leave our society and our world in an even more parlous state. New untried and untested ideas for stopping climate change in its tracks now seem to appear every other day - from seeding the atmosphere with sulphur and blocking the sun's rays with a giant cloud of moon dust, to storing frozen carbon dioxide in giant domes or creating new carbon-dioxide munching microbes. Taken at face value, it is easy to understand why some scientists find it difficult to ignore the lure of the exotic. Building a gigantic reflector in space to reduce the amount of solar energy reaching the Earth's surface does sound more exciting than making a billion homes more energy efficient. When examined rigorously, however, such schemes are invariably little more than thought exercises in which considerations such as cost, risk and potential consequences have barely been touched upon. Across the whole spectrum of technology and science, however, advances are being made that, together, can really help us to tackle climate change and adapt to its many ramifications, while driving structural changes in society and economy that will provide for a sustainable and optimistic future, without – perhaps literally – costing the Earth.

It is in the field of energy that technology and science can make the greatest contribution to winning the climate-change battle, starting with improving energy efficiency, developing new means of getting the best out of renewable energy sources like the sun, wind and water, and inventing new ways of producing energy altogether. This importance is noted by Nicholas Stern, who argues sensibly in his report that the need to tackle and adapt to our changing climate should be thought of as an opportunity rather than a burden. Stern goes on to predict that the global market for low-energy products could, by the middle of the century, be worth half a trillion US dollars; I would suggest that it could in fact be much more than this. While, to be honest, remaining pessimistic about our chances of acting quickly enough to avoid dangerous climate change, I have been somewhat heartened by how rapidly solar and wind technologies are coming on-stream, together with the pace of advances in battery technology, hydrogen power, and so-called second generation biofuels for transport, which – on a good day – make me think that all may not be lost after all. Even without climate change, oil production will start to fall off in the next couple of decades, if it hasn't started to do so already, so many of these advances would be needed even if climate change were not an issue.

On top of the more established renewable technologies, lots more are waiting in the wings; some barely off the drawing board, others nearing full-scale trials or commercial application. Giant skysails to power and guide cargo ships and oil tankers; domestic, tethered, wind turbines held aloft by helium balloons, ultra-quiet wind generators for city environments; super-efficient offshore Aerogenerators that mimic the movement of spinning sycamore seeds; tidal barrages that protect coastlines from flooding while at the same time generating electricity, and mammoth rechargeable batteries – the equivalent of ten million AAs – to store wind and solar power until it's needed; gigantic 'solar towers' half a mile high within which rising hot air heated by the sun at the surface drives giant turbines to produce electricity for 200,000 or more homes. Electricity, in the future, could even be generated in the simplest of ways, for example by squeezing water through arrays of tiny tubes or puffing gas across them, while room-temperature superconductors could ensure that hardly any energy is lost in transmission. There is even the prospect of using finely powdered metal as an alternative to petrol – boron, for example, has the potential to carry a car three times further than an equivalent top-up with petrol. Plain old iron could also be used, perhaps crushed down to form particularly cleanly burning nanoparticles, or what about using aluminium from all those recycled cans?

Outside the energy sector, greenhouse gas emissions could be reduced through pills that stop cows producing so much methane; crops could be genetically modified to require less nitrogen-rich fertilisers, a source of the greenhouse gas nitrous oxide, or to 'fix' nitrogen in the soil more effectively. 'Bio-refineries' could take anything from corn, wood or soya to grasses and algae to make oil-replacing petrochemical products for the plastic, paint, cosmetic and pharmaceutical industries. There is even research going on into how the sun's rays might be harnessed to turn carbon dioxide produced from fossil fuel burning back into useful hydrocarbons. Artificial photosynthesis might be feasible too, using renewable solar energy to convert simple carbon dioxide and water into methanol or hydrogen fuels.

In the cold light of day and faced with the harsh realities of even a green-tinged commercial climate, many of these promising gadgets and potential breakthroughs will undoubtedly fall by the wayside or fail to come up to expectations. Some, however, will flower to become important new tools for tackling climate change.

IS ENERGY EFFICIENCY THE KEY?

Even better than producing energy from sustainable sources is cutting back on the amount we actually need. This could go a long way towards slashing greenhouse gas emissions, with energy efficiency measures in the USA alone capable of cutting national electricity usage by three quarters. Some of the biggest savings can be made by generating more power in the places where it is needed – so saving losses during transmission from central generating plants to the customers – and by retrofitting old homes so that they consume less energy. This so-called 'soft-energy' route is being ardently followed by Germany, but still cuts little ice with many other governments, including that of the UK.

Energy efficiency is the poor relation of a sustainable energy policy, often taking a back seat to showier renewable energy initiatives – after all, constructing wind farms or solar power plants is intuitively more appealing than insulating lofts or putting in double glazing. In terms of tackling climate change, however, both are of equal importance –

and improving energy efficiency is often both easier and cheaper to accomplish.

Better energy efficiency is about more than just making homes cosier: it also means, for example, reducing energy loss during transmission, and developing fuels that enable vehicles to travel further on less energy. In many ways, energy efficiency is something that should be tackled before deciding that more energy is needed, but energy efficiency is not yet regarded as sufficiently important to throw serious money at – either in the UK or in many other developed countries – despite the fact that there are vast improvements to be made. Why invest more money in new nuclear power plants and coal-fired power stations instead of promoting micro-generation, when seven per cent of the electricity they generate is lost en route to consumers? Why use old-style incandescent light bulbs, when only one fifth of the energy they generate is actually light? Why stick to inefficient internal combustion engines when independent wheel-hub motors can translate nearly twice as much available energy into moving a car along? The potential savings to be made from investing in improved energy efficiency are vast. In the USA alone, for example, the California-based Electric Power Research Institute reckons that improving energy efficiency could save a staggering three quarters of the electricity the country now uses. In the UK, too, we have barely scratched the surface with respect to using energy efficiently, and still seem to be locked into the antediluvian idea that pumping out more is better than using what can already be supplied more effectively.

Energy efficiency is a critical element of what energy guru Amory Lovins, founder of the Rocky Mountain Institute (RMI), calls the 'soft-energy path', which also incorporates renewable technologies and a diversity of energy production that is matched to the needs of the end users. This contrasts sharply with a 'hard-energy path' that is characterised by large, centralised, power-generation facilities and inefficient, liquid-fuel vehicle transport. Lovins and the Colorado-based RMI, who foster interest and research into the efficient and sustainable use of resources, including energy, certainly practice what they preach, to such an extent that sunlight plus the body heat of its workers is sufficient to keep the RMI HQ at a comfortable temperature, even when it is -30°C outside. Lovins is also the originator of the 'negawatt power' concept, which holds that a market designed to trade improved energy efficiency could deliver more electricity to consumers without the need for more power plants; an idea given short shrift by many governments and much of the world's energy-generation sector, but one that chimes perfectly with the battle against climate change.

In the USA, Lovins' ideas have led to many energy companies counting energy efficiency as something they do, as well as power generation. Some, for example, offer low-interest loans to allow customers to buy energy efficiency measures, while others give away low-energy light bulbs or reward with rebates customers who buy energy-efficient white goods. The negawatt as a commodity is also becoming recognised in the UK, with the 100 per cent renewable energy company Good Energy, for example, paying customers for electricity generated from home-installed wind turbines or solar panels. Even though customers use the energy themselves, this saves Good Energy from having to supply it.

The soft-energy path is probably best reflected in Germany's energy policy and approach to cutting greenhouse gas emissions. While eschewing a new round of centralised nuclear power plant construction, the German government is instead placing much greater emphasis on de-centralised micro-power generation, as well as making homes and other buildings more energy efficient. By 2020, distributed electricity generation is expected to be a major contributor towards a 40-per-cent cut in greenhouse gas emissions. This will be backed up by an ambitious retrofitting plan that aims to dramatically improve the energy efficiency of the country's housing stock – with a target of five per cent of pre-1978 German homes every year. Not only are such measures energy- and emissions saving and climate friendly, but they also create jobs and prosperity, with the country now boasting 1.5 million so-called 'green-collar' jobs.

Australia, under Prime Minister Kevin Rudd, is also planning to follow the German ideal, presumably to at least partly make up for more than a decade of Kyoto-bashing from former premier John Howard. Not to be outdone, Hillary Clinton, at the time of writing one of the leading Democrat candidates in the 2008 battle for the White House, has also promised a one-billion-dollar fund to retrofit homes and create 100,000 green-collar jobs if she wins the election. It seems that the UK, however, is still in the Dark Ages. Inefficient centralised energy generation remains utterly dominant, with micro-generation strangled at birth by government cutbacks, to the extent that homeowners once interested in the idea have now given up in disgust. Such is the government's short-sightedness – at a time when many other industrialised countries are recognising the critical roles that improved energy efficiency measures and distributed power generation can play in cutting emissions. According to its Low Carbon Buildings website, the UK government subsidised the installation of 750 domestic solar power systems between April 2006 and February 2008, while in 2006 alone, 100,000 domestic solar power systems were installed in Germany. Some governments have not got their acts together at all.

IS NUCLEAR POWER THE ANSWER?

Despite its major disadvantages, nuclear power looks like making a comeback, with around 250 new reactors planned world-wide. Nevertheless, the technology remains risky, expensive, slow to develop, and brings with it the massive costs associated with reactor decommissioning and waste disposal. In the UK, the government is forcing through plans for ten new nuclear plants, to fill a perceived 'energy gap' that will develop over the next 15 years, even though the first reactor will probably not be on-line before 2020. The fact that the gap could be filled more quickly through improved energy efficiency and a bigger renewables drive has been conveniently ignored.

While a renewable revolution is going on in countries like Denmark and Germany, others are looking backwards to embrace an expensive, dirty and risky technology that will make little impact on energy production for decades, if at all, and, in many cases, will probably need subsidising by taxpayers. In addition to the 440 nuclear power plants already in existence, around 250 new reactors are planned worldwide, mostly in China, India and the USA, but also in Europe, Asia, Latin America and even South Africa. The most recent member of this rejuvenated nuclear club is the UK, having announced a few months ago, despite continuing opposition from both experts and the public, plans for ten new reactors. Nuclear power is even less popular in Europe, yet the EU also seems to see it as part of a future low-carbon energy mix. The logic of returning to such a technology before seriously tackling energy efficiency or fully tapping the potential of sun, sea and wind seems deeply flawed, especially barely 20 years after the Chernobyl disaster spread the equivalent of 400 Hiroshima bombs' worth of radiation across a huge area of the former Soviet Union and Europe. The European Parliament estimates that a future large-scale nuclear accident would cost between 83 billion and 5.5 trillion Euros.

The reason given by proponents for nuclear's rehabilitation is that it does not produce greenhouse gases during operation, and is therefore 'green'. Of course, emissions produced by digging the uranium ore out, processing it and transporting it halfway across the planet, those generated in building the facility, and, most importantly, decommissioning the reactor and disposing of and monitoring the waste are conveniently forgotten. Furthermore, with demand for uranium looking soon to be greater than ever, supplies of the highest-quality ore, which can be relatively easily extracted and processed, are only likely to last 25 to 30 years or so.

One of the biggest arguments against nuclear power is the radioactive waste that it leaves behind. In the UK, the clean-up programme for existing reactors is expected to cost £73 billion (up 16 per cent on just a year ago) and take an incredible 75 years, and that is without the cost of disposing of the nuclear waste itself. This is another problem that, despite study after study, has not been solved, beyond deciding it should be stuck in a hole in the ground somewhere. The UK's Committee on Radioactive Waste Management suggested in 2006 that it might be a good idea to have a competition for the location of the deep repository for the country's high-level nuclear waste. The lucky community would be rewarded with enough high-level waste to fill the Royal Albert Hall several times over, in a concrete block three hundred metres beneath their feet, where it would remain highly radioactive for many centuries. Any concerns, the Committee suggests, might be bought off with extra cash for roads, schools and the like. So, that's all right then. Similar deep repositories will be needed all over the world, to store ever greater amounts of the most radioactive waste, including more than 17,000 tonnes of the stuff waiting to be secreted away in Europe alone. Disturbingly, a recent UK Environment Agency report suggests that proposed waste containers may only last 500 years when stored deep underground, leaving an awful legacy to our descendents. The Oxford Research Group has also warned that the technology would result in the proliferation of weapons-grade plutonium and increase the potential for nuclear terrorism – and pointed out that to really make any impact on rising emissions, around 3,000 reactors would be needed. In other words, a new one every week for 60 years.

The plan to build new reactors in the UK, where 18 per cent of electricity is currently nuclear-sourced, has been pushed through by the government – undemocratically and, according to some, illegally. Certainly it has been done in defiance of a report by the Sustainable Development Commission, which concluded that by the late 2020s a new nuclear programme would save just four per cent of UK greenhouse gas emissions. The main excuse is that this is the only way to fill a so-called energy gap arising from the retirement of 20 gigawatts of electricity-generating capacity over the next 15 years. At the same time, however, little serious consideration has been given to filling this gap with improved energy efficiency, renewables and micro-generation. Energy-efficiency measures alone, such as retrofitting old homes, would save close to a third of the energy used in the UK, and far more rapidly than a nuclear 'solution'. The first reactor is not even due to come on-stream until 2018 – a date that will almost certainly slip to at least 2020. Because of the proximity of water for cooling, most reactors will be coastally located on the sites of existing nuclear plants, completely disregarding the very real threat of catastrophically rising sea levels. Some, however, may be built on the sites of old coal- and gas-fired power plants, so if you live in Brighton, Bristol or Didcot, keep your ear to the ground.

COULD THE SUN BE OUR SAVIOUR?

The sun is the ultimate power source, providing more free and reusable energy than we are ever likely to need. So far, this has barely been tapped: solar power generation worldwide equals less than one third of the output of China's Three Gorges Dam. Things are changing, however, with a solar revolution now being driven by Japan and Germany, which have between them more than half a million homes powered by the sun. A new mass production method will soon make domestic solar energy as cheap as that generated by fossil fuels, and plans for giant solar arrays in desert regions could provide much of the industrialised world's energy, slashing greenhouse gas emissions.

The sun is the source of virtually unlimited power, bathing our planet in 8,000 times more energy than we currently use. So far, however, we have barely touched this resource. The solar-power industry generated 6,000 Megawatts of electricity worldwide in 2005, which is less than a third of the generating power of China's gigantic Three Gorges Dam hydropower project. Wind generates ten times as much power, and nuclear, something like 60 times as much. Solar power, though, is expanding faster than any other energy source, at a rate of around 30 per cent each year since 2000.

The sun's rays are converted to electricity using photovoltaic (PV) cells. Japan is the world's biggest producer, but is being rapidly caught up by Germany, where the company Q Cells is now the world's second largest PV maker – and one of the fastest-growing companies on the planet. Japan aims to have solar PV generating nearly 5,000 Megawatts of electricity by 2010, which is about as much as three nuclear power plants, and wants something like 16 million homes to be powered by the sun by 2030. Germany is equally ambitious, with 300,000 homes making their own electricity from the sun's energy, and the world's biggest solar power station nearing completion. Unsurprisingly, in sunnier California, plans are afoot to install solar power systems in a million homes over the next decade, and China too is taking solar power seriously, and recently announced plans to put PV systems on 100,000 of Shanghai's six million rooftops. This is all in spite of the fact that solar power currently costs more to generate than electricity produced from fossil fuels. Not for much longer, however. The industry is expected to see explosive growth in the next few years, following the launch in 2007 of a new process that mass produces thin, flexible solar PV cells 'printed' onto rolls of aluminium film. This technique, pioneered by California-based company Nanosolar, is predicted to revolutionise the industry, with the resultant plummeting cost of solar power making it more than a match for oil, gas and coal.

One of the great advantages of solar power systems is that they can generate electricity on any scale. So far, most of the emphasis has been on micro-sized domestic systems, rather than centralised power plants, but that could change. In particular, there is growing interest in what some have called the forgotten energy system: Concentrating Solar Power or CSP. This is a tried-and-tested technology that has been around for a while, but which is only now really capturing the imagination. There are a number of different types of CSP, but all involve the use of arrays of mirrors to concentrate the sun's heat in order to generate electricity. The heat can be used to turn water to steam and drive turbines directly, or to heat oil or a similar fluid, which is then – in turn – used to generate steam. Alternatively, the heat may be used to drive a so-called Stirling Engine, which can convert it directly and efficiently into electricity. To be effective, CSP plants need lots of sun, and a small number of them have operated in sunny places like California's Mojave Desert since the 1980s. Now, however, CSP plants are planned elsewhere in the USA, and in Australia, southern Spain and Algeria. In the USA, the potential of CSP has become apparent as a result of a study published in 2006, which showed that half the country's energy needs could be supplied by CSP plants covering an area of the sunny south-west just 30 times greater than New York City. Most ambitiously, a German-led group, called TREC, has had considerable interest in building a CSP network in North Africa, linked to Europe by a high voltage power grid that results in a far smaller loss of power during transmission than existing power lines. In this way, according to TREC, a small area of the North African desert could supply Europe with all its electricity needs by 2050, as well as providing local power for seawater desalination to irrigate crops grown in the shade of the reflectors.

In addition to generating electricity, solar cells are also used to capture the sun's rays to heat water and space, and solar collectors now provide hot water for 40 million homes. China dominates the market, with 60 per cent of the world's solar heating capacity, while Europe is a strong second. Germany, for example, is installing over 100,000 solar heating systems every year, and more than two million Germans now live in homes with solar water and space heating. In Spain, the government requires that new and renovated homes have solar heating built in, while solar is also likely to form an important element in the UK government's zero-carbon homes initiative, although this is not slated to start until 2016. Currently, just 40,000 UK homes have solar heating installed – a pretty pathetic performance by any standard. Although solar heating does not generate power in its own right, it can make a significant contribution to reducing greenhouse gas emissions through the savings on fossil fuels that would otherwise be used to provide the heating.

WHAT ABOUT THE WIND, WAVES AND TIDES?

With enough wind around to provide five times the world's current energy needs, we have barely even begun to realise its potential. The world leaders are Germany, Spain and the USA, with China and India coming up fast, while the UK, which has 40 per cent of Europe's available wind, is lagging far behind. Wave and tidal power are even less developed, but wave power will feed electricity into the UK grid from 2009, and the world's first commercial wave energy farm is now being built off Portugal. Tidal power may also get a big boost if the UK government approves plans for a tidal barrage across the River Severn estuary.

In many countries the sight of wind turbines is now almost as commonplace as that of the giant cooling towers of power stations fed by fossil fuels. Worldwide, wind energy capacity has more than tripled since 2000, and it is now the second-fastest-growing energy source after solar power. Having said that, the total wind-generating capacity of the planet in 2006 was still only 74,000 Megawatts, the equivalent of 60 or so large power stations, so there is still vast untapped potential. In fact, there is enough wind around to generate five times the total amount of electricity currently needed worldwide, although not all of this could be practically utilised. In just seven years, however, wind power worldwide could be rivalling nuclear power, and it is unlikely to stop there.

Despite the perception that the USA is anti-everything-green, this is far from the truth, and for the last couple of years America has actually had the fastest-growing wind energy industry in the world, installing wind-power capacity equivalent to two large power stations in 2006 alone. To a considerable degree, this growing interest in wind is being driven by state-level concerns about climate change, with 20 states now having energy obligations in place that require wind and other renewable sources to be part of the energy mix. Most extraordinarily of all, the state of Texas, home of oil, Exxon and climate sceptics, recently overtook California to become the country's number one wind power generator.

In terms of total wind power, however, the USA remains behind world leaders Germany and Spain, both of which see wind power as critical to future energy generation and cutting emissions. In Germany, the push for wind and solar power is also a consequence of the country eschewing a revival of its nuclear power industry, so that any energy shortfall has to be covered by renewables. The pace of progress has been astounding, and shows what can be done with the right will and the right policies in place. Currently, the country has ten times the wind-generating capacity of the UK, despite the latter being a far windier place. This has mainly been accomplished by guaranteeing those domestic generators who supply renewable energy to the grid four times the market price, fixed for 20 years.

Unfortunately, the UK is dragging its feet, and – despite having around 40 per cent of Europe's available wind – currently generates just 2,000 Megawatts of electricity from this source, compared with 12,000 MW in Spain and 22,000 MW in Germany. Even India and China now head the UK in the world wind-power league. Admittedly the government did announce recently that it intended to expand offshore wind power to an astonishing 33,000 megawatts by 2020 – enough to generate a fifth of UK electricity – but this was derided by the British Wind Energy Association

(BWEA) as 'pie in the sky'. Now, however, the UK government's hand could be forced, with new EU targets announced early in 2008 demanding that the UK must generate 15 per cent of its energy from renewables by 2020. This translates into as much as 35–40 per cent of the country's electricity – a huge hike from the current figure of just under five per cent – which must involve a massive increase in wind power if it is to be met. According to the BWEA, the target can be met, but only if the government acts fast. The completion of wind farms already cleared for construction or in the planning process, including the world's biggest offshore wind farm off the Kent coast, will provide 18 per cent of UK electricity, meeting almost half of the EU obligation. The trouble is, though, that big offshore wind farms take a good ten years to build, so new projects will need to be approved within just 24 months or so.

The UK's windy atmosphere churns up some of the roughest seas in the world, and the country could generate a further fifth of its electricity by harnessing the power of the waves and the tides. Once again, however, it has been extremely slow on the uptake. Off the north coast of Cornwall, the world's first offshore Wave Hub, into which four different types of wave-power generator are plugged, will start feeding electricity into the national grid in 2009 – sufficient to power 7,500 homes – but wave energy is currently far more expensive than wind power and it will be at least a decade before it really takes off, either in the UK or elsewhere. Utilising the power of the tides may be a better bet in the short term, and a £15 billion scheme to build a 16-kilometre tidal barrage across the Severn Estuary is on the drawing board, which could produce six per cent of the country's electricity. This could be operational by 2017, just in time to meet the EU target, but has attracted understandable opposition from environmental organisations, and may struggle to get through the planning process in time. Harnessing the power of the sea, though, is at least one area in which British expertise is (so far) ahead of the game, with the European Marine Energy Centre located in the Orkneys, and the Scottish company Pelamis Wave Power building the world's first commercial wave energy farm off the Portuguese coast.

CAN THE CRAZE FOR CARS EVER BE MANAGED?

800 million cars clog the world's roads: a figure set to climb further and faster as the residents of China and India are seduced by the lure of the internal combustion engine. The transport sector produces about a fifth of all greenhouse gas emissions, with road vehicles making up the bulk of the total. Road pricing, vehicle taxation, lower speed limits and enforced fuel efficiency may slow our insatiable appetite for cars, but only new technologies can ever bring substantial falls in car-related emissions. Biofuels and electric cars both have roles to play, but ultimately the best chance of success may lie in the widespread adoption of hydrogen fuel-cell technology, or maybe simple compressed air will provide the solution.

Today, 800 million cars travel the world's roads, but in just 20 years' time, car numbers are predicted to reach one billion. The transport sector is currently producing around 20 per cent of all greenhouse gas emissions, with road vehicles making up the bulk of this. Clearly, if we are to have any chance of cutting back hard on global emissions, something must be done to reduce the impact of road transport. Different fuels are in the pipeline, with more efficient and less polluting cars coming on stream. The question is, will this be enough to counteract the spectacular growth in road transport driven by people's desire for increased mobility?

In the USA, the car is God, with an average of four for every three people. Europe is way behind: the number of cars per person is comparable to that of the USA in the 1970s, while in China, the figure is equivalent to the USA in 1912 – which shows just how much room for expansion there is in the global car market. To give an idea of the contribution American drivers are making to climate change, in 2002 their greenhouse gas emissions were actually higher – at just over a billion tonnes – than those produced by the entire Japanese economy. Hybrid cars, which complement the traditional petrol engine with an electric motor, are growing in popularity, and 200,000 a year are now selling in the USA. Toyota optimistically expects hybrids to capture 50 per cent of the US new car market by 2025, but at the moment the share is tiny. Car numbers in China are on cue to match US numbers by 2030, with the six million cars on Chinese roads in 2000 exploding to 25 million today, and projected to reach a staggering 250 million within 25 years. India also seems to be ultimately bent on a similar path, particularly with the recent launch – for the princely sum of 100,000 Rupees (£1,290) – of the People's Car. Initially, a quarter of a million of these new cars, built by Indian mega-corporation Tata, are to come off the production line every year, with numbers steadily rising – good news for Tata's profits and India's expanding middle class, but very bad news for climate change.

Even in the UK, the market is far from saturated. Government figures predict six million more cars on the roads by 2031 – enough to fill a 52-lane motorway stretching from London to Edinburgh. The problem here is that the cost of motoring has dropped 11 per cent since 1970, in real terms, while bus and rail fares have gone up by two-thirds or more. Still, the UK government feeds the car craze with schemes to make motorways ever wider – at a cost of £1,000 per inch – while doing virtually nothing to reduce traffic.

The mass car market had its centenary in 2007. It was hardly a cause for celebration, however, except among the most evangelical of petrol-heads. No viable climate-change solution will ever be possible without taming emissions from road vehicles, and that means either embracing alternative fuels, or replacing the internal combustion engine with something clean and green. Biofuels may yet provide the answer, although, as discussed later, they come with their own baggage. Road pricing, vehicle taxation and funding for public transport at the expense of roads may all have small roles to play, but without the application of new technologies it is difficult to see how car emissions can be brought under control.

The problem is that most car companies are loath to sacrifice speed and acceleration to green credentials, so legislation will likely have to play an important part in forcing their hand. The EU, for example, has infuriated European car makers by ordering them to reduce carbon dioxide emissions on all new models to 120 grams per kilometre from 2012, down from an average of 162 grams per kilometre in 2005. Future initiatives could see this cut to 95 grams per kilometre by 2020, and might even ban cars capable of exceeding 130 kilometres an hour. More than this, however, will be needed to bring about the transition to a global car fleet that produces essentially carbon-free emissions. Unless some of the more experimental biofuels, such as those manufactured from algae, come up trumps, it is unlikely that these will prove to be the main solution in the long run. Electrical vehicles are becoming more attractive all the time – evidence the sporty Tesla Roadster and the cute G-Wiz – but at the moment they are charged mainly with electricity generated by fossil fuels. Probably the best bet is renewably-generated hydrogen, initially burnt in special internal combustion engines instead of petrol, and later in fuel cells that emit steam as the only waste product. Hybrid hydrogen buses are already chugging around the streets of London, Hamburg and Barcelona, but the trick is going to be getting a more advanced version of the technology up to speed for use in cars. Alternatively, the extraordinary and recently launched oneCAT, which runs on pollution-free compressed air, could be the start of a true transport revolution.

WHAT ABOUT TAMING THE AVIATION INDUSTRY?

Aircraft emissions currently account for just a few per cent of the world's total greenhouse gas emissions, but they are forecast to cause up to 15 per cent of global warming within 40 years. Improved fuel efficiency, bigger and higher-tech aircraft, flying more slowly at lower altitude and along more direct routes, will all help to curb emissions, but their inexorable rise will continue as long as aviation fuel, ticketing and new aircraft are not taxed and flying remains cheap. With the industrialised nations seemingly not serious about tackling the aviation industry, and the growing middle classes of India and China increasingly embracing air travel, the prospects for making a real dent in predicted aircraft emission rises are bleak.

At present, the aviation industry accounts for just a few per cent of global greenhouse gas emissions, but this is set to rocket as many people around the world who don't currently have access to flying will have this opportunity in years to come. Travel and tourism are currently growing at 4.5 per cent a year and the whole business will be worth an astonishing

$9.5 trillion by 2014. Air passenger numbers – in the absence of major policy changes – are expected to continue to climb by five or so per cent every 12 months, leading to emissions rising by 3–4 per cent year on year. As the growing middle classes of China and India, in particular, embrace air travel, there is a real danger that both flying and aircraft emissions will go through the roof. Already, they are rising faster than those of any other sector, and are predicted to cause up to 15 per cent of global warming in a little over 40 years. Which is not surprising, really, when you consider that the size of China's commercial airliner fleet, alone, is expected to climb from around 800 today to close to 3,000 in 2023.

While increasing numbers of aircraft are taking to the skies, they are at least becoming more efficient. Europe's Airbus A380, for example, burns almost a fifth less fuel than any other plane currently in service, while the Boeing 787 Dreamliner, due to enter service in 2008, is claimed to be more fuel efficient than other aircraft of a similar size. Passenger aircraft built today are 70 per cent more fuel efficient than those constructed 40 years ago, and fuel efficiency is expected to rise, on average, by one or two per cent a year.

Bigger planes, such as the A380, will help by carrying more passengers, and by flying just 2,000 metres lower than they do at present, planes would burn six per cent less fuel. Flying more direct routes and avoiding stacking prior to landing could save another 12 per cent. When you consider that a single jumbo flying daily between London and Miami for a year produces 178,000 tonnes of carbon dioxide – about the same as is saved by a small wind farm – these reductions are not to be sniffed at. Flying more slowly, taxi-ing less, changing descent profiles, fitting winglets, installing lighter cabin equipment, and reducing baggage allowances can also help. Looking further ahead, radical new designs are being considered, with the intention of slashing emissions further. One example is the ecoJet prototype unveiled by EasyJet and Airbus in 2007, with open rotor engines that look a bit like old-fashioned propellers, which claims to cut emissions in half. Virgin Airlines are even proposing to use carbon-neutral biofuels, although of course these present other problems.

While improved fuel efficiency, different flying strategies, and new technologies may be able to slow the rise in aviation emissions, the only way to seriously curtail them is by cutting the numbers of flights and the numbers of passengers, and the only way to do this is by making flying more expensive. With no tax on aviation fuel, air travellers are not at the moment paying the full cost of flying. In the UK, for example, the aviation industry receives a £9-billion-a-year tax break through tax-free fuel and VAT-free transactions on tickets and new aircraft. Everywhere, governments are accepting the huge projected growth in air traffic, rather than trying to curb it: hundreds of new airports, runways and terminals are planned, with China alone looking to open 49 new airports.

Passengers could be forced to pay up each time they fly, as they are through the UK's air passenger duty. Unless swingeing, however, this is not likely to have much of an impact. Alternatively, flights can be taxed instead of passengers, as will happen in the UK from 2009, to encourage more efficient use of aircraft and discourage half-empty planes. Taxing either flights or passengers, however, makes no sense while at the same time actively expanding airports and runways. The UK government is perhaps the most disingenuous in this respect, discouraging flying with one hand while encouraging it with the other. In the UK, Europe and elsewhere around the world, emissions cuts in other sectors are in danger of being substantially wiped out by an unfettered aviation industry. In Europe, aviation emissions have risen 85 per cent since 1990 and are climbing at more than seven per cent a year. The EU is hoping to tame this rising trend by incorporating aviation into its carbon trading scheme, but this is a half-hearted measure and won't even get going until 2012: it caps emissions relative to 2004–2006 levels, which are high enough in their own right, takes no account of the extra warming effect caused by the chemical cocktail pumped out by aircraft at high altitudes, and gives away free to the airlines 90 per cent of their emissions permits, so that they don't pay anything like the true cost of the pollution they cause. If this is the best mechanism available for curbing aircraft emissions, then we really are in trouble.

IS BIOFUEL A HELP OR A HINDRANCE?

Once seen as a potential saviour in the battle against rising transport emissions, biofuel's reputation has been seriously tarnished over the last year or so. With one per cent of the planet's farmland already turned over to energy crops such as maize, soya, sugar cane and palm oil, to feed growing demand for bioethanol and biodiesel, the cost – in climbing grain and food prices, flattened forests and drained peat bogs – seems to be too high. Add to this fears that biofuel might actually lead to higher emissions, and therefore more warming, than would result from burning the fossil fuels they replace, and their future seems less than rosy.

In little more than 12 months, biofuel seems to have switched from saint to sinner in the battle against climate change. In September 2006, a *Guardian* headline asked (of palm oil or sugar cane) 'Could this crop save the planet?' Yet, just a few months later, the *New York Times* felt confident in claiming that producing a 'green' fuel caused an ecological blight, while the *Independent* reported that demand for palm oil was 'damaging the planet'. By the middle of 2007, Greenpeace, the WWF, Friends of the Earth and the RSPB were funding full-page ads in the newspapers, showing a worried orang-utan with a petrol pump 'gun' at its head, beneath the words 'tell the government to choose the right biofuel... or the orang-utan gets it'.

The initial popularity of biofuel arose from the fact that it is carbon neutral – the carbon dioxide released into the atmosphere when the fuel is burnt simply compensates for that absorbed by the source plants when they were growing. All well and good, but the reality of the situation is not quite that straightforward. While the UK government has decreed that all fuel sold by 2010 must contain five per cent biofuel, and the EU has confirmed its requirement that all transport fuels should be ten per cent biofuel by 2020, others remain unconvinced. In a report issued in early 2008, the UK's Royal Society warned that these obligations may not actually reduce emissions if large swathes of tropical forest are flattened to make room for biofuel plantations. UK MPs are also not happy, and have called for a moratorium on UK and EU biofuel targets until 'robust' measures can be put in place that can prevent environmental damage that may actually counteract their usefulness as emission-reducers. Even worse, a recent Swiss study has shown that almost half of 26 common biofuels tested, including US corn-ethanol, sugar-cane ethanol and soya-diesel from Brazil, and palm-oil diesel from Malaysia, were actually less climate-friendly than fossil fuels when deforestation and other environmental impacts were taken into account

To cap it all, the global rush to energy crops for biofuel is already pushing up the price of grain crops such as maize, wheat and rice, as competition between food and energy crop production increases and the poor suffer as a result. Environmental activists and commentators are now claiming that biofuels from crops are causing a potentially catastrophic tug-of-war between the world's 800 million motorists and the billions living on less than a dollar a day, who are just trying to buy enough food to survive. This is a line supported by the UN, who warn that the impact of the energy crop boom will be increased deforestation, the expulsion of small farmers, higher food prices and serious food shortages. One per cent of the world's fields are already devoted to energy crops, and global production is doubling every few years. In the USA alone, where a number of cities and states already require bioethanol to be mixed with petrol, one third of the 2006 maize crop went towards the production of bioethanol, pushing up worldwide maize prices by 50 per cent, and leading to tortilla rallies in Mexico. In China and India, there is even a danger that water used for energy crops will leave insufficient resources to irrigate those grown for food. A couple of dozen other countries are now also embracing energy crops, including Brazil and Indonesia, where expansion threatens the destruction of ever more rainforest. In Indonesia, peat bogs, too, are being drained to grow palm oil for biofuel, with the draining of just one hectare releasing 30 times the amount of carbon dioxide saved by burning the biofuel produced from it.

Even a cursory examination of future biofuel production trends, in the context of environmental impact, will reveal that biofuel from crops can never wholly replace petrol and diesel, or get anywhere near this. Just to meet the EU's ten per cent biofuel mix target, 40 per cent of the continent's agricultural land would have to switch to energy crops – resulting in drastic cuts in food production. Globally, for half of the fossil fuel used in transport and electricity generation to be replaced by biofuels by 2050 would require the use of between 35 and 80 per cent of all the water flowing down all the world's rivers. In addition, just to meet one tenth of the world's projected biofuel demand by 2030, all suitable land would have to be corralled into energy crop production, leaving nowhere to grow the food needed for the few billion extra new mouths that will by then have appeared. And the killer punch – the potent greenhouse gas, nitrous oxide, released after application of all the fertiliser needed to keep the crops fit and well, looks as if it might completely counteract all the gains made from replacing fossil fuels with biofuel. All may not be quite lost, however: second-generation, non-crop biofuel may be the key. Shell, for example, has just announced plans to build an experimental plant in Hawaii that will make biofuel from marine algae. The algae double their mass every day and are reportedly capable of sourcing 15 times more biofuel than rape.

DOES HYDROGEN POWER HAVE A FUTURE?

Hydrogen could power road vehicles, trains, ships and planes in a climate-friendly, post-hydrocarbon world. As a fuel, it can either be burnt in conventional engines or supply on-board fuel cells that use it to make electricity. The waste from either process is simple water, with no greenhouse gases to add to global warming. At the moment, however, there are few hydrogen-powered vehicles and just 300 filling stations on the planet. Furthermore, most hydrogen is produced using electricity generated from fossil fuels. While Iceland and California, in particular, have aspirations to develop hydrogen-based economies, it will be a while before the rest of the world follows suit.

In the past, hydrogen has had a bad name – mainly due to its tendency to explode given the slightest opportunity. A burst of popularity for the gas in the 1930s ended when the German airship Hindenburg crashed in flames in front of the cameras in New York. Hydrogen is now enjoying a serious revival, however, as the most likely green replacement for petrol. As a fuel, it has the potential to power road vehicles, trains, and even ships and planes, and is already being used in cars. Here, it can either be burnt in standard internal combustion engines or, in electric cars, used in fuel cells to produce the electricity.

Fuel cells have been around for quite a while. The first was developed by a Welsh scientist, Sir William Grove, in 1843, and they were brought to public attention in a situation reminiscent of the Hindenburg disaster, when an exploding fuel cell crippled the Apollo 13 moon mission in 1970. Fuel cells work by taking in hydrogen and oxygen and converting them into water and electricity. For use in vehicles, the hydrogen is carried either in the form of compressed gas or as liquid hydrogen, while oxygen is readily available in the air. Fuel cells of this type have been powering experimental and prototype vehicles for decades, but with technical problems ironed out they are now becoming mainstream. Fuel-cell buses are already on the streets of London, Hamburg, Barcelona, Amsterdam, Stuttgart, Stockholm, Madrid and other European cities, as part of the Fuel Cell Bus Club, and also in Beijing and in Perth, Western Australia. It is in Iceland, however, that the fuel cell as a power source for vehicles has really taken off, with the country vowing to abandon fossil fuels and power all its cars, trucks and buses using hydrogen. Not only that, but the hydrogen will be manufactured using renewable hydro-power and geothermal energy. Meanwhile, in Japan, the world's first fuel-cell-powered passenger train took to the rails in 2007, while Canada, the USA and Europe all have plans to replace highly polluting diesel engines with fuel cell-powered trains.

Hydrogen can also be used to power vehicles with conventional internal combustion engines. BMW's Hydrogen 7 version of its top-of-the-range Series 7, for example, is being driven in California by the likes of Angelina Jolie to highlight the emphasis governor Schwarzenegger is placing on hydrogen as the fuel of the future. The car is actually a hydrogen-petrol hybrid, and carries petrol as well as liquid hydrogen stored in a double-insulated tank at a chilling -253°C. It can switch seamlessly between the two fuels, which is essential with hydrogen filling stations still few and far between, even in such progressive places as California. Schwarzenegger has plans for a filling station every 20 miles across the state's road network, but there are currently just a couple of dozen in operation.

All the major car companies are working on hydrogen models, but these will never really take off until there is an effective hydrogen infrastructure to support them. This includes networks of filling stations as dense as those that currently provide us with petrol and diesel, together with the required production, transport and storage facilities. At present, there are about 300 hydrogen filling stations worldwide, mostly in Europe, Japan and North America, and to replace the US petrol and diesel filling station network, alone, is estimated to cost half a trillion US dollars. Another current problem with hydrogen is that most of it is produced using electricity derived from burning fossil fuels, so it still results in greenhouse gas emissions. For hydrogen to fulfil its promise as the green fuel of the future, it must be produced from renewables, using either electricity from a grid supplied by green sources, or electricity generated on the spot by solar cells or a wind generator. One way of speeding things up, and doing away with much of the infrastructure associated with production, storage and transport, is to carry the source of hydrogen in the vehicle with you. A company in Israel is building a prototype system that generates hydrogen by reacting water with boron – the idea being that the boron is carried in the vehicle and produces hydrogen on demand. When you fill up, therefore, all you need to put in is plain water.

Any discussion of hydrogen power would be incomplete without at least a mention of nuclear fusion – the power that drives our sun by combining hydrogen nuclei to form helium plus stupendous amounts of energy. I remember, as a small child, poring over a picture book that enthused about how our world would be transformed once scientists managed to harness the fusion process, providing us with unlimited power from the most ubiquitous resource on the planet – water. Then, a working fusion reactor was 40 years away; today, it is 40 years away. World governments have funded a £7 billion project called ITER, to build a prototype reactor in France, which could be a forerunner of a global network of fusion power stations, but don't hold your breath.

IS STORING CARBON THE ANSWER?

With coal making a big comeback, it looks as if the only way we can cope with the resulting carbon dioxide is by capturing it at source and storing it. The trouble is that this is expensive and uses more energy. Also, by the time the technology is widely available, expansion of coal use may already have pushed up emissions by a catastrophic 57 per cent. There are doubts too about whether the gas will stay put, and worries that the whole idea might be driving the new coal craze. Certainly this is far from an ideal solution, but it may well be one that we are forced by circumstances to accept.

With plans afoot for the construction or refurbishment of more than 2,000 coal-fired power stations around the world over the next two decades, the only way to prevent a huge hike in global emissions seems to be to adopt 'clean coal' technologies, such as integrated coal gasification combined cycle (IGCC), in which the carbon dioxide is removed before the coal is burnt, and carbon capture and storage (CCS) whereby carbon dioxide produced during burning is separated out, captured, and stored underground in old gas or oil fields or defunct aquifers.

The trouble with coal is that it is cheap and relatively easy to get at, which means that countries like China, India and the USA, where there are huge deposits, simply can't resist the urge to dig it up and use it. This is why nearly five and half billion tonnes of coal are now burned every year, generating one third of all carbon dioxide emissions. Capturing and storing the carbon dioxide released at coal power plants is probably the only realistic way of making the best of a bad situation, at least in the shorter term. To have any significant impact on emissions, of course, the technologies need to be applied on a huge scale, with those countries who are developing the capability, such as the UK, rapidly transferring the knowledge and technology to places like China and India, where it is most needed. Whereas the IGCC method cannot be retro-fitted to existing power plants, CCS technology can, so that is where most interest currently lies.

A number of CCS trials have already been undertaken, albeit in relation to the oil extraction business rather than power-plant operation. In the North Sea, the Norwegian oil company Statoil has, for the last 11 years, been pumping unwanted carbon dioxide gas from its Sleipner field into a layer of porous sandstone a kilometre beneath the seabed. Similar schemes are now being tried and tested elsewhere – sometimes, as at Weyburn, Saskatchewan, pumping back the carbon dioxide into an oil or gas reservoir to force out the final dregs. Returning to the North Sea, however, there is sufficient space in its senescent oil and gas reservoirs to hold all the carbon dioxide produced by European power stations over the last 60 years. Using the carbon dioxide to push out the last traces of oil could also have the added effect of extending oil production from North Sea fields by 15–20 years. This, however, rather misses the point of why we need CCS in the first place, which is to reduce greenhouse gas emissions, rather than to maximise usage of the most polluting hydrocarbons.

In relation to capturing waste carbon dioxide from burning fossil fuels, there are already plans to fit CCS to gas or coal power plants in Norway, Queensland in Australia, and Oklahoma in the USA, and one of these facilities is likely to be up-and-running in four years' time. The UK government, meanwhile, has launched a funding competition that is designed to see CCS working on at least one of its power plants by

2014. The EU has already decided that all new power plants must be ready to take CCS technology a year later, and hopes that a round dozen demonstration projects will be on the go by this time.

While concealing carbon dioxide underground may seem like a good idea, there are many who have doubts. For a start, CCS requires 20–40 per cent more energy and may increase electricity prices to consumers by up to 90 per cent. To be utilised on a large enough scale to have a significant impact on global emissions, it would require whole networks of pumping stations and pipelines, which are bound to have a detrimental impact on the environment. The storage side of the equation is also not that well understood, and despite assurances, no-one can be certain how long the sequestered carbon dioxide will remain where it's put. If it begins to leak in the decades and centuries ahead, then these carbon sinks will become sources, and we will have simply passed the problem on to future generations.

Another issue is the cost. The separating out, or 'capture' of carbon dioxide at power stations is a complex and expensive business currently costed at around US$40–60 per tonne, and this needs to fall substantially to make the technique cheap and attractive enough to retrofit the 213 new coal-fired power stations planned by India, and the 550 or so to be built in China, all of which will be built with no thought to CCS. Even in the UK, the government's short-sighted and unambitious energy policy encompasses the construction of up to eight new coal-fired power plants, ready to take CCS, but without the technology built in.

Probably the biggest concerns about CCS centre around its application being used as an excuse for a new, worldwide, expansion of the coal industry, and for a continuation of a 'business as usual' course instead of a more sustainable route that embraces renewable energy sources and modified lifestyles. The greatest worry, though, is that CCS will not be viable on a big enough scale until after 2030. By this time, according to the most up-to-date predictions, energy demand – much of it satisfied by coal – will have climbed 50 per cent on 2005 levels, forcing up emissions by a catastrophic 57 per cent.

CAN WE ENGINEER THE PLANET TO BRING DOWN TEMPERATURES?

Over the last few years we have seen plenty of mad-cap ideas aimed at stopping climate change in its tracks. Billions of tiny silver balloons or sulphur particles scattered throughout the stratosphere, giant reflectors parked in orbit, great clouds of moon dust blocking the sun, and ocean-going cloud seeders are just a few of the proposals aimed at lowering the amount of solar radiation reaching the Earth's surface. Others include storing unwanted frozen carbon dioxide in giant domes or building made-to-measure carbon-chomping life-forms. None of these schemes provides a hard-and-fast guarantee of success, which is pretty scary when the future of the planet is at stake.

We will never tackle dangerous climate change without resorting to advanced technologies, but the recent weird and wonderful ideas for stopping climate change in its tracks by geo-engineering the planet simply go too far. Not only are they panaceas that allow us to modulate global temperature while carrying on as before, but most are designed to lower temperatures without addressing associated problems, such as increasing acidification of the oceans. Ultimately, geo-engineering is all about untried and untested experiments on a global scale, the subjects of which are our world and all life upon it.

One of the earliest, wildest and wackiest geo-engineering 'solutions' to our warming climate was proposed by the late Edward Teller, 'father' of the H-bomb and alleged (by some) template for Stanley Kubrick's anti-hero Dr Strangelove. Before his death in 2003, Teller and colleagues at California's Lawrence Livermore Laboratory published plans for making a global 'sun-screen' by scattering billions of tiny, hydrogen-filled aluminium balloons throughout the stratosphere, where they would cool the planet by reflecting the sun's rays back into space. More recently, Dutch Nobel laureate chemist Paul Crutzen has suggested that tiny sulphur particles scattered throughout the stratosphere would be just as effective. As shown by the global temperature falls that follow big volcanic eruptions, such particles are very effective at absorbing and reflecting incoming solar radiation and thereby cooling things down. Just five million tonnes of extra sulphur every year, on top of what industry is already pumping out, could bring rising temperatures to heel. Then again, the oceans would continue to become more acid, the ozone layer might not like it, and who knows how it might affect our weather-systems. Even worse, more sulphur from a huge, unexpected, volcanic eruption might result in more cooling than we had bargained for.

Lowell Wood, a co-author on the balloon paper, has also proposed an alternative scheme that involves parking a 1,000-kilometre-wide diaphanous mirror in orbit, again counteracting warming by blocking out around one per cent of the sunlight heading our way. Curtis Struck at Iowa State University prefers another approach – mining moon dust to make a gigantic dust cloud that shields the Earth from the sun's warming rays – while astronomer Roger Angel, at the University of Arizona, has suggested that a cloud of silicon discs launched from Earth could do the same job. Meanwhile John Latham, at the National Center for Atmospheric Research in Boulder, Colorado, and British scientist Stephen Salter, at the University of Edinburgh, want fleets of unmanned boats to roam the seas, blasting a fine mist of seawater into the air as they go, the idea being that the billions of tiny salt nuclei will increase the number of water droplets in any clouds in the vicinity, making them whiter and therefore more reflective.

UK climate scientist Chris Rapley's idea is to tether millions of vertical pipes in the world's oceans, which would bring nutrient-rich cold water from deeper down up to the surface. Tiny algae making the most of this new food source would bloom, taking carbon out of the atmosphere as they grew, died and sank to the sea floor. The consequences for marine ecosystems, however, are not known – and in fact such a scheme might even transfer carbon dioxide from the rising water flow into the atmosphere. Alternatively, the oceans could be seeded with ground-up iron, thereby promoting the growth of phyto-plankton – the tiny, floating organisms already responsible for the removal of enormous amounts of carbon from the atmosphere. Past experiments have proved inconclusive, but this has not stopped a California-based company, Planktos, dumping 50 tonnes of haematite into the sea near the Galapagos Islands. The caper is part of a trial 'study' that has been widely condemned as unscientific, dubious and – potentially – environmentally damaging.

And the schemes just keep coming. The storage of frozen carbon dioxide extracted from the atmosphere in huge insulated domes is particularly laughable, at a time when we still don't know what we are going to do with the mountains of waste from the nuclear industry – and what a dream target for terrorists. Using a totally different approach, J Craig Venter, entrepreneurial cracker of the human genome, is looking to build made-to-measure micro-organisms to tackle climate change. Some, perhaps, could be designed to produce hydrogen or ethanol as waste products, which could be used as fuel, while another might feed on carbon. Once again, however, what happens if we lose control? In the big, wide world, the carbon-eating bugs might not stop until Snowball Earth is with us once more – the ultimate consequence of what Royal Society President Sir Martin Rees refers to as 'bio-error' as opposed to 'bio-terror'.

Messing around with the wholesale composition of the atmosphere is what has got us into our predicament, so we need more speculative experimentation on a planetary scale like a hole in the head. The sensitivity of our climate is such that geo-engineering a reduction of less than two per cent in the solar energy reaching our planet's surface would cancel out the warming caused by a doubling of greenhouse gas levels in the atmosphere; a miscalculation resulting in a few more per cent and the glaciers could be on the move again. Is it really worth the risk? If the choice lies between living a more sustainable life or taking a techno-fix gamble that could see our world in an even more precarious state than it is now, I know which will get my vote.

PART 5: IS IT ALREADY TOO LATE?

The pre-eminent oceanographer and climate scientist Wallace Broeker has famously warned that 'climate is an angry beast and we are poking at it with sticks'. Well, the beast is now stirring and has got as far as opening one bleary eye. The big question is, can we persuade it to return to its slumbers? It would seem to be touch-and-go at present, with a rapidly growing awareness of climate change and its potentially devastating consequences finely balanced against the inertia of a society and economy still stuck in the rut of nineteenth-century thinking when it comes to growth and profit. No doubt, given time, a combination of precaution and ever-diminishing resources will drive serious action to tackle climate change. Unfortunately, time is a luxury we just don't have.

With just a few years to start to bring the situation under control, it is difficult to look at the hard facts and remain optimistic. Greenhouse gas concentrations in the atmosphere are rising more rapidly than ever, as are global emissions. Almost every new piece of research suggests that climate change is going to be even worse than previously thought, with the threshold for dangerous climate change now lower than was predicted just a few years ago. Do we have any realistic chance of stabilising emissions within seven years, and bringing about a near zero-carbon world in just over four decades' time? And even if we do, will this be enough, or will positive feedback effects as our world warms take us over the edge and into climate chaos anyway?

There are so many critical factors involved that it is simply not possible yet to say whether we will win out or not. Feedbacks could be smaller or greater than predicted; the threshold for dangerous climate change could be lower than 2°C, or higher; renewable energy could become so cost effective as to leave oil and coal in the ground unused; the global economy could continue along its business-as-usual path or switch to a route that leads rapidly to sustainable growth and big emissions cuts.

Perhaps most critical of all, however, is the outcome of the climate conference that will be held in Copenhagen in December 2009. The so-called COP15 meeting[9] will be one of the most momentous in human history, with a global consensus to cut greenhouse gas emissions in line with the science providing at least the basis of a firm footing for averting dangerous climate change. Failure here, however, is almost certain to mean that time has run out – for us, and for generations to come.

JUST HOW BAD CAN THINGS GET?

It is difficult to imagine that faced with overwhelming evidence we will choose, as a global community, to do nothing about climate change. But what if we have already released such a huge quantity of greenhouse gas into the atmosphere that we have lit the fuse of unstoppable and devastating climate change? The last time the atmosphere was flooded with so much carbon was 55 million years ago, during the Eocene period, when Arctic seas were as warm as those off Florida are today and sea levels were far higher than they are now. Could it be that it is too late for us to avoid a return to the super-greenhouse of the Eocene?

Clearly the world that we bequeath to future generations will depend to a great extent upon our actions in the next few decades. But what if we do nothing, or next to nothing, or don't act quickly enough? Or, heaven forbid, we have already passed a point of no return? How bad could things get? Geologists often talk of the present being the key to the past, in the sense that we can explain much of what went on in so-called 'deep time' by recourse to the sorts of processes we see going on around us today. In the same way, the past can be the key to the future, so that by looking back to similar conditions in the geological record we can say more about what the future might hold. Looking ahead, we can best get an idea of what future generations might be faced with by looking back to so-called 'hothouse' or 'super-greenhouse' climates of the past. The Cretaceous period, for example, lasted for a good 80 million years – from the end of the Jurassic, 145 million years ago, until 65 million years ago, when a large asteroid strike or huge lava outpourings, or a combination of the two, changed the climate for the worse – at least as far as the dinosaurs were concerned. The Cretaceous was a time of bath-tub oceans, with water temperatures perhaps 14°C higher than they are now. Similar conditions were also encountered during the more recent Eocene period, which lasted from 55 million to 34 million years ago, when the Earth again basked in the warm glow of an almost planet-wide tropical climate. Hothouse climates are characterised not only by warmer oceans, but also by the complete, or almost complete, absence of permanent polar ice, so that sea levels are many metres higher than they are today. Temperatures at the poles are also far above freezing, with crocodiles living quite happily around Canada's Hudson Bay, and lemurs feeling perfectly at home in Svalbard. It could be argued that we are already on course for the return of such conditions. Certainly, the Eocene super-greenhouse conditions can be reproduced quite well using one of the more pessimistic IPCC scenarios, in which a doubling of carbon dioxide levels lead to a 4°C temperature hike. Furthermore, maintaining polar ice sheets of any great extent seems to become increasingly difficult once carbon dioxide levels get above 550 ppm or so.

During the Eocene, tropical rainforests extended as far north as 45 degrees, the equivalent of Bordeaux in France and the state of Maine in the USA, while temperatures at the north pole look as if they might have been higher than at any time in the last 100 million years. Hardly entirely surprising, then, that the waters of the Arctic Ocean were a balmy 24°C – the sort of water temperature you might expect to encounter today in the Florida Keys. The burst of heat known as the Palaeocene–Eocene Thermal Maximum (PETM) 55 million years ago has been clearly linked to a rapid release of greenhouse gas, amounting to somewhere between 1,500 and 4,500 billion tonnes of carbon, with 2,000 billion tonnes the most commonly quoted figure – but how might the two events have been connected? As mentioned earlier in the book, the best bet is that the carbon arose from a huge 'burp' of methane from clathrates in marine sediments, derived from the decomposition of plankton and other marine life. But what was the trigger that caused the clathrates to yield up their methane? One possibility is that rising magma linked to the splitting apart of the North Atlantic may have ignited organic material contained in rocks beneath the Norwegian Sea, driving off huge quantities of greenhouse gas. The story goes that this might have heated up the planet sufficiently – perhaps by just a few degrees – that the warming penetrated the oceans and destabilised the vast deposits of clathrates around the world, causing more massive methane 'burps' that contributed to even more warming. The amount of carbon released by the magma-triggered burp in the North Atlantic seems to have been equivalent to around six billion tonnes of carbon – less than human activities have released year-on-year since the late 1980s, which is disturbing to say the least. It also seems that the carbon burp occurred on a very similar time scale, with estimates ranging from 360 years down to just 35.

Might it be, then, that human activities have already flooded the atmosphere with sufficient carbon to destabilise the world's clathrate deposits? As rising temperatures lag behind increasing greenhouse gas levels in the atmosphere, this could well be the case. Even if we stopped all human-related emissions today, temperatures would continue to climb into the twenty-second century, and could at some point start to trigger the large-scale release of methane from clathrates. All that is needed is for the world's oceans to warm to deeper levels so as to bring the clathrate-bearing deposits within range. Significant warming has so far only penetrated down to about 300 metres, and most deposits are substantially deeper than this, but if the fuse has already been lit by human activities over the last couple of hundred years, all we can do is wait until the first methane starts to bubble its way towards the surface.

WILL PEAK OIL AND PEAK COAL SAVE US?

The burning of oil and coal is the main driver of rising levels of greenhouse gases in the atmosphere, but production of oil may have already peaked and coal is expected by some to do so in the next few decades. Will this help in the battle against climate change or will the search for dirtier, harder-to-get-at deposits make the situation even worse? While oil companies seem intent on following this route, difficulties in getting out much of the coal currently classed as 'reserves' could sharply curb emissions and keep atmospheric concentrations of the gas from climbing above 470ppm.

Nothing lasts for ever, and in the case of oil, coal and gas, this is no bad thing. Climate change or not, the one thing we can be certain of is that the oil age is coming to an end, with coal and gas to follow. For years, various doom-mongers have warned of the imminent arrival of 'peak oil', the point at which the world's consumption of oil outstrips discoveries of new oil so that we begin to eat more and more into known reserves. Unsurprisingly, the timing of peak oil is a moving target, with those with a vested interest in the resource constantly playing up reserves and playing down their demise. In its 2007 Statistical Review of World Energy, therefore, BP suggests that there are enough proven reserves to support current levels of consumption for 40 years. This contrasts utterly, however, with the findings of London's Oil Depletion Analysis Centre, which announced recently that the peak for easily accessible oil was reached in 2005. They have also warned that the global production of all oil will peak by 2011 before starting to slide steeply. Going one better, the German-based Energy Watch announced in October 2007 that oil production actually peaked in 2006 and would fall by an extraordinary 50 per cent by 2030. If this is true, falling supply will not be able to match rapidly increasing demand, especially from China, leading to soaring prices and a global economic crash. Energy Watch estimates that worldwide production by 2030 will be just 39 million barrels a day, compared with 82 million today, but the International Energy Agency estimates that demand by this time will be at least 113 million barrels – a recipe for catastrophe as countries fight to keep their economies afloat.

While the predicted rate of oil supply collapse may sound dramatic, it chimes with what has been seen before. In the North Sea, for example, UK oil production reached its peak as recently as 1999, and has already fallen by 40 per cent. As David Strahan, author of *The Last Oil Shock: a Survival Guide to the Imminent Extinction of Petroleum Man*, points out, the oil business is having to run flat out just to stand still. It now spends close to half a trillion US dollars every year in the quest for new reserves, yet the output of both Shell and BP is currently lower than in 2005. Production is falling in two thirds of the world's 98 oil-producing countries, while reserves in the giant Middle Eastern fields are suspected of being massively inflated.

But surely this is good news for climate change? Well, considering that fossil fuels have almost single-handedly caused the problem, it would be intuitive to think so. Unfortunately, though, it's not quite that simple. As any mineral resource becomes scarcer, its price rises. This in turn makes it economic to spend more money ferreting out those remaining deposits that no-one was interested in when prices were lower. The problem is that extracting oil from such deposits, which include oil shales and tar sands, is dirtier and uses a great deal more energy than just pumping up liquid oil. It would be nice to think that the higher cost of getting these deposits out of the ground would encourage petroleum companies to expand investment in renewables. Unfortunately, they seem determined to stick to what they know best – extracting oil. Separating heavy crude from a mixture of sand and water in Alberta is set to become Canada's biggest contributor to global warming, with emissions close to those of the whole of Denmark, as a consequence of exploiting less than ten per cent of the total reserves. Getting at the rest will cost more money, use more energy, produce more emissions and cause more warming. The bottom line remains: if we burn all available fossil fuels, including the clathrates in marine sediments, then global temperatures are likely to reach 13°C above pre-industrial levels.

There is another worry, too, which is that as the oil supply plummets and prices go through the roof, so governments will look to coal to keep their economies from falling apart. The World Energy Council reports that there are 847 billion tonnes of known coal reserves, enough to supply current needs for nearly a century and a half. Closer examination reveals, however, that reserves of high-quality coal that can be dug out without financial pain are considerably lower; combined with massively rising demand this is likely to mean that 'peak coal' is closer than we think. In fact, Energy Watch are predicting its arrival as soon as 2025, with production falling into terminal decline thereafter. A study by David Rutledge of the California Institute of Technology suggests it might come even sooner, largely because higher coal prices do not seem to be driving the exploitation of hard-to-get-at deposits. While another hammer blow for the global economy, Rutledge's prediction, if correct, could be a godsend for the climate, leading to a cut in total fossil fuel emissions and atmospheric carbon levels peaking at just 470 ppm by 2070. Not quite enough, on its own, to prevent dangerous climate change, but a big step in the right direction.

IS A ZERO-CARBON WORLD ACTUALLY POSSIBLE?

A zero-carbon world by the middle of this century will probably be needed if we are to stand a chance of staving off dangerous climate change, and is possible with the right will and motivation. Some countries, including New Zealand, Norway, Iceland and Sweden, are already heading down this path, while in the UK, the Liberal Democrat party has produced a detailed blueprint for a zero-carbon Britain. A carbon-free world would be powered by electricity from renewable sources and fuelled by clean electrical energy, hydrogen and environmentally-friendly biofuels. The destruction of the rainforests would have been reversed and the world's mostly urban population would live in eco-cities. International trade would still flourish, but the buzz-word would be 'localism'.

Is there any real chance that, in a little over 40 years, we can transform our society from one defined by energy profligacy, redundancy, waste and disposability into one that is sustainable and produces no carbon whatsoever? With Andrew Weaver and his colleagues at British Columbia's University of Victoria predicting that even a 90-per-cent cut in emissions by 2050 will not be sufficient to keep our descendents from the clutches of dangerous climate change, it seems that we have no choice. In the past, economies and societies have been successfully transformed, almost overnight, to face and defeat new threats – the UK's stand against Nazi Germany and the US transition from depressed state to war economy in the 1940s spring to mind. So far, only war and the threat of war seem to provide urgent enough incentives for such realignments, and nothing less than a war-footing will enable the world to achieve zero-carbon status within half a century. But where do we start?

A mechanism is needed to ensure that sacrifices are made and emissions reduced in a manner that is fair and equitable, and Contraction and Convergence would seem to be the only one in the frame. In line with the scientific consensus, a timetable needs to be determined by international agreement that would see the emissions of all the world's nations converge on a common per capita figure that is ultimately reduced to zero by around 2050. It is worth being mindful of the fact that based upon current population growth predictions, the goal will be to produce no emissions from a world of nine billion people – half as many again as today.

Industrialised countries will need to work far harder than those whose emissions barely register anyway, but this is as it should be. Furthermore, the USA and EU member states have both the cash and the know-how to do the job. Just imagine how much progress could be made if even half of the USA's half-trillion-dollar military budget were siphoned off into the battle against climate change – or, for that matter, the £55 billion thrown by the UK government at the ailing Northern Rock Bank. China, India and other rapidly developing countries will also need to pull their weight, and accept that for them to follow development paths along the lines of the UK, USA, Germany and Japan is a physical impossibility on a small planet with finite, and fast-depleting, resources. At least they should be helped by massive hikes in the price of oil and coal and a global economy for which this is likely to mean a sustained period of recession, if not depression, in coming decades.

The zero-carbon concept is already beginning to gather pace and is official policy in some of the world's smaller nations. New Zealand, Norway and Costa Rica have all pledged to become carbon-free, while Iceland is well on its way to developing a hydrogen economy and Sweden is on course to phase out oil by 2020. In the UK, the Liberal Democrat party has committed itself to a zero-carbon, non-nuclear Britain by 2050, with fossil-fuel powered cars phased out by 2040, a new high-speed rail network, distributed and renewable electricity generation, and a change in the taxation system so that you 'pay as you burn' for everything you eat, drink or do that involves adding carbon to the Earth's atmosphere. The 2007 Liberal Democrat report Zero Carbon Britain also stresses the importance of a big push to transfer climate-friendly technologies to poor and industrialising countries, without which a zero-carbon world simply cannot happen.

So what could a successful, mid-century, carbon-free society be like to live in? Far from a world of do-it-yourself haircuts, home-spun clothes, home-grown root vegetables and smelly armpits, a zero-carbon Earth could be a high-tech heaven. The world's population would be almost entirely urban, with most people living in green eco-cities such as those already being constructed outside Shanghai and in Dubai. Clean power would come from the wind, waves, sun and waste, while efficient, silent cars, buses and trains would be fuelled by renewable electricity, hydrogen, compressed air or environmentally-friendly biofuels. Planes would still criss-cross the skies, but they would be powered by hydrogen or algae-based biofuel made in a 'bio-reactor'. The relatively low cost of renewables and the use of 'bio-refineries' to make substitute petroleum products would ensure that substantial reserves of oil and coal remained underground, where they could do least harm. With deforestation in Brazil and Indonesia halted by financial incentives, a massive programme of reforestation would have restored to the great tropical rainforests at least some part of their former beauty and wonder.

While international trade would thrive, albeit at a lower level, much would be locally sourced: this would certainly not be a world where, as in 2006, the UK exported 15,000 tonnes of chocolate-covered waffles and imported 14,000 tonnes of – you guessed it – chocolate-covered waffles.

Zero-carbon Earth is not pie-in-the-sky, it is a world there for the taking if we – both citizens and governments – want it badly enough. The alternative is an increasingly-down-at-heel global society in a state of perpetual depression, haphazardly powered by the dregs of oil and coal, along with expensive nuclear energy; a world shaken by war and civil strife and increasingly at the mercy of a catastrophically changing climate and an ever-more degraded environment.

QUE SERÁ, SERÁ

What will be, will be. I must admit that in the course of writing this book I have become a little more optimistic – or at least a little less pessimistic – about our chances of saving the planet as we know it. From the perspective of March 2008, it is impossible to say whether we will achieve this or not, but the door is not yet closed. Climate change is now at the top of the world agenda and is beginning to shape the policies of national governments.

Admittedly, the latest science has revealed that the emissions cuts we need to aim for are even tougher than previously thought, while emissions are still on the up, but we now know that we have the tools to do the job – without resorting to the wild, wacky, and downright scary wholesale engineering of the planet. We know that using the sun, wind, waves and other renewable sources we can generate sufficient carbon-free energy, at some 2.3 million times our current usage, even for a population of nine billion, and the technologies to do this are maturing and growing at an astonishing rate. When it becomes apparent that a relatively small area of the Sahara Desert, covered with solar reflectors, can provide all the world's current energy needs, the true potential of renewable energy systems really hits home. Similarly, alternative methods of powering the world's cars, and even aircraft, are looking increasingly promising.

More and more, business and industry are seeing the opportunities afforded by tackling climate change, rather than the problems. This is hardly surprising when you consider that in 2005 the US environment sector generated more than US$340 billion in sales and 5.3 million jobs, with one economist predicting that by 2030, 40 million Americans could be working in the renewable energy and energy-efficiency industries alone. The UN reckons that investment in renewables has already reached US$100 billion – 18 per cent of all new investment in the global energy sector – and could approach US$2 trillion by 2020 – now that's big business.

However huge the green business boom, though, it must not detract from the fact that our small planet and its dwindling resources simply cannot support nine billion people living the unsustainable, consumer-driven lifestyles that we in the UK, the USA and Europe have become accustomed to. Professor Rod Smith of Imperial College, London has determined that an annual growth rate of just three per cent means that economic activity doubles every 23 years. This rate of global growth over the next three decades or so would consume more resources than in all of prior human history. Clearly, this can't happen. Consequently we either make a reasonably orderly transition to a sustainable lifestyle, which also happens to be a climate-friendly one, or attempt to continue with business as usual, even though it has to end in tears. On a finite planet with finite resources, a sustainable and more equitable economic system can be the only way forward. This isn't communism, it's common sense.

One way or another, we need to find an alternative and better way of measuring progress other than how many weekend breaks we can manage in Venice or how many different models of mobile phone we can get through in a year. Radical environmental campaigner and journalist George Monbiot has called for a complete reappraisal of what progress actually means, if not simply ever-faster economic growth. Ah, but he would demand that, I hear you say. Not so easily dismissed, however, are the thoughts of Adair Turner, ex-head of the UK Confederation of British Industry and vice-chairman of investment bank Merrill Lynch. In an essay in a recently published anthology entitled *Do good lives have to cost the Earth?*, this big-business hi-flier also expresses doubts that business success can be measured purely by growth at a time of environmental crisis, and argues that growth for the hell of it needs to be 'dethroned' as the be-all and end-all of progress.

Avoiding dangerous climate change, then, requires an end to the Western consumerist lifestyle and the enlightening of those in industrialising countries who aspire to it. Not only will this save the planet, but it will also make us a good deal happier and healthier. Mental illness in the UK,

USA and Australia almost doubled between the 1980s and the start of the new millennium, much of it attributed to 'affluenza', which is sometimes defined as a sustained addiction to economic growth, but more perceptively labelled on Wikipedia as 'the bloated, sluggish and unfulfilled feeling that results from efforts to keep up with the Joneses'. If we are serious about sustainable life on a small planet, we could also – to be honest – do with a lot less Joneses around, and although it is a topic that many environmentalists tiptoe around, population growth is the elephant in the living room when it comes to addressing resource depletion and climate change. Put simply, the more of us there are, the bigger our race's ecological footprint is likely to be and the more difficult we will find it to achieve the sort of sustainability needed to defeat climate change. At present, only one country, Cuba, provides a decent standard of living for its people without consuming more than its fair share of resources, which really highlights just how far we have to go before we can live at one with the planet and its climate.

I think we all know now that we can't carry on the way we are doing. If we were bacteria in a Petri dish we would have committed auto-genocide by now; if we were any other mammal species, our unsustainable way of life would long ago have set us on the road to extinction. The big difference between *Homo sapiens* and all other species, however, is that we have the means within us to address the problems we have caused, to tackle them, and to solve them. This is the reason why we have become so successful at the expense of the rest of the planet, why we are still here, and why our numbers are still climbing. Now, we face the greatest challenge of all, and one that is entirely of our own making. Can we overcome it in time? Can we be bothered to try – even for our children's sake? Only time will tell.

NOTES

1 The term 'dangerous climate change' is incorporated in the 1992 UN Framework Convention on Climate Change (UNFCC) – the seminal Earth Summit in Rio de Janeiro that propelled climate change into the limelight of world politics and public awareness. Specifically, the framework called for the stabilisation of greenhouse gases to 'prevent dangerous anthropogenic interference with the climate system' and that this must be accomplished within a time-frame that ensures food production is not threatened, that gives ecosystems sufficient time to adapt naturally, and that allows economic development to continue in a sustainable manner. In 2004, the European Climate Forum highlighted some more specific indicators of dangerous climate change, including the extinction of iconic species (eg. the Polar Bear), the loss of entire ecosystems or human cultures, a threat to water resources and a significant rise in mortality rates.

2 Oil equivalent is a standardised measure used to compare fuels, based upon the energy produced when they are burnt.

3 A more technical definition for the climate of a given location is the weather, and its variation, averaged over a period of at least 30 years.

4 Emissions due to human activities are also sometimes expressed in terms of just carbon, rather than carbon dioxide. The total amount of carbon in the atmosphere today is around 800 Giga-tonnes. Since the Industrial Revolution really picked up steam in the mid-eighteenth century, the burning of fossil fuels, together with cement production, has released 305 billion tonnes of carbon into the atmosphere, with half of this total released since the mid-1970s.

5 One Giga-tonne is equivalent to 1 billion tonnes.

6 An 'extreme flood' is a flood of a magnitude expected to occur once in 100 years or more.

7 Later searches revealed that the expedition's two ships had been stuck in the ice for a year and a half before being abandoned. The survivors ultimately died of starvation and exposure after – according to some accounts – being forced to resort to cannibalism.

8 A megacity is a metropolitan area with a population of ten million or more inhabitants.

9 COP stands for 'Conference of Parties' and is the highest body of the UN Climate Change Convention, which meets once a year to address issues related to the convention. The climate change summit in Kyoto was COP3, and the one in Bali, COP13. The conference planned for Copenhagen in December 2009 is COP 15.

ACKNOWLEDGEMENTS

Writing a book on climate change is like trying to pin down a rapidly moving target, with almost daily new findings and observations requiring continuous updating and constant modification. As a result, the compilation of *Seven Years to Save the Planet* has been not so much a labour of love as one of enormous stress and strain, although certainly worth the struggle by any measure. I would like to thank all those who have encouraged, cajoled and pushed me towards the conclusion of the project, most notably my agent, Vivienne Schuster of Curtis Brown, and Michael Dover and Debbie Woska of Weidenfeld and Nicholson. Not least, I must say a heartfelt thanks to my wife Anna, who has supported me throughout, and to my four-year old son, Fraser, who must sometimes have wondered how and why his relaxed and smiling daddy had been transformed into a 'grumpy old sod'.

USEFUL WEB LINKS

Boat and train options
www.nofly.co.uk

Buy Less Crap
www.buylesscrap.org

Calculate and reduce your carbon footprint
www.terrapass.com

California Consumer Energy Center
www.consumerenergycenter.org

California solar power
www.gosolarcalifornia.ca.gov

Car sharing – North America
www.carsharing.net

Car sharing – worldwide
www.pickuppal.com

City Car Club
www.citycarclub.co.uk

Climate Change kids
www.epa.gov/climatechange/kids/index.html

Climate Change News Digest
www.climatechangenews.org

Climate Outreach and Information Network
http://coinet.org.uk/materials/carboncalculations

Eco-friendly Kids
www.ecofriendlykids.co.uk

Eco-friendly Weddings
www.eco-friendlyweddings.co.uk

Eco Schools
www.eco-schools.org

Electricity Information – UK
www.electricityinfo.org

Energy Quest (kids energy website)
www.energyquest.ca.gov

The Energy Saving Trust
www.eta.co.uk

Global Warming Kids
www.globalwarmingkids.net

Gold Standard Carbon Offsetting
www.cdmgoldstandard.org

Good Energy
www.good-energy.co.uk

Green America
www.globalgreen.org

Green and sustainable lifestyles
www.treehugger.com

Green driving
www.ecodrive.org

Green energy – Australia
www.originenergy.com.au/1544/Green-electricity

Green Energy – UK
www.greenenergy.uk.com

Green energy and green lifestyles
www.motherearthnews.com

The Guardian: Climate Change
www.guardian.co.uk/environment/climatechange

Hybrid cars
www.motortrend.com/new_cars/27/hybrid_cars/

Intergovernmental Panel on Climate Change (IPCC)
www.ipcc.ch

Micro-generation – North America
www.homepower.com

Natural Death Centre
www.naturaldeath.org.uk

The Owl wireless energy monitor
www.theowl.com

Pledge to stop or limit your flying
www.lowflyzone.org

RealClimate: Climate Science from Climate Scientists.
www.realclimate.org

Renewable energy – Canada
www.web.net/~cfre/

Resurgence Carbon Calculator
www.resurgence.org/energy/index.htm

Royal Society: Climate Change
www.royalsociety.org/landing.asp?id=1278

Saving energy
www.ase.org

The Sierra Club – green and climate change issues
www.sierraclub.org

Sustainable learning
www.sustainablelearning.info

Tumble drier alternatives
www.pulleymaid.com

UK Climate Impacts Programme
www.ukcip.org.uk/default.asp

United Nations Environment Programme (UNEP)
www.unep.org

United Nations Framework Convention on Climate Change (UNFCCC)
http://unfccc.int/2860.php

What Green Car?
www.whatgreencar.com

WWF Climate Program
www.panda.org/about_wwf/what_we_do/climate_change/index.cfm

Yurt Holidays – UK
www.yurtworks.co.uk/holidays/index.htm

FURTHER READING

Brown, Lester R *Plan B 3.0: Mobilising to Save Civilisation* Norton, 2008

Goodall, Chris *How to Live a Low-Carbon Life: the individual's guide to stopping climate change* Earthscan, 2007

Heinberg, Richard *Peak Everything: Waking up to the Century of Decline in Earth's Resources* Clairview, 2007

Henson, Robert *The Rough Guide to Climate Change* Rough Guides, 2006

Hillman, Mayer *How we can Save the Planet* Penguin Books, 2004

Houghton, John *Global Warming: the Complete Briefing* Cambridge University Press, 2004

Maslin, Mark *Global Warming: a Very Short Introduction* Oxford University Press, 2004

McGuire, Bill *A Guide to the End of the World: Everything You Never Wanted to Know* Oxford University Press, 2002

McGuire, Bill *Surviving Armageddon: Solutions for a Threatened Planet* Oxford University Press, 2005

McGuire, Bill *Global Catastrophes: a Very Short Introduction* Oxford University Press, 2005

McGuire, Bill, Mason, Ian and Kilburn, Christopher *Natural Hazards and Environmental Change* Hodder Arnold, 2002

Monbiot, George *Heat: How we Can Stop the Planet Burning* Penguin, 2007

Intergovernmental Panel on Climate Change (IPCC) *Climate Change 2007: the Physical Science Basis* Cambridge University Press, 2007

Intergovernmental Panel on Climate Change (IPCC) *Climate Change 2007: Impacts, Adaptation and Vulnerability* Cambridge University Press, 2007

Intergovernmental Panel on Climate Change (IPCC) *Climate Change 2007: Mitigation of Climate Change* Cambridge University Press, 2007

Leggett, Jeremy *Half-Gone: Oil, Gas, Hot Air and the Global Energy Crisis* Portobello, 2006

Lynas, Mark *Six Degrees: Our Future on a Hotter Planet* Fourth Estate, 2007

Meyer, Aubrey *Contraction & Convergence: the Global Solution to Climate Change* Green Books, 2000

Stern, Nicholas *The Economics of Climate Change: the Stern Review* Cambridge University Press, 2007

Strahan, David *The Last Oil Shock: A Survival Guide to the Imminent Extinction of Petroleum Man* John Murray, 2007